Preaching in Arduous Times

© 2020 Summum Academic Publications - Kampen
www.summumacademic.com

Interior design: Gewoon Geertje
ISBN 9789492701152

All rights reserved

Maarten Kater and Ferdi Kruger

Preaching in Arduous Times

Outline of Perspectives from
the Hebrews Sermon on Preaching

Summum

Research Justification
This book is meant for academics in the fields of theology and homiletics reflecting on preaching that should communicate with listeners in arduous times. This research is undertaken by two scholars from the Netherlands and from South-Africa and is based on homiletics from the viewpoint of the Hebrews-sermon aimed at addressing the challenge that preachers are experiencing when it seems like that their sermons do not have a profound impact on their listeners. It is the aim of both authors to stimulate an on-going discourse within theological research of scholars interested in the Letter to the Hebrews and to preachers within ministry concerned with preaching to listeners that are experiencing challenges in daily life. The shared interest of both authors is to emphasise the idea that preaching has to bring new perspectives to listeners because preaching based on the Gospel has to do with a living voice that should be voiced. The authors also share the theological premise that God is present in this world. In the kingdom of God, believers are encouraged to participate in the listening process in order to experience profound hope for challenges experienced in daily life. This book roots theological research and reflection in the real life of the listeners and wants to stimulate on-going transdisciplinary research focusing on a homiletical praxeology that deals with both the fact that God is speaking through His Word and with listeners living in arduous times like for example a post-pandemic world.

The publisher certifies that this book was evaluated according to review process. An initial election process by the editorial board has reviewed the proposed research in order to determine whether it could be published. An in-depth peer review process was adhered to where a specialist has participated in the peer review process. The comments of the reviewer were integrated, revised by the authors and eventually verified by the editor. We can certify that the recommendations which have been made and responded to by the authors have improved the quality of this manuscript.

TABLE OF CONTENTS

Preface   XI
Introduction
Maarten Kater and Ferdi Kruger   1

CHAPTER 1
On speaking terms*Preaching and the voice of God*
Maarten Kater   25
  1.1 The gift of the human voice - a phenomenological exploration   26
  1.2 Communication is relation   30
  1.3 The Voice of God   33
    1.3.1 Mediated speech   34
    1.3.2 Embodied speech   36
    1.3.3 Acoustic symbiosis   36
  1.4 God speaks 'today'   38
    1.4.1 The present from within   38
    1.4.2 The present from the future   38
    1.4.3 The present contains more than the past - a surplus of meaning   39
  1.5 Preaching and the Voice of God   40
References   41

CHAPTER 2
A multitude of chords needed in enabling listeners to actively listen to the voice
Ferdi Kruger   43
  2.1 A polyphony of voices in the Hebrews sermon   46
    2.1.1 The kaleidoscope of various concepts for preaching   46
    2.1.2 The dimension of admonishing and encouraging - παρακαλειν   47
    2.1.3 Preaching as intelligible dialogue - λαλειν   50
    2.1.4 Preaching the good news and remembrance- Ευαγγελιζ ω   52
    2.1.5 Hearing of the Word that brings no good - ὠφέλησεν ὁ λόγοςτῆς ἀκοῆς ἐκείνους   53
    2.1.6 Preaching as witnessing- μαρτυρειν   55

2.2 The multitude of voices of preaching intertwined with the
    listeners' attitudes (the notion of the intrinsic voice) 56
2.3 A polyphony of voices in voicing voice- homiletical
    perspectives 60
2.4 Conclusion 62

CHAPTER 3
Servant or master? Preaching and rhetoric
Maarten Kater 67
3.1 Phenomenological exploration - Augustine's voice 68
3.2 Hebrews from rhetorical perspective 70
3.3 Imagination as an instrument 74
3.4 Preaching with *pathos* 77

CHAPTER 4
The inseparable intertwining of the preacher's and the listeners' attitudes in the act of preaching
Ferdi Kruger 83
4.1 Speak-for-itself concepts in the Hebrews sermon
    related to attitudes 85
    4.1.1 *The attitude of the preacher in addressing the attitude
    of the listeners* 85
    4.1.2 *The listeners' attitudes in need of to be altered* 86
    4.1.3 παρρησια -boldness (Hebrews 3:6, 4:16,
    10:19 and 10:35) 86
    4.1.4 θαρουντθας (boldness) - Hebrews 13:6 89
    4.1.5 σπουδαζω [diligence to act] 91
4.2 Widening attitude dimensions in sermons illustrated from
    Hebrews 92
    4.2.1 *The attitudinal dimension of sermons* 93
        4.2.1.1 *Do not drift away (Hebrews 2:1)* 93
        4.2.1.2 *Laziness to listen - Hebrews 5:11* 94
        4.2.1.3 *Through faith and perseverance/ endurance* 95
        4.2.1.4 *Longing for - Hebrews 11:16* 95
    4.2.1.5 *Persevere like one seeing the invisible* 96
        4.2.1.6 *Not grow weary and lose heart* 97
        4.2.1.7 *Not making light the Lord's discipline* 97
        4.2.1.8 *Strengthen your feeble arms and weak knees* 98
        4.2.1.9 *Let us be thankful and so worship* 99
    4.2.2 *The preacher's attitude in addressing the listeners'
    attitudes* 100

4.3	Homiletical perspectives on the functioning of attitudes	102
4.4	Conclusion	105

CHAPTER 5
Preach as you teach
Maarten Kater *111*

5.1	Short phenomenological exploration on listening	112
5.2	The lex orandi - lex credendi- rule (LOLC)	115
	5.2.1 State of the art - 'what's going on'?	*116*
	5.2.2 Historical background	*118*
	5.2.3 Perspective from Hebrews	*120*
5.3	Remedies leading to recovering	123

CHAPTER 6
Persuasive preaching's pertinent focus on the changing of attitudes that impede the interrelationship between listening and doing
Ferdi Kruger 127

6.1	Persuasive communication and the importance of the use of language	130
6.2	Deliberateness in preaching enables listeners to stand firm in their faith.	132
6.3	Persuasion to change attitudes	135
	6.3.1 Rhetorical devices underlining the essence of persuasion	*135*
	6.3.2 Persuasiveness in the light of the serious crisis experienced by listeners	*138*
	6.3.2.1 Logos or logical argumentation	*139*
	6.3.2.2 Ethos (character)	*140*
	6.3.2.3 Pathos (emotion)	*141*
6.4	Persuasive preaching to promote a change in attitude	142
	6.4.1 The importance of the construction of the community of faith - Hebrews 10:19-25	*142*
6.4.	The importance of the liturgy of daily life	144
6.5	Persuasive preaching and a change in attitude - homiletical perspectives	146
6.6	Conclusion	148

CHAPTER 7

Preaching on Abel as an exemplum
Living example or just a predecessor?
Maarten Kater   153
7.1   Abel's place in God's speech   155
     7.1.1   Abel in the letter to the Hebrews   155
7.2   Abel as *exemplum* and contemporary   156
     7.2.1   'By faith' is to learn to look through the eye of God's love   157
     7.2.2   Not morality   157
     7.2.3   *The function of the exempla*   159
     7.2.4   Contemporary   160
7.3   Abel as predecessor and passer-by   161
7.4   Some homiletic notes on preaching exempla   164

CHAPTER 8

Remembrance as propellant for the act of seeing in persuasive preaching that evokes a change in attitude
Ferdi Kruger   167
8.1   The influence of memories on listeners' difficulty in understanding a problematic praxis of temporality   171
8.2   Remembrance as a set of perspectives for encouragement as found in the Hebrews sermon   173
     8.2.1   *Anamnesis (remembrance) of familiar things* - Hebrews 10:3 and Hebrews 10:32   175
     8.2.2   *Remembrance of Christ as Mediator of the new covenant (memoria Christi)* - Hebrews 12:24   178
         8.2.2.1   Preaching as the revisiting of the storehouse of memories   178
         8.2.2.2   Remembrance of the Mediator of the new covenant-memory of the old and cognizance of the new   179
8.3   Homiletical perspectives on the importance of remembrance   183
     8.3.1   *The preacher should share remembrances with listeners*   183
     8.3.2   *Remembrance as propellant to stir memories in preaching*   185
     8.3.3   *The power of remembrance in preaching*   186
8.4   Conclusion   189

CHAPTER 9

Hearing and being in church Preaching in worship services
Maarten Kater 195
9.1 A phenomenological exploration 196
    9.1.1 Capturing the complexity of the in-church worship experience 196
    9.1.2 Some descriptions of in-church worship and corporality 199
9.2 Some key elements characteristic of being in church 202
    9.2.1 The congregation of the LORD 203
    9.2.2 The presence of God 204
    9.2.3 On earth as it is in heaven 205
9.3 Preach while they have come 207
9.4 Homiletical lessons to be learned again and again 210

CHAPTER 10

The determining dimension of encouragement as part of the eschatological dimensions in the Hebrews sermon
Ferdi Kruger 215
10.1 Colourful eschatological dimensions of the rainbow of the Hebrews sermon 217
    10.1.1 Active listening to the message of Christ in these last days (Hebrews 1:1-3) 219
    10.1.2 The eyes focussed on the reality of the sabbath-rest - Hebrews 4 222
    10.1.3 Fixed eyes on God's promises needs perseverance - Hebrews 10:19-39 225
    10.1.4 Warning against refusing of the living God who speaks - Hebrews 12:14-29 228
10.2 Homiletical perspectives on the eschatological dimension in preaching 229
    10.2.1 Interest in the concept of prophetic preaching with an eschatological outlook 229
    10.2.2 The eschatological dimension of preaching 231
10.3 Conclusion 233

CHAPTER 11
    Homiletical headlines from Hebrews
    Maarten Kater and Ferdi Kruger   237
    11.1 Directions for a homiletical theory to consider and to process are: 237
    11.2 Reflections in broader perspective   240
    11.3 Relevance of the Hebrews sermon for the discipline of homiletics   241

Preface

> 'When I really listen *with* the other to what he himself,
> as he speaks, is listening to or has listened to, then it is really
> *he* to whom I am listening.'
> (Jean-Louis Chrétien, *The Ark of Speech*, 10)

This homiletic study is offered as fruit of putting into practice this aforementioned saying from Chrétien as well as we could. First of all, in listening to the text of the Hebrew sermon itself which invites us not to be just spectators considering many treasures hold in it intellectually, but being involved as participants in these marvellous realities with the deepest veins of our existence. Doing theology is always an existential exercise or it is just daydreaming. Listening consists of attentiveness of a voice to be heard. God in Christ, the Word, has taken a human voice and takes human voices by calling them. The living Word once in human form, Christ, comes now to us in the living words of Scripture. By means of listening we receive new sights and we see the voice while hearing.

Secondly, in listening to all others who have done such work before us as all the footnotes record as an acknowledgement to them.

Thirdly, in listening to each other as two theologians from different parts of the world, one in the North and one in the South, and nevertheless we met each other from 2014 on in both studying on Hebrews from a practical-theological and especially homiletic perspective. We really share the great joy of cooperation between our universities, the North West University of Potchefstroom and the Theological University of Apeldoorn.

It is our privilege to acknowledge several man and women who have been of great help in publishing our study. Every page, not to say every single word, has been carefully read through by Etienne Terblanche (CUM LAUDE Taalversorging) after the texts have been formatted by Ferdi's 'better half', Celia Kruger. She used her creative gifts by designing the book cover. Before one will read one single letter in this book his or her eyes are attracted by the wonderful image as painted and printed on the front which shows the kernel of the sermon: speaking attractive and hearing attentive. We want to express our gratitude to the peer reviewers who contributed essential improvements and every imperfection which will be still there is for our own account. During the last stage of our project we looked for an academic book publisher and we are happy with Pieter Rouwendal's *Summum Academic Publications* (Kampen, The Netherlands) who was willingly to include this study in the list of books already published by him.

Spring 2021
Apeldoorn/Potchefstroom
Maarten Kater
Ferdi Kruger

INTRODUCTION
THERE IS NO TIME LIKE THE PRESENT

A word of encouragement to listeners looking or meaningfulness in arduous times

Maarten Kater and Ferdi Kruger

This book engages multi-dimensional perspectives from the Hebrews sermon that resonate with the praxis of preaching to listeners in the grip of rapid changes in their lives. In practice, when people's comfort zones are shaken due to the inescapable ripple-effects of drastic changes, they are compelled to search even deeper into the meaningfulness of acts of faith.[1] Arduous circumstances challenge people to seriously reconsider whether things they normally do as Christians still add value to the realm of life. Browning refers to the concept of practical reasoning within a practical theological approach as indication that thinking processes related to this challenge also have to do with the deeper meaning behind human actions, also called *habitus* thinking.[2] This notion of *habitus* is inextricably linked to the nuanced, much-discussed social and philosophical ideas of Bordieu. Bordieu is convinced that the key to analysis of any practice within a field is to examine the ways in which people organize and interact with one another, often unconsciously. [3]*Habitus*-focussed thinking is an everyday experience requiring an understanding of the dynamics behind it, because within the praxis of being human the quest for meaning or purpose in life after all determines all forms of praxis thinking. In other words, people need to make sense of concrete events in their lives, a process that is called someone's cognition. The danger of losing hope and the questioning of meaningfulness in

---

1 D.J. Louw, "Preaching as Art (Imaging the Unseen) and Art as Homiletics (Verbalising the Unseen): Towards the Aesthetics of Iconic Thinking and Poetic Communication in Homiletics," *HTS Teologiese Studies/Theological Studies* 72, no. 2 (2016): 18, a3826, http://dx.doi.org/10.4102/hts.v72i2.3826.
2 Don S. Browning, *A Fundamental Practical Theology: Descriptive and Strategic Proposals* (Minneapolis: Fortress, 1996), 55.
3 P. Bordieu, *The Weight of the World: Social Suffering in Contemporary Society* (Oxford: Polity, 1999), 7.

everyday life is after all much more than a mere theoretical- or even fictitious problem. While finalizing this book, the Covid-19 pandemic has induced far-reaching consequences, putting in stark relief the view that people look for meaningfulness in a time of troublesome uncertainty. Homiletics, as the study of the art of preaching, is inevitably forced to rethink how preaching could contribute to this and other intrusive matters around how people could possibly deal with everyday experiences that are ostensibly essential and that simultaneously contradict what listeners used to be familiar with.

For practical theology, reflection on the spiralling functioning of doubt that starts with a feeling of isolation amidst the exposure to uncertainty is pivotal--because of the centrality of communicative acts within the focus of this discipline while people are globally confronted with a unique kind of reality leading to an awareness of impotence and resulting in a distorted outlook of an immutable Christian future[4]. The importance of this is that there is more to life than waiting for death, because a liveable life exists. Without piercing hope for current circumstances and without an anchor of hope for the future, most people will struggle to find meaningfulness in listening to sermons and meaningfully participate in worship services[5].

The risk involved in hopelessness is that it most probably suppresses enthusiasm in participating in meaningful acts within their faith-lives.

For example, Robinson published an essay on the overwhelming power of feelings of fear in the Western World (2015)[6].

She describes how this fear, caused by rapid changes, subtly permeates social reality and settles into the lives and minds of ordinary people. Feelings of fear seamlessly take over feelings of trust and frequently give way to feelings of anger, caused by loss of economical certainty, safety and hope for the future. These feelings of fear are part of the so-called *zeitgeist* or spirit of the times and can be compared to a dangerous virus which, when unnoticed, by and by affects the whole body, in this case the whole fabric of society. The fear and drastic measures around restrictions on daily routines as well as the revolving social effects of the Covid-19 pandemic offer accurate illustrations of how fear could unexpectedly

---

4 J.M. Beach, "The Real Presence of Christ Preaching of the Gospel: Luther and Calvin on the Nature of Preaching," *Mid-America Journal of Theology* 10, no. 1 (1999): 89.
5 Louw, "Preaching as Art," 18.
6 M. Robinson, "In principio erat sermo," in *Viva Vox Evangelii: Reforming Preaching*, Studia Homiletica 9, eds. J. Hermelink and A. Deeg (Leipzig: Evangelische Verlaganstalt, 2015), http://www.nybooks.com/articles/2015/09/24/marilynne-robinson-fear/. Robinson shortly refers to her lecture at the Conference of Societas Homiletica at Wittenberg, Germany.

paralyze people's convictions around their immediate expectations of all meaningful segments of being human. The fear for contagion and the spread of the virus will in all likelihood change people's everyday experiences and their interaction with others for a considerable time to come. People could also become even more distrustful of strangers, especially when quality of life becomes limited. The challenge for preachers within this particular praxis is to determine an effective way of preaching to listeners that struggle with the existential issue of vulnerability and difficulties that arise around meaningfulness of life, while they are rudely awakened by fears induced by the pandemic.

We argue against this background that there is a significant resemblance between current circumstances and the concrete context of the listeners to the Hebrews sermon. God speaking in Christ in the midst of a changing world is an intriguing aspect to think of within these challenging circumstances. The Hebrews listeners who received this letter within the first century were experiencing something very similar to what Christians often experience within a changing world that evokes uncertainty. The listeners to the Hebrews sermon had already experienced the change from temple-centred- to Jesus-centred worship. They had grown up in Judaism, centred in its temple in Jerusalem, the one special place on earth where, in keeping with his promise through Moses, God had placed his name (Deuteronomy 12). Such worship was carried out by means of things they could visibly see and touch. They knew that there had been a sacrifice for sins because people brought a sheep or a calf and watched the priest slaughter it[7].

But what did this act, taken concretely, mean for their worship within their current circumstances? Was it the proverbial case of memories that were only a mere 'blast from their past'? There was no longer a golden altar, no majestic temple, no priests with rich vestments, no shed blood to tell them that their sins had been covered. A feeling of powerlessness and emptiness resulted in a lack of meaningfulness. Under these circumstances they finally met in homes and their faith was fed on what they could not see and could not concretely touch. They were dependent on listening to the Word of God, which their preachers taught them. Their faith was now to be fed to grow strong not on visible and tangible things, as mentioned, but through what they heard about the good news of Jesus Christ, who was victoriously raised from death and who ascended to heaven. The seemingly untouchable message of the final sacrifice and the forever-priest who prays for his people at God's right hand in heaven, were

---

7 D.E. Johnson, *Him We Proclaim: Preaching Christ from all Scriptures* (New Jersey: P&R Publishing, 2007), 269.

something of a distant 'pie in the sky'. The far-off message about Christ offered difficulties to listeners around their understanding of being *in* this world but not being *from* it. On top of this, their circumstances were extremely challenging and certainly did not offer the proverbial 'walk in the park'.

Memories of the past (the 'good old days') were tempting for the listeners to the Hebrews sermon and the danger was that they would turn back to the old ways, to the ways in which you could see and touch in order to get near to God. This centred on finding a sense of security in the midst of their uncertain world and an audible message about Christ that did not bring thorough relief to this intense longing. That is exactly the reason why this letter was written, namely to assure listeners that they have indeed a more secure source of security in Jesus Christ. This security about Him that always remains the same, is more secure than anything in the visible, touchable temple, or even of anything else in this visible, touchable world, could possibly offer[8]. To do this, a purposeful strengthening and development or formation process that relates to the memories of the past, but with the fuller picture of a past that was fulfilled in Christ, was needed.

It is our conviction that the purposeful structuring of the Hebrews sermon is furthermore providing dynamic perspectives to preachers that are simultaneously reflecting on the burning-issue of connectivity to listeners in a postmodern or one could say a post-everything world. Although the variegation of aspects of engaging with a postmodern culture offers time to reflect on various aspects thereof we are in need of a praxis of preaching that realises the value of active listening whether within a worship service or following preaching via the online environment. The Hebrews sermon is enabling us to realise that preaching, the preacher as well as listeners are involved in a sensitive interrelationship that could easily be skewed and become distorted when one aspect is emphasised at the expense of the other. The Hebrews sermon is furthermore assisting us to realise the importance of God's voice within *the today* of our existence as well as to recognise the responsibility that something should be responsibly done by listeners with the good news of the Gospel they have received. The Hebrews sermon wants to avoid the pitfall of a mere hearing without a proper response and consequently leads to the hardening of listeners' hearts (see Hebrews 3:7). In listening to preaching within the *today* could be called the most important day that concomitantly provides a dimension or sense of an urgency to the act of preaching.

---

8 Johnson, *Him We Proclaim*, 371.

Hebrews as example of a first century sermon
Hebrews could be regarded as a sermon with a unique conclusion of a typical ancient letter[9]. The purpose of this sermon was to enable listeners to see that the message of Christ, even within the culmination of problematic circumstances and challenges that emanate as a result thereof, has relevance for them. Preaching according to the Hebrews sermon deals with the persistent process of providing essential nutrients for the strengthening and development of listeners in order for them to build themselves up. It could be further illustrated from the Hebrews sermon where a deliberate approach of development by means of a three-dimensional sermon is utilised. This sermon deals with a systematic approach of persuasion for people to gain understanding around dealing with their perceptions and with memories that ostensibly contradict the meaningfulness of life. This sermon does not over-simplify by telling listeners rather to forget about their memories of the past. Instead, the Hebrews sermon starts with the vivid memory that God has spoken many times and in numerous ways, while in the last days he has spoken through his Son, purposefully and in a planned manner. The memory of a communicative God that always remembers what he has communicated through the ages is central.

Hebrews is written or preached to people who have vivid memories of the past but became disheartened due to their concrete circumstances. Uncertainty regarding what their understanding had to contain in difficult circumstances prompted them towards the question as to whether it was at all still worth it to be a Christian in the contemporary world[10]. Hebrews could therefore be regarded as a thoughtful three-dimensional sermon[11] that touches on these fears and turbulent times, as illustrated in the schematic presentation below.

---

9 Donald Guthrie, *Hebrews*, Tyndale New Testament Commentaries (Grand Rapids: Eerdmans, 1996), 117; cf. Tomasz Lewicki, *"Weist nicht ab den Sprechenden!" Wort Gottes und Paraklese im Hebräerbrief* (Paderborn: Ferdinand Schöningh, 2004), 23-27, especially n. 66, 23; Jonathan I. Griffiths, *Hebrews and Divine Speech* (New York: Bloomsbury T&T Clark, 2016), 12-27, who's exposition does refer to a huge of literature and the classis study: H. Thyen, *Der Stil der Jüdisch-Hellenistischen Homilie* (Göttingen: Vandenhoeck & Ruprecht, 1955).
10 Simon J. Kistemaker, *Hebrews*, New Testament Commentary (Grand Rapids: Baker House, 1984), 5.
11 J.C. Coetzee, *Gedagtestruktuur van Hebreërs [Thought structure of Hebrews]* (Potchefstroom: Fakulteit Teologie, 1986), 5.

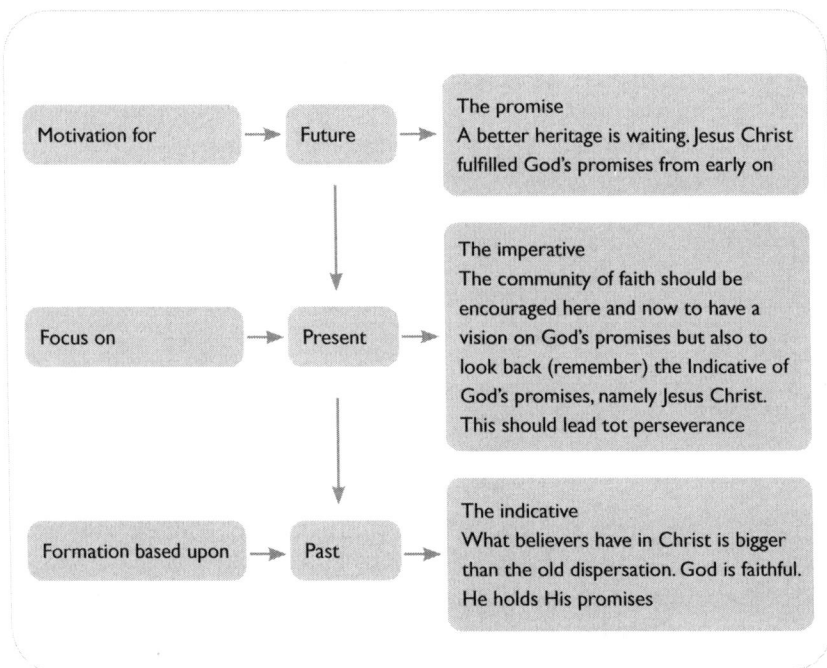

In the Hebrews sermon, the preacher avoids hiding behind the common idea expressed these days in the idiom stating that 'when the going gets tough, the tough gets going'. After all, the easiest manner to address listeners who seemingly show signs of decline in their faith-lives would be to urge them to work even harder. Legalistic preaching could easily be utilised to offer a 'solution' to a problematic praxis. On the contrary, in Hebrews 13:22 the preacher describes the real intention of this sermon, namely to act as a word of encouragement instead of mere nit-picking around a *do it yourself* solution. The preacher of this sermon in fact aligns it with the unique circumstances of the listeners. The pastoral concern of the preacher for the listeners' challenges supposes that he offers a word of encouragement. Johnston[12] goes as far as to say that this expression of a '*word of exhortation*' is synonymous with our understanding of what a sermon should be. The unique functioning of systematic doctrines or doctrinal matters within this word of encouragement, is remarkable. The phrase "*word of exhortation*' enjoyed a specific meaning in the context of first-century Hellenistic Judaism[13]. It is an idiomatic expression for

---

12 Johnson, *Him We Proclaim*, 172.
13 D.E. Johnson, *Preaching to a Postmodern World* (New Jersey: P&E Publishing House, 2006), 172.

homily or strengthening and development from designated portions of the Gospel, and is typical of a sermon expounding and applying it to listeners. Quotations from the Gospel to indicate the persuasive influence of the Word itself, is also remarkable. It is emphasised that God is speaking and encouraging listeners in the present difficult reality of their lives. The reason for this has to do with the fact that difficult circumstances in daily life influenced listeners so that they became tired and eventually the danger emerged to turn or fall away from God[14]. This word of encouragement of the sermon has a specific aim, namely to develop and strengthen the believers to be followers of Christ in all aspects of daily life. At the heart of the argument and the encouragement lies renewed or sharpened focus on Jesus Christ. Profound encouragement is after all integrated in the message about Christ and his reconciliation. No preaching could offer encouragement without the foundation of a message that is related to the adequate fulfilment of Christ. A sermon is according to this Hebrews sermon not just a human enterprise. God is somehow actively involved in the act of preaching and the Hebrews sermon provides important perspectives on this matter. This is a striking sermon with a specific message, also for contemporary listeners who experience doubt about numerous matters or, one could also say, it contains a message for listeners who became disheartened due to difficult and arduous circumstances in their lives.

Thoughtful and planned structuring of the Hebrews sermon to exhort listeners to persevere

VINES[15] as well as Long[16] underline the importance of a thoughtful structuring of the sermon. Three immediate purposes of sermon-structuring which are also related to the Hebrews sermon can be identified:

- It promotes the power of a sermon.
- It cultivates the cohesion of the various elements in a sermon.
- It enables the sermon to move (progress) in a given direction.

14　Anrie du Toit, *Hebreërs vir vandag [Hebrews for today]* (Vereeniging: CUM boeke, 2004), 23.
15　J. Vines, *The Believers Guide to Hebrews* (New Jersey: Loizeaux, 1993), 104.
16　Thomas G. Long, *Preaching from Memory to Hope* (Louisville: John Knox Press, 2009), 29.

The Hebrews sermon applies the powerful structure of explication and application to indicate an arrow-movement of the Gospel that should be noticeably present in daily life. Guthrie[17] highlights the benefit of this approach in saying that it provides balance. Two pitfalls are therefore avoided, namely moralism where the imperative is preached without an anchor of the indicative, and the danger of preaching the indicative without any imperative. The danger of preaching only the indicative without reflecting on the imperative will result in a praxis of folding arms and sitting back, because the Gospel is then presented as though it has no penetrating influence for daily life. The attitude of listeners could emerge that they are mere passengers, because God is doing everything anyway, and this could easily be cultivated. The latter danger inevitably leads to a situation of fatalism in which listeners only receive the message that the Gospel has no implication for daily life, so that answers to daily challenges should be sought elsewhere. On the other hand, preaching only the imperatives without relatedness to the indicative could lead to legalistic moralism. The reality of God that enables listeners to act and respond could become an irrelevant matter. Typical formulations of this kind of practice will become audible, namely 'do not do this' or 'do not do that'. A structure of *'you must'* AND *'you must not'* will surface and this will discourage listeners, mainly because of the realisation that no matter how hard they try, they could not reach a perfect outcome. This kind of preaching would surely not offer any hope and encouragement, because the harder listeners try to satisfy the preacher, the more the realisation of imperfection will emerge.

Within the balanced thought-pattern of the Hebrews sermon, however, an overarching theme is found in that believers have already inherited wonderful things in Christ and should consequently persevere like heirs of the God's glorious promises[18]. This sermon offers a good example of the interrelated aspects of Christ-centred preaching with its balanced and profound focus on listener-orientated communication. The words of exhortation that the Hebrews sermon speak are firmly anchored in the good news and in God's unlimited grace. This is a further indication of what one could describe as the grace of obedience and the grace of changing your attitude according to what the Gospel says. The indicative here could be defined as God's grace for and in us and, without proper communication of this foundation, the act of preaching could be skewed

---

17 Guthrie, *Hebrews*, 139.
18 Cassie J.H. Venter, "Die Gees, die Woord en die bedienaar van die Woord," in *Koninkryk, Gees en Woord*, red. J.C. Coetzee (Pretoria: N.G. Kerkboekhandel, 1988), 371.

in the direction of unilateral communication of the preacher's views. The Hebrews sermon gives insight into of God's planned communication through the ages, namely that preaching of the Gospel '*today*' indeed enjoys important consequences for listeners, because they are confronted by the reflection of what the Gospel asks from them around the concreteness of their lives. One therefore overlooks the interplay between human- and divine aspects in preaching at one's peril. The Hebrews sermon provides further insight into the reasons why a sermon could be regarded not as a mere human speech but rather as divine discourse[19].

The unique structure of the Hebrews sermon seems to evoke interest from scholars. Griffiths[20] for example reflects on the eleven cycles he has discerned that consist of a threefold pattern of exempla, explanation/application, and exhortation. The importance of Old Testament passages that could be described as the known content to the listeners to the Hebrews sermon is therefore being underlined. The authors will discuss this matter later on in this book in chapter 7. Guthrie[21] continues in this vein and submits a schematic representation of the way in which divine- and human acts[22] are connected, therefore shedding light on the concrete flow of the interrelatedness between explication and application, namely:

---

19 Gerrit Immink, "Naming God's Presence in Preaching," *HTS Teologiese Studies/Theological Studies* 75, no. 4 (2019): 30, a5453, https://doi.org/10.4102/hts.v75i4.5453.
20 Jonathan I. Griffiths, *Hebrews and Divine Speech* (New York: Bloomsbury T&T Clark, 2016), 29-32.
21 Guthrie, *Hebrews*, 128-134.
22 Griffiths, *Hebrews and Divine Speech*, 12.

Exposition	Application
Introduction (Hebrews 1:1-4) God has spoken to us in His Son.	**Application** (Hebrews 2:1-4) Pay careful attention to what you have heard in order not to drift away.
Hebrews 3:1-6 Jesus the apostle and high priest whom we confess.	**Application** (Hebrews 3:7-19) The people who turned away from God died in the dessert. Hold firmly till the end.
Hebrews 4:3-11 A sabbath-rest for the people of God.	**Application** (Hebrews 4:12-13 en 14) Everything is uncovered and laid before God to whom we must give account.
Hebrews 5:11-6:3 Situation of listeners, namely they are slow to listen and to learn.	Application Listeners are slow to listen and therefore slow to obey God.
Hebrews 6:4-8 Hebrews 6:9-12 The preacher's trust in listeners.	Application Hebrews 10:26-32 Show diligence to the very end to make your hope sure.
Hebrews 11:1-40 Positive examples of people in history - faith-pioneers	Application Hebrews 12:1-2 en 3-17 Perseverance and endurance are needed in the race. Strengthen your feeble arms and weak knees.
Hebrews 12:18-24 The blessing of the new covenant and eschatological hope.	Application Hebrews 12:25-29 Let us be thankful and worship God with reverence and awe. **Hebrews 13** - concluding exhortations.
Conclusion- Hebrews 13:22-25: Sermon of encouragement.	

This shows that preaching of the Gospel indeed has an address, namely the listeners. The expression of *'you've got an attitude'* seems to be applicable in the case of listeners. They have observed a major change in their way of worshipping and their difficult circumstances were indeed challenging. This resulted in the emergence of attitudes regarding numerous aspects in their lives. The emphasis on what is heard is therefore unavoidable and should be put into practice by listeners. This is further motivation for sermons that should be grounded in concreteness and that should not function as shots fired in the air merely to scare listeners. The preacher of the Hebrews sermon is well aware of the extent of the attitudinal problem and gives special attention to the listeners' situation in a variety of coherent exhortations that address diverse areas of life including peace-making and sexual purity (12:14, 16-17; 13:4), brotherly love and generous hospitality (13:1-2, 16), compassionate identification with the suffering (13:3) and contentment grounded in the assurance of God's constant presence and provision (13:5-6). It is noteworthy, though, that the Hebrews preacher utilises hortatory subjunctives in the first person plural to exhort the listeners. The preacher obligates himself to the listeners. The notion of a pastoral perception of ethical challenges should not be overlooked when considering homiletical perspectives from the Hebrews sermon. These exhortations are, after all, not simply generic commands: they are specific applications of the call to persevering faith and are designed to fit listeners' circumstances and spiritual needs[23]. The preacher of the Hebrews sermon simultaneously enables contemporary listeners to sermons to understand that the current circumstances of believers are anchored in the past of God's promises, which have been fulfilled already in Christ. Therefore the future is inherently linked with God's eternal heritage for his children, entailing that listening to sermons is an inherently hopeful act that should enable listeners to see matters differently. Consider that listening and seeing can therefore not be separated in the Hebrews sermon. Listening to God's voice is in fact so dynamic that it opens listeners' ears to have fixed eyes on Jesus Christ (see Hebrews 12). The act of listening to sermons is directed towards a new perspective on daily life and the listeners' faith-lives.

Methodological approach of this book
When designing a theoretical framework for practical theology as an academic discipline, consideration should be given to the *theological nature* of this discipline as well as its focus on the element of *praxis*. As a theological discipline, practical theology differs to a certain degree from the approach of other disciplines in the humanities. As a praxis-oriented discipline, it differs from those that work strictly with conceptualizations and do not deal with the interaction between theory and praxis. As a praxis-oriented science, then, practical theology is concerned with the forces that move human beings to action and guide them in certain directions. The subject matter is studied not only with respect to its factuality but also with consideration for its potentiality[24], that is, what must be done to bring about change in a desirable direction. In short, practical theology is not only a *descriptive* science that explores empirical matters (discerning *what* "), but also a *normative* science that offers a

---
23 Johnson, *Him We Proclaim*, 78.
24 J. Firet, *Spreken als een leerling: Praktisch theologische opstellen* (Kampen: Kok, 1987), 123.

vision for how the world should be and suggests ways to make it so (prescribing" *ought*).

The planning and framing of a research project are crucial. The end must be in mind when the project starts. A research statement, a topic, a specific, theologically-defined question are necessary with the eye on framing the research. For the purpose of framing and specifying a research project of this nature, the following overarching research question has been formulated by us for the purpose here:

> ***What kind of perspectives could an investigation***
> ***of the Hebrews sermon offer to the homiletical praxis***
> ***of people living in arduous times?***

What follows will be organized according to a qualitative literature study, acknowledging existing materials offered by research in this field[25]. The latter will be organised and critically interpreted in light of the research problem. We recognize the inter-disciplinary approach of the social sciences as well as an intra-disciplinary approach, and references will be made to various disciplines[26][27]. In practical theology, research focuses on communicative acts, which dovetails with other sciences that have the same focus. Heitink's[28] distinction between two different concepts or kinds of understanding of praxis is important in this respect. He wrote that theory and praxis are twin moments of the same activity.

In short, research in practical theological research has to do with *hermeneutical interaction between theory and praxis*. In its most basic form, practical theological research consists of observing human actions and considering these actions with the goal of designing descriptive, interpretive and strategic theory for improving the human condition. Bearing in mind that the research is focused on events in the process of unfolding in a certain direction, the relationship between theory and praxis cannot be visualised as a static relationship. The theoretical indicators designed for renewal of praxis are met with a certain reaction in praxis that calls for re-interpretation of various movements and re-alignment of the way in which strategic theoretical elements are articulated.

---

25 Y. Bothma et al., *Research in Health Sciences* (Cape Town: Pearson, 2003).
26 M.J. Cartledge, *Practical Theology: Charismatic and Empirical Perspectives* (London: Paternoster, 2003), 15.
27 Hennie J.C. Pieterse, *Preaching in the Context of Poverty* (Pretoria: UNISA Press, 2001), 13.
28 G. Heitink, *Practical Theology* (Grand Rapids: Eerdmans, 1999), 21.

Therefore, practical theological research is seen as cyclical, in that it constantly re-assesses its results as new information and insights emerge.

Refers to the mediation of the Christian faith (praxis 1) in the praxis of modern society (praxis 2). Much of the confusion regarding the unique object of practical theology has to do with the failure to make a logical and methodological distinction between the two. Praxis 1 indicates that the unique object of practical theology is related to intentional, more specifically, intermediary or mediative, actions, with a view to changing a given situation through agogics. Praxis 2 emphasises the context, where these actions take place, as a dynamic context in which men and women in society interact, whether or not their actions are religiously motivated while pursuing various goals (emphasis ours).

Heitink admits that the two praxes interrelate constantly and that their interconnectedness must be adequately stressed. By emphasising that practical theology focusses on the mediation of Christian faith, his work interlocks with Firet[29], who says: *'God's coming to humanity in the world is a constant and ever-recurring event that takes place through the intermediary of human ministry'* (our emphasis).

The encounter between God and human beings as mediated by the communicative act of preaching takes place within the existential realm and context of everyday living: this is called the praxis of life. This encounter and intervention have traditionally been referred to as the covenantal encounter between God and human beings. In terms of practical theological terminology, one can translate this covenantal encounter as the praxis of God[30].

As it were, practical theology does not only consider what it can contribute to interdisciplinary discourses regarding transformation, but also what lessons can be learnt through these discourses[31]. We purposefully want to link up with the approach of critical correlation according to the description of Ballard and Pritchard[32], since it allows us to set up a dialogue between questions related to ministry, that is, homiletical praxis on the one hand, and perspectives that come forth in the Hebrews sermon on the other. A theological perspective will be offered that indubitably leads to a homiletical theory at the end of the book. To this end, interrelatedness between the Hebrews sermon and present reality will be kept

---

29 Firet, *Spreken als een leerling*, 31-32.
30 Louw, "Preaching as Art," 175.
31 Rick R. Osmer, *Practical Theology: An Introduction* (Grand Rapids: Eerdmans, 2008), 164-166.
32 P. Ballard and J. Pritchard, *Practical Theology in Action: Christian Thinking in the Service of Church and Society* (London: Ashford Colour Press, 2006), 63-66.

in mind throughout. We further intend to integrate these perspectives throughout. Hermeneutic overlapping among chapters will be kept in mind to arrive at a homiletic theory at the end of this book. Although this book comprises of various sections, we will ensure that these sections will function in the mode of interconnectedness. Above, we have commenced already with the descriptive aspect of what has been occurring in the midst of arduous and challenging circumstances. Furthermore, theological perspectives from the Hebrews sermon will be examined towards the homiletic theory to be formulated.

Delineation of perspectives from the Hebrews sermon should start with the notion of its beauty, which is anchored in a God who always stays the same. Everything in the world is subjected to change, but this sermon finds solace in the fact that God is constant. By elaborating on the Old Testament passages, the preacher of the Hebrews sermon brings home the bottom line that God always stays the same, and what he has done, is doing and will do in future, while speaking in Christ or what one could term *Christopraxis*[33]. Based on this important consideration, the book will be outlined as follows:

- In accordance with the methodology set out by Ballard and Pritchard (discussed above), the book will comprise three sections. A dialogue between homiletical matters and the Hebrews sermon will firstly be offered. A second section, namely theological perspectives, will then be offered and, subsequently, a homiletical theory will be arrived at.
- In the first four chapters, typical homiletical aspects will be addressed that will include an examination of a deeper-seated attitudinal problem that was influential in necessity to deliver this sermon. It will also be indicated that preaching (communication) of the Gospel could be regarded as an important manifestation of persuasive communication. Persuasive preaching should not be confused with a manipulative approach towards preaching.
- Within chapters 6-10 the importance of active listening to sermons to persevere and to live in an ethical manner will be addressed. The important features of the Hebrews sermon to develop and strengthen listeners will also be scrutinized to provide a homiletical theory at the end of this book. Listening also entails seeing and finding delightful meaningfulness in listening to sermons will also be addressed.

---

33 Johnson, *Him We Proclaim*, 86.

We aim to provide a perspective on a homiletical praxis that has to deal with guidance to listeners who experience agonizing uncertainty in daily life due to arduous circumstances. Listeners who fear their circumstances could easily yearn for things, even things from the so-called good old days, that they believe will negotiate their paralyzing apprehensions[34].

In such a context, preaching should not only describe and name the reality of paradoxes, but also has to be influential in creating a different and hopeful reality, an aspect that the above mentioned author described as wholeness[35]. We have to acknowledge the existing of an underlying field of tension in this regard. Preaching has to open new perspectives and indeed has to be influential in picturing new horizons towards understanding the purpose of life, but it should also be acknowledged that people often mistrust sermons, especially ones on the end times, because of a fear that it is manipulative.

We will therefore try to provide a perspective from a sermon that was once communicated to listeners who also doubted numerous things and even the functioning of the message about Christ. The Hebrews sermon could for the same reason also offer insightful perspectives to people who reflect on how to engage with listeners in arduous times. In addition to the aspects mentioned, two aspects deserve particular attention, as discussed briefly below.

Descriptive perspectives on the relevance of the Hebrews sermon for present realms of life

Grethlein[36] states that preaching also centres on reflecting on the communication of the Gospel to listeners within the present realms of daily life. The interplay between life and meaningfulness has increasingly come into play over the past years. Communication of the Gospel should inevitably enable listeners to cope with demands of daily living and the idea of *helfen zum leben* [assistance for life] should be regarded as important[37]. Preaching that deals with life-help or life-support is worth reflecting on. For example, pandemics and trauma that occur within the realms of daily life have the potential to reshape people's experiences in society.

---

34 B. Goudzwaart, M. van der Vennen, and D. Van Heemst, *Hope in Troubled Times: A New Vision for Confronting Global Crises* (Grand Rapids: Baker Academic, 2017), 57.
35 J. Müller, "Mense, verhale en struktuur: Armoede narratief benader," in *God in 'n kantelende wêreld*, eds. F.G. Immink and C. Vos (Pretoria: Protea, 2009), 23.
36 C. Grethlein, *Praktische Theologie* (Berlin: De Gruyter, 2012), 12.
37 Grethlein, *Praktische Theologie*, 166.

As mentioned above, Covid-19 has rapidly thrown the world into a cyclone of fear and chaos. Preachers deliver their sermons either within the empty space of a church-building or by streaming their messages to a virtual audience. The burning issue of participating in liturgy and the act of preaching given the constraints of the physical absence of the community of believers poses intriguing challenges worthy of debate. The fundamental issue of caring for other people without enjoying contact with them offers a difficult and awkward puzzle. It seems that Covid-19 invokes further reflection on how to act around the challenge of physical absence in which a praxis of being in close contact with a faith-community is suddenly altered. The lasting effects of engaging in alternative ways to worship and preach will become known only in future.

According to Rosenberg[38], epidemics unfold as social dramas in three acts. The earliest signs of an epidemic are subtle. Whether influenced by a desire for self- reassurance or a need to protect economic interests, citizens ignore clues that something is awry until the acceleration of illness and deaths forces reluctant acknowledgment[39]. Recognition of the seriousness of an epidemic launches the second act in which people demand and offer mechanistic and moral explanations. The explanations, in turn, generate public responses and further increase feelings of fear and uncertainty. These can make the third act as dramatic and disruptive as the disease itself. Epidemics eventually resolve, whether by succumbing to societal action or having exhausted the supply of susceptible victims. As Rosenberg puts it, *'Epidemics start at a moment in time, proceed on a stage limited in space and duration, follow a plot line of increasing revelatory tension, move to a crisis of individual and collective character, then drift toward closure'*[40] (our emphasis). This drama has been playing out around Covid-19, first in China and now in many countries worldwide[41]. People are suddenly confronted by intense pressure in how to react against contagious diseases that tenders the challenge of a ban on social gatherings. The extent of this tension offers dynamic opportunities to reflect on matters that people value as important[42].

Keeping a safe distance between people, including limited opportunities to worship with other people, has inevitably changed people's thinking processes about the essence of preaching. Fears about what should be

---

38 C.E. Rosenburg, "Pathologies of Progress: The Idea of Civilization as Risk," *Bulletin of the History of Medicine* 72, no. 4 (Winter 1998): 7.
39 D.S. Jones, *History in a Crisis: Lessons for Covid-19* (Cambridge: Harvard, 2020), 3.
40 Rosenburg, "Pathologies of Progress," 6.
41 Jones, *History in a Crisis*, 1-2.
42 Jones, *History in a Crisis*, 2.

changed to manage the catastrophic effects of the coronavirus furthermore play an underlying role in shaping people's attitudes at a time of social distancing. The new way of being in the world and of being apart of a community of faith are pivotal aspects to reflect on. The lifestyle involving the presence of others has changed to a reality of being absent; this could go along with an attitude of comfort around not attending sermons.

It therefore seems likely that numerous topics addressed in the Hebrews sermon confront today's listeners. For instance, keeping social distance could provide dynamic opportunities to profoundly reflect on connectivity to listeners via the online environment. It seems likely that people have to engage in new avenues to connect and this quest will surely influence homiletical praxis. The longing for the good old days where listeners could have encouraged each other in a visible manner while being present within a liturgical space of a church building, could in future become a prominent phenomenon and this is also why the Hebrews sermon could offer informative perspectives on preaching to listeners in arduous times.

Gerrit Immink, a much-discussed homiletic scholar, announces an intriguing that 'the preaching practice is rooted in a reciprocity between the gathered community and the preacher. There would be no preaching without a gathered community and without the interaction between the community and the preacher'[43] (our emphasis). The reality of a lockdown persuades one to revisit the Immink's accepted principles around being together and dynamic interaction between preacher and listeners. Theory and practice once again experience a field of tension here that calls on acute reflection on uncertainty, even when it comes to theological definitions of concepts. Within the framework of Immink's distinction one could once again note something of a difficult problem, also called conundrum. The essence of Immink's view has been put under the spotlight by practical experience around uncertainty within a period of extreme measures of social isolation. Interaction between preacher and listeners as well as profound community are focal aspects to be reflected on when listeners and preachers are dependent on communication via the online environment. It is clear that, without thorough planning, preaching can degenerate into a hit-and-miss affair in which no depth and growth in a specific direction are accomplished. Without good planning, the preacher can lose touch with the full extent of the life that the congregation is embedded in. God is under way with each congregation and the minister of the Gospel should continually be occupied with a thorough examination of the spiritual condition of the congregation. He

---

43 Immink, "God's Presence," 3.

should try to determine the aspects around which spiritual equipment is needed to lead the congregation to maturity in Christ as well as what is needed to achieve God's purpose for that particular congregation in the particular community where he has called him or her to.

The importance of sermon analysis and sermon discussion before the sermon as well as an analysis of preaching afterwards could contribute towards an environment of collaborative preaching to mediate the field of tension identified above, especially when listeners are limited to the online environment only.

Descriptive perspectives on the relevance of the Hebrews sermon and the realms of daily living in the space where God's presence is experienced

In the previous sections, we refer to listeners of the Hebrews sermon that longed for the good old days where God's presence in the temple was visible. Space as such created challenges to listeners of this sermon. Within their circumstances they were confronted with the message of Christ's victory. They could not see and were not able to touch upon the reality of this message within a particular holy space. They became disheartened and suddenly doubted the meaningfulness of acts of faith.

The reminder within the Hebrews sermon that meaningfulness is integrated within a Person, namely Christ, calls on further reflection on the value of religious spaces for worshipping. This concern especially emerges within countries that are forced to engage in a lock-down situation where churches are confronted with the issue of how to interact with the people who belong to a community of faith. The present book endeavours to demonstrate that the church building should not be confused with the actual church[44]. The place of worshipping, namely the liturgical space of a church building, nonetheless remains functional for participants in liturgy to assemble. The true identity of the church however remains in people and not in buildings[45]. Having said this, one should simultaneously remember the importance of liturgical space in functioning as a powerful communicative medium. Through embodiment in a church building the danger of disembodiment is minimized[46].

The drastic steps of the lock-downs as well as the emphasis on social distancing challenge local churches mainly because of the conviction that

---

44 P. Post, *Place of Action: Exploring the Study of Space, Ritual and Religion* (Leuven: Peeters, 2008), 39.
45 R.H. Roberts, *Space, Time and the Sacred in Modernity/Postmodernity* (Leuven: Peeters, 2001), 340.
46 Roberts, *Space, Time*, 340.

the place of worship should be regarded as holy. This holy place is regarded as apart from the routine of responsibilities of daily life. Throughout history, evidence is found that believers were challenged by concrete circumstances and the importance of homes were emphasised[47]. People's homes were adjusted to have a new function to communicate the essence of worshipping. This became even truer during times of persecution and of epidemics in history. It is important to realise that people rather than buildings should always be seen as pivotal. It seems that churches worldwide are being challenged to alter spaces, including their buildings, to develop and strengthen listeners within a changing context. The challenge for churches will be to elaborate on the principle that form should follow function[48]. A renewed focus on the liturgy of a local congregation and a sharpened vision on how liturgy could enable listeners to participate in their liturgy should realise be established. It should be emphasised that this kind of reflection is needed not only during a time of social distancing but constantly.

A decrease in the mobility of all people, not restricted to elderly people, has been occurring. The possibilities of what could be called a virtual church is indeed challenging in its essence. Church buildings are provide the privilege of experiencing the sacred within a visual space and with communion among participants in liturgy[49]. The senses of listeners are therefore cultivated within a space where the message is audible and visible. Noll[50] underlines that the interest of people in the internet is increasing on a daily basis. The unprecedented potential of offering instant messages and effective connection with listeners calls for examination on a more substantial basis[51]. At a time of self-isolation, connectivity to other people and of social networking could still proceed via this powerful tool. People are in fact already connected to people within a global village.

---

47 M.F. Schoombie, *Staila Liturgy: Exploring Space as an Active Element in Liturgy* (Pretoria: Protea, 2015), 15.
48 F. Viola and G. Barna, *Pagan Christianity? Exploring the Roots of Our Church Practices* (New York: BarnaBooks, 2012), 38.
49 Duncan Stroik, "The Church Building as a Sacred Place: Beauty, Transcendence, and the Eternal," Free Enterprise Institute, February 2, 2013, http://www.theimaginative conservative.org/2013/02/the-church-building-as-sacred- place.html.
50 M.A. Noll, *Turning Points: Decisive Moments in the History of Christianity*, 3rd ed. (Grand Rapids: Baker Academic, 2012), 23.
51 Noll, *Turning Points*, 25.

Howard and Magee [52] are in favour of increasing investment in online communication, which underlines the importance of church buildings that enhance face-to-face meetings, while it simultaneously emphasises the value of the internet in creating or producing interactive life experiences to those who would otherwise not be able to communicate. The use of technology not only serves as catalyst in bringing friends together in virtual social settings, but introduces strangers who have a commonality of purpose, views or belief systems[53]. The final outcome of the Covid-19 pandemic is not known to us, but it seems to indicate already that reflection by practical theologians is urgently necessary. The impact of a virtual community rather than a gathered community within one building should receive attention. To our mind, one thing should be clear. Whether participants assemble in a building or interact within a virtual environment, an inviting hospitality should be evident. God's presence through His Spirit and the profound message in Christ should be the igniting factors here.

The Hebrews sermon is, after all, an indication that people search for something they could touch and see. The challenge within arduous times will be to utilise all available resources to communicate in such a manner that listeners could hear in order for them so see that God has indeed spoken to them within the last days. Response to difficult life situations is often challenging because there are no prescribed texts with immediate, instant answers to the difficulties posed. What is most needed in preaching is the creativity to probe new or different options[54]. The Hebrews sermon provides a framework to engage in exactly this endeavour. Preaching as God-talk evokes God's presence and his voice. This will always be a mystery, namely that preachers could dare to speak about God and that listeners have the expectation that preachers should do exactly this.

---

52 M.C. Howard and S.M. Magee, "To Boldly Go Where No Group Has Gone before: An Analysis of Online Group Identity and Validation of a Measure," *Computers in Human Behaviour* 29, no. 5 (2013): 13, DOI: 10.1016/j.chb.2013.04.009 2013.
53 Howard and Magee, "Boldly Go," 15.
54 Louw, "Preaching as Art," 17.

REFERENCES

Ballard, P. and J. Pritchard. *Practical Theology in Action: Christian Thinking in the Service of Church and Society.* London: Ashford Colour Press, 2006.

Beach, J.M. "The Real Presence of Christ Preaching of the Gospel: Luther and Calvin on the Nature of Preaching." *Mid-America Journal of Theology* 10, no. 1 (1999).

Bordieu, P. *The Weight of the World: Social Suffering in Contemporary Society.* Oxford: Polity, 1999.

Bothma, Y., M. Greeff, F.M. Mulaudzi, and S.C.D. Wright. *Research in Health Sciences.* Cape Town: Pearson, 2003.

Browning, Don S. *A Fundamental Practical Theology: Descriptive and Strategic Proposals.* Minneapolis: Fortress, 1996.

Cartledge, M.J. *Practical Theology: Charismatic and Empirical Perspectives.* London: Paternoster, 2003.

Coetzee, J.C. *Gedagtestruktuur van Hebreërs [Thought structure of Hebrews].* Potchefstroom: Fakulteit Teologie, 1986.

Du Toit, Anrie. *Hebreërs vir vandag [Hebrews for today].* Vereeniging: CUM boeke, 2004.

Firet, J. *Spreken als een leerling: Praktisch theologische opstellen.* Kampen: Kok, 1987.

Goudzwaart, B., M. van der Vennen, and D. van Heemst. *Hope in Troubled Times: A New Vision for Confronting Global Crises.* Grand Rapids: Baker Academic, 2017.

Grethlein, C. *Praktische Theologie.* Berlin: De Gruyter, 2012.

Griffiths, Jonathan I. *Hebrews and Divine Speech.* New York: Bloomsbury T&T Clark, 2016.

Guthrie, Donald. *Hebrews.* Tyndale New Testament Commentaries. Grand Rapids: Eerdmans, 1996.

Heitink, G. *Practical Theology.* Grand Rapids: Eerdmans, 1999.

Howard, M.C. and S.M. Magee. "To Boldly Go Where No Group Has Gone before: An Analysis of Online Group Identity and Validation of a Measure." *Computers in Human Behaviour* 29, no. 5 (2013). DOI: 10.1016/j.chb.2013.04.009 2013.

Immink, Gerrit. "Naming God's Presence in Preaching." *HTS Teologiese Studies/Theological Studies* 75, no. 4 (2019): a5453, https://doi.org/10.4102/hts.v75i4.5453.

Johnson, D.E. *Him We Proclaim: Preaching Christ from all Scriptures.* New Jersey: P&R Publishing, 2007.

Johnson, D.E. *Preaching to a Postmodern World.* New Jersey: P&R Publishing, 2006.

Jones, D.S. *History in a Crisis: Lessons for Covid-19*. Cambridge: Harvard, 2020.

Kistemaker, Simon J. *Hebrews*. New Testament Commentary. Grand Rapids: Baker Book House, 1994.

Lewicki, Tomasz. *"Weist nicht ab den Sprechenden!" Wort Gottes und Paraklese im Hebräerbrief*. Paderborn: Ferdinand Schöningh, 2004.

Long, Thomas G. *Preaching from Memory to Hope*. Louisville: John Knox Press, 2009.

Louw, D.J. "Preaching as Art (Imaging the Unseen) and Art as Homiletics (Verbalising the Unseen): Towards the Aesthetics of Iconic Thinking and Poetic Communication in Homiletics." *HTS Teologiese Studies/ Theological Studies* 72, no. 2 (2016): a3826, http://dx.doi.org/10.4102/hts.v72i2.3826.

Müller, J. "Mense, verhale en strukture: Armoede narratief benader." In *God in 'n kantelende wêreld*, edited by F.G. Immink and C. Vos. Pretoria: Protea, 2009.

Noll, M.A. *Turning Points: Decisive Moments in the History of Christianity*. 3rd ed. Grand Rapids: Baker Academic, 2012.

Osmer, Rick R. *Practical Theology: An Introduction*. Grand Rapids: Eerdmans, 2008.

Pieterse, Hennie J.C. *Preaching in the Context of Poverty*. Pretoria: UNISA Press, 2001.

Post, P. *Place of Action: Exploring the Study of Space, Ritual and Religion*. Leuven: Peeters, 2008.

Roberts, R.H. *Space, Time and the Sacred in Modernity/Postmodernity*. Leuven: Peeters, 2001.

Robinson, M. "In principio erat sermo." In *Viva Vox Evangelii: Reforming Preaching*. Studia Homiletica 9. Edited by J. Hermelink and A. Deeg. Leipzig: Evangelische Verlaganstalt, 2015.

Rosenburg, C.E. "Pathologies of Progress: The Idea of Civilization as Risk." *Bulletin of the History of Medicine* 72, no. 4 (Winter 1998).

Schoombie, M.F. *Staila Liturgy: Exploring Space as an Active Element in Liturgy*. Pretoria: Protea, 2015.

Stroik, Duncan. "The Church Building as a Sacred Place: Beauty, Transcendence, and the Eternal." Free Enterprise Institute. February 2, 2013. http://www.theimaginativeconservative.org/2013/02/the-church-building-as-sacred-place.html.

Venter, Cassie J.H. "Die Gees, die Woord en die bedienaar van die Woord." In *Koninkryk, Gees en Woord*, edited by J.C. Coetzee. Pretoria: N.G. Kerkboekhandel, 1988.

Vines, J. *The Believers Guide to Hebrews.* New Jersey: Loizeaux, 1993.
Viola, F. and G. Barna. *Pagan Christianity? Exploring the Roots of our Church Practices.* New York: BarnaBooks, 2012.

CHAPTER 1
ON SPEAKING TERMS

Preaching and the voice of God

Maarten Kater

Hebrews has been called 'the Cinderella' of New Testament studies. At least during the middle part of the 20th century, she had her admirers, though comparatively few. Yet, at the dawn of the 2first century, she seems to have come out of obscurity and be - like Cinderella - on her way to the ball, that is, she has of late been invoking a steady stream of commentaries, monographs and articles. Dissertations on the book seem to be on the rise. Nevertheless, no volume has been published on the lessons to be learned from this part of Scripture around the area of practical theology in general and, more specifically, of homiletics.

One of the most important characteristics of Hebrews is the phrase right at the beginning that reads: 'God has spoken'. This canonical sermon thus emphasises a theology of language, of the gift of communication by means of verbally speaking, using our voices. However, before we humans utter one single word, God has spoken in the past and - as Hebrews tells us again and again - God speaks in the present. This 'sermon' - divine speech - comes first, and only after that does homiletics as the scientific research on and consideration of our sermons comes into play. 'The most basic, widespread concept with which the texts identify themselves is divine speech […] since thereby the Bible incorporates both "personal" and "propositional" aspects in its self-presentation', as Treier eloquently states.

It is of course very clear that preaching - delivering a sermon - mainly consists of speaking, although everyone knows that using words is not all that communication is about, because important non-verbal aspects of communication create meaning even when no word is uttered when there is nothing but silence. However, in this chapter I would like to investigate primarily what Hebrews says, not so much about our voices, but the reality of the 'voice of God' and what this means for preaching. We hear in preaching that Divine Voice in the very words of Scripture while listening to a sermon from the mouth of the preacher as he voices the message of a canonical text.

What does this chapter offer with a view to this focal motif in Hebrews? First, it performs a brief phenomenological exploration on the gift of the human tongue (language), the ability and power of using our voice to communicate. Second, the connection of communication and communion will be discussed to see what communication *of* and even *in* God means when one speaks of the voice of God. Third, with reference to Hebrews, that which is meant by the Voice of God will be examined, and, finally, I end up with reflections on the *praesentia realis*. Indeed, God speaks to us in the present time, today. 'Today, when you hear His Voice', as the saying goes. All of this will be engaged to reflect theologically on preaching as part and parcel of homiletics.

1.1 The gift of the human voice - a phenomenological exploration

Considering the human voice theologically is to open the book of creation as related in Genesis humanity. Our capacity to speak in verbal sounds, using names and verbs in many timbres, stems from and is part of being created in or after the image of God. It is important, then, to see that the human voice is a gift for being called to respond to - as his creature - the voice of God. Our voice must even represent - as the image of God - his voice. Succinctly put, humanity is *homo respondens*. 'In the beginning' (Gen. 1:1) sounds the creative voice of God, and only by his voice was Adam given the power of speech to give names to all animals (Gen. 2:19). Adam received, so to speak, the dictionary and grammar of the Spirit of God. Any human being ultimately lives on the breath of God's voice to speak in wisdom, love and truth. All words, then, are created realities. 'Words are those realities by which the Holy Spirit enables created intellects, sometimes, when and as God pleases, to articulate the truth of the creator and his creation'. However, after the fall, humanity still had the ability and great privilege to utter meaningful words, but their language suffered from sin and no longer was fundamentally pneumatological at all. We hear Adam and Eve speaking harsh words to each other, their son Cain speaking bitter words from a jealous heart and Lamech uttering oppressive words merely for the sake of oppressing. So, then: 'Human beings are fallen beings who can articulate the truth, either of the world or of God, only by a kind of redemption of their created faculties'.

Of course, Scripture on many occasions gives insight into what a voice does, for bad or for good. Acquiring a modicum of sensitivity for the gift of speech and the responsibility humanity has for its tongue, I give examples from the book of Proverbs in which daily- and spiritual life are united in the fear of the Lord as the beginning of wisdom. In the life of a *wise* man - one who fears the LORD - Proverbs distinguishes between the power, the character and the source of words. A word has the power

- even of life and death (12:6;13:14;15:4;18:21);
- to heal and to wound (11:9,11;12:18;15:4,30;16:24).

What a voice is able to prompt in the life of the one who is addressed, is remarkable. Everybody experiences the reality that human words are not just neutral sounds that disappear after a few vibrations of the air.

Surely, though, there are limitations to what words may achieve:
- they cannot alter the facts (26:23-26);
- they cannot compel response (29:19;
- they are not a substitute for deeds (14:23).

As far as the character of words is concerned, Proverbs makes clear that words from the wise man are honest, not false (12:22, 16:13), few, not many (10:19), not boastful (27:2), not contentious (29:9) and not gossip (10:18, 11:13, 20:19, 26:20-22). Wise words are not emotional but rational (15:28;17:27), gentle and peaceable (15:1,18) yet persuasive (25:15), and apt, not untimely (15:23;25:11). The source of words is the heart (4:23): one utters - or at least indicates - what is in his inner being. True words are revealing.

As part of practical theology, homiletics will listen to other disciplines in thinking about language. A very instructive perspective has been given from a phenomenological philosophical point of few by the Jewish-German historian and sociologist Eugene Rosenstock-Huessy (1888-1973). In my opinion his theory (philosophy) of language, known as speech-thinking, gives us an astute illustration of how one is able to bridge the gap between the reflection on the relation of the Word and words of God on the one hand, and human speech on the other - and that is one of the considerable questions in homiletics - by what is called speech-thinking.

I subsequently consider one or two aspects of this manner of thinking. Formal speech is what creates us as human beings. 'It intends to form the listener into a being which did not exist before he or she was spoken to. Human speech is formative and it is for this reason that it has become explicit and grammatical [...] [L]anguage can name a place, Tipperary in Ireland, and a child, Dorothy, the gift of God. This, animals cannot do'. If, as Rosenstock-Huessy reasons, we are formed by speech, the most basic hypothesis is that through understanding the structure of speech we can improve understanding of the nature of our humanity. It would follow that speech reflects our social health and is the path towards social regeneration. 'Forms of language move people who speak and who listen, into the field of correspondence and out of it again. Speech is movement'.

According to Rosenstock, the four root sentences - 'answer me,' 'may I have an answer,' 'I have answered you' and 'he is answering you,' -enjoy a logical sequence. Imperative must precede optative, which must precede the narrative, which must precede the indicative. However, the vocative has the ultimate priority. We should not start with the 'I' at all. Long before I have developed self-consciousness and can say 'I', I have been addressed as a 'You' and heard my name. In his most famous work entitled *Die Sprache des Menschengeslechts* (1962-1963) [*The Language of Human Race*] in four volumes (1962-1963), Rosenstock put it summarized this way. One has given me an own name, therefore I am. Being is to be addressed by one's name. According to Rosenstock a human being is first 'you' and only then 'I'. The vocative precedes, followed by the imperative, as the authentically creative *Modus der Verwandlung* [mode of transformation].

Just one more illustration from Rosenstock's thoughts to demonstrate how much homileticians and preachers can learn from his insights when they would like to speak seriously of speech. Our speech is posited in and is the origin of what Rosenstock calls the 'cross of reality' consisting of the dimensions of time and space:

- When we speak we are connected through the millennia with the dawn of humanity because we try to use the *proper* words;
- We look forward to the future (in Rosenstock's words, 'the completion of its evolution') because we combine the heritage of the ages in an *answerable*, that is, a new way;
- We *express* the inner man's intentions and emotions, and thereby complete them and 'get them out of our system' as everyday parlance says;
- We register the external processes that touch our senses, and we are not satisfied before our sensations have been *clarified* in scientific language.

Whenever we speak, we assert our being alive because we occupy a centre from which the eye looks backward, forward, inward and outward. To speak means to be placed at the centre of what he called the cross of reality.

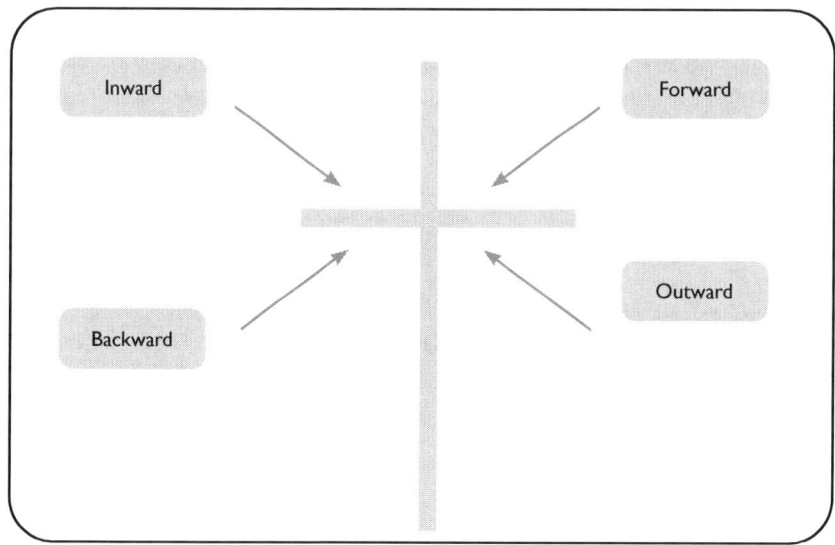

Here a human being speaks from an inner space to an outer world and from an outer world into his own consciousness. And *now* he speaks between the beginning and the end of times[1]. Rosenstock shows in any case how strongly communication is connected with the intense relation between a speaker and his or her listeners.

It's a small exploration, but it carries some important homiletical implications:
- Seen from the book of creation:
- The necessity of a theological view of speech and language as a means of communication, given by our Creator, ultimately in and through his Son and exercised by his Spirit by the renewing of our minds.
- From the perspective of the book of Proverbs:
  ° The immense power of just a single word (, that is, naming!) and the exercise of becoming wise before one becomes a preacher. However, words and their use in writing and speech also reveal ambivalences and discrepancies. The intoxication of words with framing and equivocation, with cacophony and euphemism, with fake news and rumour, with propaganda and agitation, lurches resoundingly between truth and untruth, between orientation and seduction, between words of life or death. Words encourage or hurt, bring joy or fear, enlighten or manipulate, open up meaning or indoctrinate.

---

1 E. Rosenstock-Huessy, *Speech and Reality* (Norwich: Argo Books, 1970), 51-52.

- ○ True words are revealing: God speaks, that is, we hear his heart beat and so does a preacher when he ministers the Word.
- From a phenomenological / philosophical point of view:
  - ○ Being addressed by one's name is being called to live and to love.
  - ○ A theological interpretation in the field of homiletics from Rosenstock's 'cross of reality' with men in the centre is, for example, to flip the arrows in the scheme above: God addressed men from inwardly ('in his Son'), and outwardly (by the prophets and apostles) and he does so by speaking from the front (resurrection as the breakthrough of the future) and the back (history of Israel and especially of Christ).

1.2 Communication is relation

Real communication is a matter of communion (Lat. *communio*) between a speaker and the person addressed. If there is no communion, the speaker does not seem to have any respect for his hearers. Vice versa, without communion every communication will be fruitless or in the worst case only evoke envy and anger. The purpose of real communication is to institute or evoke a relationship. Long before the word 'homiletics' came into use, the art of preaching was referred to not only as *ars preadicare*, but also as *ars concionandi*. The verb *concionare* has to do with the *contio* (abbreviation of *conventio*), which refers to a people's assembly, convened by a magistrate to make some kind of announcement, generally for all public and religious acts of officials and priests, to promulgate edicts, or to debate any subject matter. And this *contio* was the result of *convenire* (coming together) and is related to a *convention*, an agreement between a speaker and the public. So, the area of homiletics is about the *ars concionandi* as many homiletical works were called throughout the 16th to the 18th centuries. Real *homilein* is about having a dialogue, as shown in the beautiful and instructive example on the Road to Emmaus (Luke 24).

According to Christian Grethlein, the communication of the Gospel is the central theme of practical theology in general[2]. He outlines practical theology as consisting of hermeneutical framework, empirical conditions and theological foundations. In thinking theologically about communication -of which preaching is an important part- Hebrews shows us first of all the communication in God or God in communication within

---

2 Christian Grethlein, *An Introduction to Practical Theology: History, Theory, and the Communication of the Gospel in the Present*, trans. U. Rasch (Waco: Baylor University Press, 2016).

himself. The idea of 'God as Communion' (Zizioulas)[3] certainly contains the danger of tritheism, but actually does justice to what Scriptures teach us about the One God in three Persons. God never has been a lonely Subject as Father, Son and Holy Spirit. First and foremost, Hebrews brings us to a wonderful communication within the communion of God.

Indeed, Hebrews underscores a conspicuous fact about this. The voice of God - and for the time being I am using this indication for the speaking of God in words - has not sounded 'to us' in this cosmos in the first place. I am not referring to the 'after' as the conjunction that expresses the priority of 'the fathers' (1:1). The voice of God sounded before there was any human ear to capture these creative sounds. According to Hebrews, this creative speaking is explicitly connected to the Son 'through Whom He created the world' (1:2). Speaking 'in these last days' (1:1) happens *in* the Son, but it is therefore emphatically connected with God's speech in creation. This speaking is the deathblow for every form of middle-platonic thinking, a thinking from 'down here it is not'. For 'down here,' He came as a human being and still is by means of his word: 'He carries all things by His mighty word' (1:3).

So, then, the first word turns out not to be addressed 'to us'. It sounded even earlier than the moment of creation. When did it ring earlier? The answer is 'before all times', namely, as the word of the Father to the Son and the answer of the Son to the Father. So it was a two-way conversation, a dialogue! The extent to which Christology and theology, then, are connected in the speaking of God is shown first of all by this conversation from the Father to the Son and from the Son to the Father. All quoted words from Scripture, the so-called *qatena* in 1:5-13 (seven quotes from the Psalms!), sound as words directly from the mouth of the Father to the Son. Likewise this is also the case a few more times in the remainder of the sermon concerning the appointment of the Son as High Priest: 5:5-6 (quote Ps. 2:7) and 7:17, 21 (quote Ps. 110:4).

Conversely, the words from Psalm 22 (2:12 v.) and Psalm 40 (10:5-7) in this sermon sound as the very words from the mouth of Christ the Son to the Father. So, then, the claim of the Father is followed by an answer from the Son. God's claim is always *dabar JHWH*[4] - which is indicating the unity of word and deed - or, to put it in the terms of the familiar speech-act theory, a philosophy of language, it is *performative* in nature; it does have some effect. Jesus is Son and High Priest, because he is

---

3 John D. Zizioulas, *Being As Communion: Studies in Personhood and the Church* (Darton: Longman and Todd, 1985).
4 See '*dbr*' in: William A. van Gemeren, ed., *New International Dictionary of Old Testament Theology and Exegesis*, vol. 3 (Carlisle: Paternoster Press, 1996), 912-915.

addressed and appointed by God. My conclusion is that God's speaking is essentially Christologically determined. That aspect has always been decisive for the timbre of God's voice.

Now the question of course arises how all these Psalms can be quoted without the arbitrary use and filling in of texts? Just by following the rabbinic methods of exegesis? Surely, the author of Hebrews does so (as is discussed elsewhere in this volume), but for him all of the Old Testament's words are living words of the living God, words through which he speaks today (further reflections follow in the next section). Hebrews accentuates this by mentioning the human author only once. Quotations are also not introduced, as is quite the case in Paul's writings, and are indicated not by phrases such as 'as is written', but by the phrase 'as is spoken/said'. This underlines how full Hebrews is of the theology of the glory of God. The use of these somewhat vague indications should be heard in that light. '*Someone* has said something' (2:6) refers to what David says in Psalm 8, but apparently that does not matter at that time. God speaks through these very words. Likewise, when Genesis 2:2 is quoted, it reads: 'He spoke *somewhere* OF THE SEVENTH DAY' (4:4). *Where*, then, are we inclined to ask? Where is that written? The answer to these questions is: 'He has spoken, and so He speaks'! The vivid character of the words of God take shape in the quotation from Psalm 95 as the title of this speech, namely by his voice and by the use of the word 'today', as we will see.

God speaks, but does God have a real voice? When we make the transition from 'speaking' to 'voice', something occurs, something changes. After all, what does hearing a voice do? A voice has something in it of the personal and relational, the uniqueness or particularity of someone. The metaphor of the *voice* keeps together content and sound, including *what* is said, *who* says it (the relational aspect) and the sound/ timbre of the voice, *how* something it is said. Against this background, consider Webb's assertion that the idea that we are most present to each other in sound is also true about God's relationship to us. Only the sense of hearing can do justice to the way God is simultaneously with us and beyond us. Put another way, the voice of God reveals God's innermost purposes without exposing God to our objectifying gaze. Sound is the medium that best carries a supernatural message, because it delivers something external without putting us in control of its source[5].

This seems to me to be an essential aspect of speaking about the voice of God: this Voice reveals God's interior without exposing God to our objectifying gaze. Reading Scripture in this way also makes the claim much more personal: I do not read a letter, but hear the voice of God.

---

5 Webb, *Divine Voice*, 39.

The notion of the 'present' will be discussed later, but now we see that, according to Hebrews, it is connected with the 'present', which the Father speaks to the Son, 'the eternal today of the divine eternity' ('Today I have generated You.'). This manner of theological interpretation reads the texts as *acts of communication* with God as the primary author[6]. Such communication is first and foremost a matter of the communion of Father, Son and Spirit. This determines the theological content of the sermon. Thus, the trinitarian character of the preaching will be expressed, not only when it comes to the application of salvation, but also around when its acquisition is articulated. Moreover, it is not only about what God has done, but most of all about who He is.

Speaking *in* the Son (1:1) in Hebrews belongs to a perspective of speaking *to* the Son (see Col. 1:16). Similarly, Christ was given the Psalms in his mouth in response to the speaking of the Father in the Psalms to His Son, the Kingly High Priest. Thus, Psalm 22 and Psalm 40 sound to us from Jesus' own mouth, and are not arbitrary matters, but are grounded in the depths of the Father's pleasure and gracious will (Matthew 11:25-27).

It is clear from what we have seen around the perspective of a homiletic theology , that is, a theology of sermons, that the speaking of God by means of this voice of God '*to* the Son' with its timbre carrying the reality embodied by the phrase '*in* the Son', are of decisive significance for preaching today. Only by listening to this voice of God can we speak of a full theological homiletics.

1.3 The Voice of God
God speaks *to us*! His communion - as He has in himself as the triune God - is open to humanity. His communication is not just in himself, but reaches out to us. That communication has as its gracious purpose and invitation, to persuade, to evoke, to press by love and many other purposes. God seeks a relation with the world which was shattered by the misuse of language by Satan and humanity's abuse of its own ears. So, then, after the fall, God had to raise his voice to get our attention, not to kill us but save us. Although Hebrews starts so gently and sweetly with 'God has spoken' (1:1), full of grace in his justice and mercy, our distorted senses can make God sound fearsome and menacing (see Gen. 3:8). But again and again His voice rather than hvoice to grant his fallen creatures a place in his communion. Ultimately, He has spoken in his Son, the Word that existed already before the creation of the world. This is the overture Hebrews starts with, creating the background where our hearing

---

6 John Webster, *Holy Scripture: A Dogmatic Sketch* (Cambridge: University Press, 2003), 69.

the voice of God finds itself to be part of a symphony with the beautiful *cantus firmus* contained in the melody of the greatness of Jesus Christ.

1.3.1 Mediated speech
According to the dedication of this sermon (1:1), we hear God's voice in or through others. First of all, the fathers and prophets are mentioned. It is through them that the voice of God sounds and resounds. Also, the present tense is emphasised. There is not a single word that dies in the speaking of God. The 'after' of today and to us - as the other part after the word 'previously' directed at the fathers and the prophets - will not and cannot in any way give the impression that there is a kind of so-called substitute theology in Hebrews. It is very striking, after all, that Hebrews makes focusses intensely on the use of opposites, but in this case there is no mention of a conjunction that suggests even the slightest contradiction between the 'former days' and these 'last days'. On the contrary, this appears to be obvious when, in speaking 'in the Son', the content of the whole world marked by the word 'previously', as found in the *Tanak*, is heard. Certainly, there is also talk of 'how much more around speaking in the Son in 'these last days', but that is based on the continuing line of the indication that 'God has spoken'. Moreover, in the course of this proclamation along this continuum, the example (Hebrews 11) will take its place as the 'cloud of witnesses' (12:1) of the past for the present (see chapter 7).

This recurring phrase, 'how much more' (*kreitton*), or the similarly repeated 'so much better' (*kreitton*), is significant. This *kreitton* sounds with the wonderful *cantus firmus* on Jesus throughout Hebrews[7]. Precisely these expressions of 'more' and 'better' point to a relationship between the Old Testament and New Testament that does justice to both aspects: there is a superlative and therefore also a similarity. The superlative - and there is an antithetical element in it - is expressed rhetorically in the *comparatio* (more on this in chapter 3). A similarity is struck by the preliminary image with which the comparison is made. The example expresses the equivalence between the two members of the comparison. Both modes of argumentation are found in Hebrews. The connection with the Old Testament is also shown by the fact that this sermon makes use of the Jewish-Hellenistic style of sermons. This shows that, from the perspective of the first hearers (Jewish Christians), the connection was also sought by means of the style of sermons.

According to Aristotle, the peculiarity or hallmark of using the *comparatio* is that it 'assumes the actions as undisputed, so that only their

---

[7] Cf. Gudrun Holtz, "Besser und doch gleich: Zur doppelten Hermeneutik des Hebräerbriefes," *Kerygma und Dogma* 58 (2012): 159-177.

size and beauty must be added'. That is why the *Steigerung* (that is, increase) is most suitable for a so-called *epidectic* speech (that is, occasional or festival speech). This means that for this mediated speaking 'in the Son': the 'better' and 'more' of Jesus Christ are based on what is confessed in short sentences in the first verses (1:1-4). This proclamation cannot be reduced to saying something new - it was apparently not necessary to witness this use of a rhetorical means - but, instead, entails singing the praises of Jesus Christ, exalting the greatness and beauty of his deeds. Hebrews can be heard as a eulogy. And it is precisely this eulogy that appears to be closely related to the *paranese*. The 'word of exhortation' (13:22) - as the ultimate purpose of this sermon - may be heard in the sound of 'how much more'. Thus the exhortation in 2:1-3 sounds like a penetrating warning, but it sounds all the more penetrating because at that moment the hymn of praise of the first chapter resounds. A homiletic theology therefore thinks along the lines of salvation history from Old Testament to New Testament, from then to now, and is of a doxological nature.

The mediated speaking carried by the phrase 'in the Son' (1:1) has been preceded by the speaking of God by the fathers and prophets. Typical of the whole sermon is the part of the sermon in which Psalm 95 sings (3:7-4:13). Intentionally it is not said that just the single verse of Psalm 95:7 resounds, because when a verse is quoted the whole context - in this case a Psalm - sounds along with such a verse according to Hays (2014)[8]. In God's speech to both parts of his people - 'then' Israel and 'now' the church - there is first and foremost a fundamental similarity in Hebrews, as mentioned. Therefore, in the 'present', the congregation can be addressed by (means of) the example of the desert generation of Israel. Put otherwise and preferably, addressed 'in' this example, as if they were contemporaries of these people today, addressed in warning and promise. In this way the Christian congregation is also taken *to* or even *in* - which is preferable - the 'cloud of witnesses' that follows in chapter 11. As they were and behaved, we profoundly are and behave[9].

---

8 Richard B. Hays, *Reading Backwards: Figural Christology and the Fourfold Gospel Witness* (Waco: Baylor University Press, 2014).
9 P.M. Eisenbaum, *The Jewish Heroes of Christian History: Hebrew 11 in Literary Context* (Atlanta: Scholars Press, 1997), 82-83.

1.3.2 Embodied speech

God's speaking 'in the Son' has taken on flesh and blood, is embodied in the concrete history of salvation. Thus, in an entirely unique way, the voice of God takes on a very personal character. Thus, when we speak this, the words also acquire vibrance in what we perceive as the Word of God. The 'living and powerful' (4:13) characterization of the speaking of God takes on special meaning when we do what is exhorted (3:1): 'pay careful attention to the High Priest and Apostle, Jesus Christ'. He is the Word in which we hear and see the heart of God. His voice sounds in all kinds of tones, including that of a 'loud cry and under tears' (5:7). He stood out in fear of death, fear was His part, and you can hear that, a definite embodiment of God's compassion! This Voice of God - even in those cries and tears - also belongs emphatically and empathetically to God's speaking 'in the Son' (1:1)[10].

With this embodied speaking belongs a small homiletic turn. Our voice is embodied by our body. 'I see a Voice' seems to me to be an excellent indication of this. That 'seeing' is more than just seeing with one's own eyes or because one obtains insight through the voice in the mind: it amounts to no less than that the word 'seeing' speaks[11]. Therefore, I refer to the fact that the voice is not separately available. How true is this corporeality of our voice when we search for words or when the words occupy us so that we cannot utter one single word and we start to stammer! Then, at that moment, more than our vocal cords vibrate in what we say. In other words: in our vocal cords something of our whole existence resounds, in joy and sorrow, when we sing from the top of our voices and when we stammer in search of words. Our speech does not transmit our inner life, but it *is* our inner life in public form. This will be audible in proclamation. And this, too, deserves theological reflection: how our voice is connected to our sound. Not a play on the pulpit or the stage, but an 'embodied' speech, articulated in mimicry and gesture. That is why it makes a considerable difference whether we hear someone speak or see someone speak. Above all, let us not separate our voices from our hearts. When 'strings of the soul' vibrate, our vocal cords join in.

1.3.3 Acoustic symbiosis

What follows describes what happens when we start reading and especially reading out loud. What happens when the reader is drawn into

---

10 Thomas G. Long, *What Shall We Say? Evil, Suffering, and the Crises of Faith* (Grand Rapids: Wm. B. Eerdmans, 2011).
11 Edith M. Humphrey, *And I Turned to See a Voice* (Grand Rapids: Baker Academic, 2007), 175-178.

the text, also affectively involves participation in the text, and the text is drawn into the reader. The well-known Dutch professor of spirituality, Kees Waaijman, discusses these matters questions in his influential handbook on spirituality *Spiritualiteit. Vormen, grondslagen, methoden* (*Spirituality: Types, Foundations, and Methods*). In my opinion, the following is of great importance for the process of the service of preaching. This more or less involves a phenomenological description of the relationship between voice and body:

> *The text comes to sound in the voice, which is driven by the breath. Voice and breath give the text pitch and melody, drive and power. The breath divides the text into breathing units of shorter or longer duration (the so-called cola) and gives it a more fluid or jolting character. The breath and the voice complete the text saying, reciting or singing. The text is articulated by the throat, the uvula, the tongue, the teeth and the lips. Within each breathing unit they give shape and colour to the syllables [...]. Accentuation and tempo are also determined by breathing. The text is amplified in the sound cavities of the head, chest, abdomen and limbs, which form the primary sound space of the text that is brought to sound*[12].

Then there is the question of rhythm in the length of sentences, sound such as vowels and consonants, repetition- in the form of rhyme, parallelism or paronomasia - and the *melos* that is, circling around a certain tone.

Embodied speech also includes the fact that we use a certain language and that - at least for most people - we find language best if we use our mother tongue. It is language at the moment of communication that really matters.

In sum: within homiletics we deal with God's Voice as mediated and embodied speech, involving mediated speech 'in' or 'through' other media such as fathers, prophets and especially the Son; in this sermon the preacher himself is the medium, embodied speech as our speech does not transmit our inner life, but actually becomes our inner life in public form while our body is connected with our voice as a resonance box physically and emotionally.

---

12 Kees Waaijman, *Spiritualiteit: Vormen, grondslagen, methoden* (Kampen: Kok, 2000), 736 (my translation).

1.4 God speaks 'today'

'Today, if you hear his voice', says Hebrews. How can words from the past become present? And then it does not involve the question of how it can seem *as if* they are becoming present, but really about the *reality* that those words are present. What the present exactly is, nobody seems to know in our four-dimensional space-time[13]. Although this may be true, in this paragraph just two theological aspects are mentioned which are of great importance when dealing with the 'present' in our worship.

1.4.1 The present from within

I start with an image. According to Hebrews, texts can be seen as windows on God's speaking in history, and thus bear witness to what the Spirit wants to say in the present. Looking through the window - that is, listening to the Word - we do not see ancient history but our place in this speaking in the present. In a sense, the text disappears when the interpreter outside the text becomes part of the world within the text, while that world within the text is seen as the past of the world outside the text[14]. So, there is a homiletic theology from within, a thought from within. And then the 'present' also sounds from within, because we ourselves become part of the world within the text. That is the first characterization of what 'present' means.

1.4.2 The present from the future

But there is also an inverse movement. Speaking 'to the fathers' remains a speaking 'to us'. A permanent salvific remains present. Living under the promise that we may enter into His rest calls for the surrender of faith. If it fails because of a 'depraved heart, full of unbelief' (Hebrews 3:12), 'hardened by the temptation of sin' (Hebrews 3:13), there is the imminent danger of 'falling away from God' and ultimately not being allowed to enter into his rest (Hebrews 3:19). This embraces the desert generation to the time of David - entering Canaan cannot be the actual sabbatical rest! - to today's situation, which is eschatologically qualified by the repeated 'present'. For today, there is still a new 'present', because God continues to speak. In and with that speaking the future makes its way to the present. Thus there is a homiletic theology from 'ahead', from the future. And with that the 'present' also sounds from the future.

---

13 Alister E. McGrath, *A Theory of Everything (That Matters): A Brief Guide to Einstein, Relativity and His Surprising Thoughts on God* (Carol Stream: Tyndale Momentum, 2019).

14 Schenck, "God Has Spoken," 321-336, 323.

So what happens to the enunciation of Psalm 95 in this sermon (3:7-4:14)? What is going on around the many other quotations of direct claims of God - words of God from the past - in Hebrews? It appears there is no separation made between then and now, time and eternity, below and above. Hebrews places the congregation in one of the aspects of the four-dimensional space-time of acting and speaking of God. In that space, we become contemporaneous with the time and place of 'the fathers' (Hebrews 1:1) and are carried away from the tabernacle to the heavenly sanctuary (Hebrews 9:1-12), from Sinai to Mount Zion (Hebrews 9:1-12). 12:19-24), from the desert to the rest that remains for the people of God (Hebrews 3:7-4:11), in the pilgrimage procession to the city of fundaments and the heavenly homeland (Hebrews 11) and the career of faith (Hebrews 12:1-3). It is in this light that these words resound: 'Jesus Christ is yesterday and today the same and forever' (Hebrews 13:8).

1.4.3 The present contains more than the past - a surplus of meaning
Perhaps as western theologians finding ourselves at a time after the Enlightenment, we suffer in from an apparent way of *thinking exactly* along the lines of time, and from bottom to top. Have we forgotten too much about how much language affects our conception of space and time? That does not mean, however, that we should not explain the word 'present' in its theological meaning and soteriological value. We certainly should, as long as we do not forget that the word 'present' sounds like the 'present' with some kind of power of attorney. There is also something about preaching that re-presents the Word of the living God.

'The call to enter God's rest comes now, not at any given moment in redemptive history, but at the very recitation of God's Word, with increased intensity and richer theological valence in this final, climactic dispensation'[15]. This involves a way of reading and listening that we may need to learn again in our age. Perhaps this will save us from unnecessary sighs and struggles around the interpretation of the message of the texts that speak to us when we read them. I am referring to what has been emphasised over the last decade around the way of listening to the scriptures as it was done in the early church. As early as 1980, the Dutch theologian H.W. de Knijff gave the following characterization of the historical-metaphoric sentence: 'The biblical words and biblical history are recognized as bearers of the reality of God's actions'[16]. Both aspects -

---

15 G.W. Lee, *Today When You Hear His Voice: Scripture, the Covenants, and the People of God* (Grand Rapids: Wm. B. Eerdmans, 2016), 178.
16 W.H. de Knijff, *Sleutel en slot: Beknopte geschiedenis van de Bijbelse hermeneutiek* (Kampen: Kok, 1980), 35.

words and actions - are important, and this is how we encounter them in Hebrews.

We do not arrive at Christ through a flat plane and along straight historical lines. The text itself has its own dynamics, as can be seen, for example, in the quotation from Psalm 95. A text like this appears to have a surplus of meaning, as found, for instance in the quotations from Psalm 8, 40 and 110. The text itself has a width and depth and thus forms a space. Certainly, it is a space with walls - we stay within the 'fence' of the letter line. In this sense one could also speak of a 'space for grace', because of the graciousness of words and texts. In summary, each and every text forms a space to which we are invited when we hear the word of God from within this space in time and from ahead when we become aware there is much more in it than we see at that very moment.

1.5 Preaching and the Voice of God

Following are some short remarks around what has been shown in this chapter from Hebrews to demonstrate that it actually is instructive for our reflections on preaching within the homiletical field; certainly and even more so when we endorse the so-called 'Bullinger's rule' from a reformed perspective.

It is helpful to connect this rule with the sermon of the Hebrews. Henrich Bullinger wrote this much-quoted sentence in his 2nd *Helvetic Confession* (1566):

'*The preaching of the Word of God is the Word of God*' (Latin, praedicatio verbi Dei est verbum Dei).

This is a forceful statement that, within a reformed homiletics, expresses the deep conviction that there is a reality - , that is, of 'God speaks' - a speech of God through the human voice. Much comes down to how one understands the word 'is' in this confessional statement. Anyone who believes that he as a preacher has this 'is' under his own power suffers from overconfidence and pride. This word 'is' never comes in the hands (mouths) of preachers, but receives its value and its content only from God. He hold this whole world of the 'is' in His hands. The well-known German homiletician, Bohren, says: 'Admittedly, in my sermon teaching I have nothing else in mind but to explain these three letters [that is, those found in the German word *ist*] for our time'[17].

When we keep in mind this explanation of the word 'is' as expressed in Bullinger's rule, we have in sum what Hebrews tells us:

---

17 R. Bohren, *Predigtlehre* (Gütersloh: Gütersloher Verlaghaus, 1993, 1971), 51.

- The gift of the human voice is used when God speaks;
- Preaching and communication is relational as the voice of God seeks our hearts and minds for a relationship in love and faith;
- The voice of God is mediated- and embodied speech;
- God speaks in the present tense to us where we find ourselves within our four-dimensional space-time.

REFERENCES

Bohren, R. *Predigtlehre*. Gütersloh: Gütersloher Verlaghaus, 1993, 1971.

De Knijff, W.H. *Sleutel en slot: Beknopte geschiedenis van de Bijbelse hermeneutiek*. Kampen: Kok, 1980.

Eisenbaum, Pamela M. *The Jewish Heroes of Christian History: Hebrew 11 in Literary Context*. Atlanta: Scholars Press, 1997.

Grethlein, Christian. *An Introduction to Practical Theology: History, Theory, and the Communication of the Gospel in the Present*. Translated by U. Rasch. Waco: Baylor University Press, 2016.

Gunton, Colin E. *Act and Being: Towards a Theology of the Divine Attributes*. London: SCM Press, 2002.

Guthrie, G.H. "Hebrews in Its First-century Contexts."
In *The Face of New Testament Studies: A Survey of Recent Research*, edited by S. McKnight and G. Osborne, 414-443. Grand Rapids: Baker Academic, 2004.

Hays, Richard B. *Reading Backwards: Figural Christology and the Fourfold Gospel Witness*. Waco: Baylor University Press, 2014.

Holtz, Gudrun. "Besser und doch gleich: Zur doppelten Hermeneutik des Hebräerbriefes." *Kerygma und Dogma* 58 (2012): 159-177.

Humphrey, Edith M. *And I Turned to See a Voice*. Grand Rapids: Baker Academic, 2007.

Lee, G.W. *Today When You Hear His Voice: Scripture, the Covenants, and the People of God*. Grand Rapids: Wm. B. Eerdmans, 2016.

Long, T.G. *What Shall We Say? Evil, Suffering, and the Crises of Faith*. Grand Rapids: Wm. B. Eerdmans, 2011.

McCullough, J.C. "Hebrews in Recent Scholarship." *Irish Biblical Studies* 16 (1994): 66-86, 108-120.

McGrath, Alister E. *A Theory of Everything (That Matters): A Brief Guide to Einstein, Relativity and His Surprising Thoughts on God*. Carol Stream: Tyndale Momentum, 2019.

Rosenstock-Huessy, E. *The Origin of Speech*. Norwich: Argo Books, 1981.

Rosenstock-Huessy, E. *Speech and Reality*. Norwich: Argo Books, 1970.

Schenck, Ken. "God Has Spoken: Hebrews' Theology of the Scriptures."

In *The Epistle to the Hebrews and Christian Theology*, edited by Richard J. Bauckham, Daniel R. Driver, Trevor A. Hart, and Nathan MacDonald, 321-336. Grand Rapids: Wm. B. Eerdmans, 2009.

Treier, D.J. and D.E. Lauber, eds. *Trinitarian Theology for the Church: Scripture, Community, Worship*. Nottingham: InterVarsity Press Academic, 2009.

Van Gemeren, William A., ed. *New International Dictionary of Old Testament Theology and Exegesis*. Vol. 3. Carlisle: Paternoster Press, 1996.

Waaijman, Kees. *Spiritualiteit: Vormen, grondslagen, methoden*. Kampen: Kok, 2000.

Webb, Stephen H. *The Divine Voice: Christian Proclamation and the Theology of Sound*. Grand Rapids: Brazos Press, 2004.

Webster, John. *Holy Scripture: A Dogmatic Sketch*. Cambridge: University Press, 2003.

Zizioulas, John D. *Being As Communion: Studies in Personhood and the Church*. Darton: Longman and Todd, 1985.

CHAPTER 2

A MULTITUDE OF CHORDS NEEDED IN ENABLING LISTENERS TO ACTIVELY LISTEN TO THE VOICE

Ferdi Kruger

Chapter 1 identified preaching as an act of voicing to address listeners' present and concrete circumstances. Preaching is surrounded by expectations around the preacher as well as listeners to hear God's voice, as indicated further. God has spoken and he wants listeners to consider his voice carefully: this was found to boggle the mind. It emerged further that the proclaimed Gospel is a voice in itself where intriguing interaction between acts of speaking and listening manifest[1]. To preach after all denotes that the harmonious voice of God's Word should be announced audibly. Voicing the living voice supposes organic functioning of a multitude of essential elements inevitably playing their underlying role. *It could be compared with music where the harmonic function describes the role that a particular chord plays in creating a larger harmonic progression.* Various elements are interdependent for preaching to voice the voice of God's Word. Arising from the realisation that preaching has to with God's speaking, one has to admit that preaching of the living Word is a complex religious act[2]. One has to be clear about which aspect or distinct aspects are relevant in debating the phenomenon of preaching. Considered overall, text and context are, for a start, always interwoven. Stott[3] rightly pleads for a double act of listening which comprises listening with directedness to the Bible as well as the situation of the listener.

---

1 J. Hermelink, "Preaching as a Language of Hope," in *Theological Understanding of Preaching Hope*, eds. C.J.A. Vos, L.L. Hogan, and J.H. Cilliers (Pretoria: Protea Book House, 2015), 16.
2 Gerrit Immink, *The Touch of the Sacred: The Practice, Theology, and Tradition of Christian Worship* (Grand Rapids: Wm. B. Eerdmans, 2014), 163.
3 John R.W. Stott, *The Contemporary Christian* (Leicester: Inter-Varsity Press, 1992), 28.

This situation also calls renewed attention to Dietrich Bonhoeffer's important, disturbing notion of a religionless Christianity. Pugh[4] emphasises Bonhoeffer's profound question regarding what a church, a sermon, liturgy and Christian life as such mean in a religionless world. Bonhoeffer therefore raises the matter of how preachers and Christians speak about God within a context where the umbilical cord of religion has been cut. For Bonhoeffer this issue requires a new kind of speaking and a new language, namely the language of truth about a new righteousness[5]. Preaching about a living Person rather than getting caught up in 'once upon a time' will make the difference. It seems that Bonhoeffer's words are imperative within the context of perspectives offered by the Hebrews sermon to listeners who live in arduous days. It offers us with a new insight into what it means to participate in the suffering and the victory of Christ in relation to the concreteness of life[6].

In this chapter, various concepts for preaching that surface in the Hebrews sermon will be elucidated. After all, Hebrews has to do with a sermon on faith-responsibility and the importance of a God who has communicated in various ways to listeners at various times. Intentional reference to God's voice as uttered by angels, signs, wonders, miracles and prophets (Hebrews 2) further emphasises this idea. God has indeed spoken in a meaningful manner for the listeners to have the impression that they should not ignore this voice within the listening process. The various modes of voicing the voice will furthermore be described here to understand the purposefulness of the act of preaching. The preacher in the Hebrews sermon is above all aware of the many times and the various ways in which God has spoken in the past. But the preacher is always aware, too, that this voice has not been lost. Comforting and reprimanding based on the spoken voice within the present entails the giving of careful attention. The Hebrew preacher's purposeful and constructive approach entails that the concrete context of the listeners requires the appropriate form of sermon aimed at connecting with the listeners amid their experiences. A creative interrelationship between instruction (doctrinal aspects) and application is noticeably present in providing new perspectives to the listeners of this sermon (see Hebrews 5-10). The sermon consistently applies explanatory sections to the context of the listeners.

---

4 J.C. Pugh, *Religiousless Christianity: Dietrich Bonhoeffer in Troubled Times* (London: Clark, 2008), 33.
5 Pugh, *Religiousless Christianity*, 41.
6 Pugh, *Religiousless Christianity*, 44.

Hebrews is, after all, written to be preached to people in a context where they became disheartened due to the severity of their daily circumstances, as indicated. Concomitantly, uncertainty about what the meaning of these difficult circumstances should be prompted them towards the question as to whether it still was worth being a Christian in the contemporary world[7]. This centred on wisdom *(phronesis)* regarding the appropriate action.

The phenomenological issue of understanding what it entailed to be *in* the world but not *from* it had become a burning issue for listeners. They tended steadily to decline mentally. They had lost their sense for vitality and enthusiasm and, consequently, despondency was part and parcel of their new frame of reference. One of the core problematic aspects in their understanding was their perception of God's voice in various ways at many times (see Hebrews 1:1). According to some of the listeners, God's presence was clearly visible by means of constructive activities and sacrifices performed in the temple. Within the old dispensation, they could easily refer to something that provided visible handles in handling challenges. Rituals and symbols offered a visible framework in their understanding of reality. The new dispensation in Christ and the difficult challenges in society gave rise to immense questions regarding the meaningfulness of fixing their eyes and thoughts on him[8].

The purpose of this sermon was to enable its listeners to see the message of Christ even amidst these problematic circumstances and challenges. Hence, formation, that is, a becoming or constructive activity, is a deliberate approach within the Hebrews sermon. The sermon could therefore be regarded as a thoughtful three-dimensional text, as illustrated in the preface to this book. In Hebrews 4:1-2, the preacher raises the concern that the message about Christ has no value for the listeners, because it is not combined with faith. Hearing and believing the Word of God are inseparable in active listening. Considering this kind of outcome of the sermon the listeners needed a purposefully constructive approach to the process. Within the constructive formation of a community of faith using a sermon, Christ's functioning as Priest or Liturgist (Hebrews 8) stands central. The choice of the sermon utilised in Hebrews has to do with persuading people to gain understanding within their own and unique situation. In Hebrews 3, Jesus is himself described as the One who is building (forming) his house, and preaching is regarded as an important

---

[7] Simon J. Kistemaker, *Hebrews*, New Testament Commentary (Grand Rapids: Baker Book House, 1996), 15.

[8] F.F. Bruce, *The Epistle to the Hebrews*, New International Commentary of the New Testament (Grand Rapids: Eerdmans, 1990), 5.

act in this regard. In close connection with building or preparation is the idea of the equipment of his house. As has been indicated, the construction (formation) of the community of faith in Hebrews has the dual meaning of preparation as well as of equipping. Within God's house, Jesus Christ is the builder and Moses or human servants only act as servant-therapists (θεραπων). This concept of acting as a servant has to do with someone's humble attitude regarding service and could even denote assistance to someone or faithfully conducting one's duties.

Based on this idea, the listeners to the Hebrews sermon are regarded as people who share in the heavenly calling. The concept of μετοχοι is notable. This concept could even denote the idea of being a partner or companion. The listeners to this sermon are, within the mind of the Hebrews preacher, companions of the King, Jesus Christ. The concept of calling is evident here and provides a theological framework towards understanding the essence of this sermon. In preaching, a called servant is, after all, announcing the living voice of God to called servants (listeners). The idea of a merciful exchange is furthermore striking. In Hebrews 2:14, it is mentioned that Christ has shared in our humanity. Now it is said that His followers have become His companions in this world. It seems that the notion of Thomas Long[9], that preaching contains a shared story among companions in this world, is of importance to the Hebrews sermon. The five concepts utilised within the Hebrews sermon furthermore highlight that sermons should be directed or even related to shared struggles and circumstances of the listeners within a local congregation. In this vein, Hermelink[10] convincingly indicates that the Gospel and preaching of the Gospel indeed include a multitude of voices. Preaching not only has to do with the outpouring of a multitude of voices, but should also be answered in a multitude of voices in the listening process. I will subsequently focus on the purposeful manner in which the Hebrews sermon is constructed around voicing the voice.

2.1 A polyphony of voices in the Hebrews sermon
2.1.1 *The kaleidoscope of various concepts for preaching*
The concepts that are utilised for preaching emphasise that preaching should not be a monologue, but should rather be regarded as a polyphony of voices that includes the acts of proclaiming and active listening. The Hebrews sermon concerns the God who speaks[11]. The emphasis is on God who spoke in the past but continues to speak in the present. The

---
9   Thomas G. Long, *Preaching from Memory to Hope* (Louisville: John Knox Press, 2009), 4.
10 Hermelink, "Language of Hope," 22.
11 W.L. Lane, *Hebrews 1-8* (Dallas: World Books, 1991), 3.

emphasis on the communicative God as well as the importance recognition that listeners should listen actively, that is, respond, is sustained through the outline of this sermon (see Hebrews 2:-14, Hebrews 3: 7-19 and Hebrews 13). It is imperative to listen to the living voice of God in the here and now of the listeners' lives. The God who is speaking in the present time is freshly and dynamically addressing the contemporary situation of the listeners. This can be inferred from the multitude of concepts that are utilised for the act of preaching in this particular sermon. The idea of words of exhortation (Hebrews 13:22) requires a meaningful approach to provide new perspectives to listeners who may doubt the meaningfulness of what they are experiencing.

The multifaceted character of listeners in the Hebrews sermon is therefore part of the focus of the preacher. The following concepts for preaching are utilised in the Hebrews sermon:

- παρακαλειν
  Hebrews 3:13, Hebrews 6:18, Hebrews 12:5, Hebrews 13:19, Hebrews 13
- λαλειν
  Hebrews 2:2, Hebrews 2:3, Hebrews 2:5, Hebrews 6:9, Hebrews 12:25,
  Hebrews 13:7
- ευαγγελιζω
  Hebrews 4:2, Hebrews 4:6
- ὠφέλησεν ὁ λόγος
  Hebrews 4:2
- μαρτυρεῖν
  Hebrews 10:15

2.1.2 The dimension of admonishing and encouraging - παρακαλειν
Louw and Nida II[12] indicate that this concept of παρακαλειν could be seen against the background of the semantic sub-domain of *asking* or *requesting*. The concept could also be used to describe the activity of a military commander who motivates soldiers to have confidence for battle[13]. Here, the idea of preaching as exhortation attracts attention to

---

12 J.P. Louw and E.A. Nida, *Greek English Lexicon of the New Testament (II)* (New York: United Bible Studies, 1989), 407.
13 J. Brown, *Hebrews*, Geneva Series of Commentaries (Edinburg: The Bath Press, 1999), 88.

importance of earnestness in listening to sermons. The idea of the sermon as an earnest plea should also be distinguished[14]. This idea resonates with the idea to be found in other passages, that preaching should echo the earnest notion of letting yourself be reconciled with God. The coin of this particular concept has two sides, namely admonishing as well as encouraging[15]. It is important, though, to realise that preaching of the indicative of consolation in Christ also includes the imperative of taking care for what is being heard[16] [17]. Therefore, encouragement is concomitantly closely related to the preaching of the message of salvation in Christ. In other words, preaching as exhortation and encouragement is aimed at profound transformation[18].

The Hebrews sermon focusses on mutual pastoral care and attention[19]. Christians need each other. In this sermon, spiritual help is expressed by the verb παρακαλεῖν [admonish, encourage]. In Hebrews 3, the bad example of the disobedient generation in the wilderness is applied to each congregation member individually. Added to that admonition is the positive appeal to encourage one another from day to day: *'See to it, brothers, that none of you has a sinful, unbelieving heart that turns away from the living God. But encourage one another daily [...] so that none of you may be hardened by sin's deceitfulness. We have come to share in Christ if we hold firmly till the end the confidence we had at first'* (Heb. 3:12-14; my emphasis). Since believers are on their way to God's glorious kingdom, that is, the yet but not-yet dimension of preaching, such spiritual support should be a daily practice. We also find the term παρακαλεῖν in Hebrews 10:24-25: *'And let us consider how we may spur one another on towards love and good deeds'* (my emphasis). In this text, a more specific word is παροξυσμός [to sharpen]. Literally speaking, we need to keep each other sharp when it concerns the demonstration of love and doing well[20].

In Hebrews 13:19 and 22 the meaning of the word παρακαλειν has to do with exhortation. It is interesting that the role of prayer in praying for

---

14 Louw and Nida, *Greek English Lexicon*, 185.
15 Hennie J.C. Pieterse, *Verwoording en prediking* (Pretoria: N.G. Kerkboekhandel, 1985), 9.
16 Cassie J.H. Venter, "Die Gees, die Woord en die bedienaar van die Woord," in *Koninkryk, Gees en Woord*, red. J.C. Coetzee (Pretoria: N.G. Kerkboekhandel, 1988), 14.
17 Koos M. Vorster, "Vernuwing in die prediking in die lig van hedendaagse lewensbeskoulike tendense," *In die Skriflig* 29, no. 3 (Maart 1995): 460.
18 D.T. Williams, "After the Order of Melchizedek: Pre-Existence and Salvation in Hebrews," *The South African Baptist Journal of Theology* 5, no. 1 (1996): 4.
19 P.H.R. van Houwelingen, "The Epistle to the Hebrews: Faith Means Perseverance," *Journal of Early Christian History* 3, no. 1 (2013): 110, DOI: 10.1080/2222582X.2013.11877278.
20 Van Houwelingen, "Epistle," 110-111.

spiritual leaders and for people who are presiding stands central here[21]. It is clear that preaching within the framework of admonishing and encouraging is not one-sided. Preaching as *paraclesis* has to do with the crux of preaching, namely to speak in such a manner about God that he himself speaks[22]. In this sense, we can say that preaching is an instrument through which God transforms people's lives. Preaching as *paraclesis* emphasises that within the Trinitarian nature of preaching, the importance of God's act in Christ is a profound plea. In the Hebrews sermon, this very idea stands central. In fact, the over-arching theme of this sermon could also be described as Jesus Christ, the superior High Priest[23]. Preaching as *paraclesis* enables listeners to determine what this message in Christ will entail for their lives. Pieterse[24] has indicated that preaching as *paraclesis* takes its ground within the concrete lives of people, but with the purpose to encourage and to exhort. Therefore, preaching needs responsiveness or reaction from the listeners.

The Hebrews sermon explains the meaningfulness of life in the new dispensation in Christ (also referred to as the last days). One could say that wonderful privileges in the new dispensation (Hebrews 1:1-2) have considerable responsibilities as their matching part. Preaching as *paraclesis* should open up windows for sustained hope as well as eschatological insight. Preaching on biblical texts indeed enjoys the power to release what Brueggemann calls a *'counter-imagination'*, a way of seeing the world that is an alternative to consumerist, militaristic, death-obsessed imagination of the culture[25] (my emphasis). Hermelink[26] responds to this idea and sees the aim of preaching as a preaching of hope and an attempt to construct, that is, build up, listeners who will also speak hopefully amid their concrete lives. From that point onwards, the listeners have to speak in their own voices. As witnesses of what they heard, they have to learn to become responsible. Preaching amidst the paradoxes of life also reckons with the surprising act of hope, against hope, of the citizens of God's Kingdom. To name the realities of hopelessness, fear and anger in

---

21 B.B. Barton, D. Veerman, and L.K. Taylor, *Hebrews*, Life Application Bible Commentary (Wheaton: Tyndale House, 1997), 245.
22 Johan H. Cilliers, *Binne die kring-dans van die kuns: Die betekenis van estetika vir die gereformeerde liturgie* (Stellenbosch: Sun Press, 2007), 46.
23 Van Houwelingen, "Epistle," 103.
24 Pieterse, *Verwoording en prediking*, 9.
25 W. Brueggemann, *The Word Militant: Preaching a Decentering Word* (Minneapolis: Fortress Press, 2010), 2.
26 J. Hermelink, "The Theological Understand of Preaching Hope," in *Preaching as a Language of Hope*, Studia Homiletica 6, eds. C. Vos, L.L. Hogan, and J.H. Cilliers (Zoetermeer: Boekencentrum, 2007), 43-44.

preaching should not be separated from the starting point of the victory of Jesus Christ and the living faith in Christ. This does not mean relativizing real fear where people have to deal with realities, but to recognise the power of fear and the power of living hope from the perspective of God's supremacy above everything. The proclamation of the new life in Christ offers frames that become real hope[27].

2.1.3 Preaching as intelligible dialogue - λαλειν

Long[28] underlines Augustine's much-discussed idea that the purpose of the sermon is to teach, delight and persuade. The content of the biblical passage according to Augustine's understanding should in other words be taught in a delightful manner to be persuasive. In the Hebrews sermon one is struck further by the use of the word λαλειν for preaching. This word is utilised six times in the sermon. It is normally used to indicate the most familiar way in which people communicate and also an informal kind of conversation[29]. This is the opposite of a complex lecture. In ancient Greek, for instance, the verb λαλέω normally refers to informal communication such as chatter or prattle - the opposite of normal, rational speech (λέγειν). This word simply refers to the act of talking, specifically God's speech. In a sense, by using this verb the preacher of the Hebrews sermon is echoing the many references in the Old Testament to God's speech[30] [31].

The opening words of the sermon to the Hebrews holds a fascination for Bruce [32] who says that the initial words about God who has spoken is basic to the sermon and to Christian faith itself. Mentioning God who has spoken is sometimes referred to as the foundation of the Hebrews sermon[33]. In establishing a communication network with people in despair, the sermon contrasts two dispensations with each other. It could be described in the following manner:

---

27 F.W. de Wet, F.P. Kruger, and C. Stark, "Around Capes of Good Hope God's Wind Never Subsides," in *Preaching Promise within the Paradoxes of Life*, Studia Homiletica 11, eds. J.H. Cilliers and L. Hansen (Stellenbosch: African Sun Media, 2019), 246.
28 Long, *Preaching*, 5.
29 Louw and Nida, *Greek English Lexicon*, 397.
30 A.J. Coetsee, "The Unfolding of God's Revelation in Hebrews 1:1-2a," *HTS Teologiese Studies/Theological Studies* 72, no. 3 (2016): 4, a3221, http://dx.doi.org/10.4102/hts.v72i3.3221.
31 P. Ellingworth, *Commentary on Hebrews*, New International Greek Testament Commentary (Grand Rapids: Eerdmans, 1993), 92.
32 Bruce, *Epistle*, 45.
33 Kistemaker, *Hebrews*, 27.

Old dispensation: Earlier times	New dispensation: Last days
Various times	Once and for all (Aoristus tense)
Many ways	
God spoke	God spoke
In earlier times	Now in the last days
To our fathers	To us
By the prophets	In His Son

The similarity between the earlier dispensation and now (the last days) centres on the fact that God has spoken. The preacher can only speak because God has spoken. The issue at stake is God's Word in audible language. Mentioning of that God that has spoken πολυμερῶς καὶ πολυτρόπως underlines that he has done so in many portions or many parts and in manifold forms. It is evident that God's words are not aimed at a vacuum but at a concrete situation and are directed at concrete listeners amid the challenges of daily life. The concrete circumstances of the listeners that are addressed in the Hebrews sermon allow us to realise that *Zachtreue* and *Menschtreue* [focused on the matter as well as interest in people] are not opposites in the act of preaching. God's Word always includes people as well as their real situation. God has not spoken all at once, but rather in a purposeful manner. As can be inferred from the Hebrew sermon, one has to acknowledge that preaching is not a hit-and-run act, but it should, on the contrary, be purposefully planned and delivered. In Hebrews 1, the relation to the Son, Jesus Christ, as orientation-point in a purposeful approach stands central.

In Hebrews 2:1-4 the implication of listening to the proclamation of Jesus Christ is explained. The listeners are encouraged to pay careful attention to what they have heard and not drift away. Preaching as speaking (voicing) enjoys as its content God's Word, and this very fact urges listeners to pay attention to what they have heard. Long emphasises that the preacher shifts the instruction about Christ in Hebrews 1 to instruction about Christian life in Hebrews 2:1-4. In other words, preaching not only aims at the reality of eternal matters, but also daily life, and therefore the danger of drifting away is abated. It seems likely that the words of Maarten Luther echoes in the Hebrews sermon, namely *nihil nisi Christus preadicandus* (proclaim nothing but Christ). It is clear that the concept of λαλειν underlines the importance that preaching has to proclaim God's deeds in a readily understandable manner for listeners to be surprised by the hope and new perspective offered by the passage. It has been indicated that a multitude of voices is present, namely the voice of the text, the voice of listeners in concrete circumstances and, through the voice of the preacher, God's voice. When these voices become one voice, preaching is indeed the living voice of God. It is the privilege of the preacher to help listeners listen to God's voice.

2.1.4 Preaching the good news and remembrance- Ευαγγελιζω

The concept of ευαγγελιζω (preaching of the good news) is utilised in a specific context in Hebrews 4. The concept of good news occurs fourteen times in the book and the verb itself four. The word literally denotes the idea of the conveyance of the good news. Louw and Nida II therefore rightly place this concept within the semantic sub-domain of informing and information. The Hebrews sermon has a strong forward-looking focus which arranges all earthly realities in the right perspective. In chapters 2-4, and based on Psalm 95, the author demonstrates that the Christian congregation lives towards the fulfilment of God's promise of rest for his people. That is an eternal Sabbath-rest, praising and adoring God without end. To enter this rest, one needs to follow the heavenly call (Heb. 3:1) to be *en-routed* to the city-to-come (Heb. 11:13-16; 13:9-14). The preacher applies the truth of what Christ is offering in terms of two powerful applications in Hebrews 3:12-4:1-11, namely an unbelieving heart that turns away from God and the danger of hearing good news that has no value. This particular concept, of ευαγγελιζω, is utilised in the New Testament to indicate the good news regarding Jesus Christ.

A lengthy quote around Psalm 95, which refers to the Israelites' experiences in the desert, is also offered. Therefore, preaching as proclaiming the good news also has the dimension of helping listeners to be careful. Certainty about God's promise of rest does not allow for a practice of taking things easy. The idea of the appropriation of God's promises surfaces here. EMPHASIS is laid on listeners that have indeed heard the good news. The good news has been preached to them for a considerable time, but the danger is that it can do them no good, mainly because they fail to pay attention. The connection between reminding and listening to the good news is striking especially when one reflects on the idea of remembering while listening to the preaching of good news.

As part of his manner of introducing an important focal point gradually and in a structured way, the preacher in the Hebrews sermon utilises Old Testament quotations at least on 35 occasions. This preacher therefore utilises vivid memories of the past to provide dynamic perspectives for the present. For instance, the author enumerates various figures from the Israelite tradition to encourage first listeners or readers to remain loyal themselves. Hebrews 2:1 emphasises that listeners should take heed of things that they have heard because they are linked to salvation in Christ. Hebrews 3 underlines the importance of regarding *today* as the most important day. Within the calendar of listeners, today is emphasised as the most important day, because the voice should be taken seriously. The reference to Psalm 95:7-11 is striking in this context: it highlights the lesson from history that one ignores God's communication at one's peril. The message is clear, namely that God's communication has to do with the fact that he himself is speaking. Listening to God's voice today means to listen decisively. Hebrews 10:3 builds on this idea when it employs the concept of αναμνησις in close connection with Old Testament sacrifices (see chapter 8). People have been reminded of their sins and reconciliation in Christ. Long rightly explains the stark contrast between something that should have happened regularly in the past and the message that Christ did something of significance, once and for all. Johnston therefore connects Christ's reconciliation with daily and frequent remembrances of the meaning of what Christ has done. The interrelationship between knowledge of sin and reconciliation should be remembered frequently and on a daily basis, while preaching the good news is functional in this process.

2.1.5 Hearing of the Word that brings no good - ὠφέλησεν ὁ λόγος τῆς ἀκοῆς ἐκείνους

Louw and Nida II place the concept of listening (ἀκοῆς) within the semantic sub-domain of communication. In this sense, it denotes the Word of God and includes the message regarding Jesus Christ. One can also say that this concept refers to the events that have as content the message regarding Him. Listening to preaching requires a high level of concentration and energy and should not be separated from the principles of profound communication. Basic aspects such as effective communication so that listeners will understand it should be taken into account. The performative aspect of sermons emerges here, because, surely, preaching aims at cultivating various phenomena within listeners' minds and hearts. The reference to hearing has a distinct meaning in the sense that it is closely related to a reaction or even the appropriation of what is heard. Acknowledgement of profound understanding of what is heard is important. The cognizance of the church as an *ecclesia audiens* (that is, a listening church), as Karl Barth once described it, should be acknowledged. According to Barth, a community of believers is called upon to proclaim God's Word but fails in achieving this responsibility when they fail to listen. This is why scholars sometimes refer to the lost skill of listening.

To listen has to do with much more than hearing mere sounds. The act of listening as an integral activity has to reckon with the acts of hearing, understanding, remembering, evaluating and responding to messages. Listeners require the stirring of memories while remembering, even in partially concealing, past experiences (see chapter 8). In fact, in every worship service, participants in the liturgy (especially in listening to sermons) remember the good message regarding Christ's death and his resurrection. All people have memories of their relationship with God, of previous sermons about the same passage as well as of reality created by messages they have been exposed to. It is important to note that people are incapable of paying attention to all the data they receive. This could explain why people who listen to the same message about Christ's death and resurrection remember different aspects of this. People harmonise and invent detail to make a memory harmonious with their current beliefs. Schlinger therefore takes the idea of *sursum corda* one step further when he argues that listeners eventually act dialogically as speakers themselves when they submit to listen -, respond - and react to sermons daily life. In short, the act of listening to words retrieves vivid images from people's memories.

The importance of listening within the Hebrews sermon framework has to do with the fact that active listening means what is heard should be translated into obedience. The person who listens diligently is therefore also diligent when it comes to obeying God. The phrase is only mentioned once in the Hebrews sermon, namely in Hebrews 4:2. It is utilised within the context of an attitude of unwillingness to obey the proclaimed message. To illustrate the close relationship between what is being heard and the activity of the listeners, a striking metaphor is used. A word that it is often connected with the mixing of paint is utilised. It is also sometimes used to describe how water and wine are mixed. The conjunction και [for] denotes that the promise that was given to the Israelites, as it was preached to the Israelites in the desert, is still valid. The irony is that the Israelites had the good news proclaimed to them but the hearing of the good news brought no lasting benefit to them. The reason for hearing the Word that brings no good was that they did not appropriate the good news by faith when they heard it. In spite of various undertakings by fathers and leaders, the Israelites did not obey this voice and not mixing of faith and hearing realised.

It is, after all, not mere hearing of the Word that brings salvation, but its appropriation by faith. This argument is elaborated on in this sermon, namely Hebrews 5:11-6:2. This pericope sketches the interrelationship between preaching, listening and obeying. The writer to the Hebrews has to interrupt his discourse, because the listeners became slow to listen, even tardy. He is concerned, because the listeners are infant-like in their attitude and their knowledge of God's Word. They are like babies who want to function on milk alone. The problem of slow growth is created by a lack of interest and diligence. The slowness of the listeners to hear and to grow makes it difficult for the preacher to proclaim the full extent of the Gospel to them. Therefore, the preacher is afraid that the listeners will not comprehend what is being proclaimed. Guthrie underlines that this centres on the Word of God that was heard audibly and that listening should lead to commitment.

Active listening is a combination of hearing what another person says and a psychological involvement with the person speaking. Preachers should be attentive to the fact that they will not automatically concentrate and listen to sermons. Mitchell indicates that, to boot, people's ability and their way of listening to sermons have changed due to the influence of electronic and audio-visual communication. A transfer of ownership of the sermon should take place where listeners should be able to say '*Amen*' based on what they perceived. They can then walk out and say: 'This is my sermon, because it is internalised'. Immink highlights that listeners of the sermon are not mere addressees, but are obliged to make their own contribution while listening. They should also connect the essence of what they have heard with daily life. Eventually, the deeper and ultimate reality of listening in an active manner to sermons is that listeners live *Coram Deo,* in the presence of God. Buttrick refers to the symbolic-reflective modus in the listening process where critical assessment and thoughtful reflection about practices in life take place. When listeners are mere hearers who refrain from active listening, which includes remembrance of the living Christ, they will be endangered by hearing a Word that brings no good. Preaching should help listeners to remember their own experiences with God and their own faith experiences so that the past, present and future can interact in a vivid manner.

2.1.6 Preaching as witnessing- μαρτυρειν
Homileticians have been interested in the witness-metaphor for preaching mainly because giving testimony has apparently given rise to the impression of aggressiveness towards people listening to it. The preacher is, after all, the first addressed person, mainly because of thoughtful preparation of the sermon. He or she does not function as a person merely delivering mail at people's addresses. It is the preacher's responsibility to convey the truth of God's voice to the listeners. The concept of μαρτυρειν is derived from the legal environment and denotes a witness appearing in a courtroom. This implies that the preacher is one who bears witness. In calling the preacher a witness, it is important to realise that authority

does not lie in the preacher but in what the he or she has heard, seen and appropriated. In preparation of the sermon, the preacher has wrestled with the text and has tried to listen to the voice of the text by emptying him- or herself from subjective preferences. The authority to preach grows out of the preacher's seeing of and listening to the text. Witnesses testify to events and, in this instance, the encounter between God and his people. The questions of listeners are in the mind of preachers when they listen to God's voice. After listening to this voice, the preacher turns to the listeners to tell them the truth.

The witness (preacher), one should realise, is not a neutral observer. In being a witness, the preacher's involvement stands central. In the Hebrews sermon the preacher refers to the witnessing or assuring activity of the Holy Spirit. In this process he or she allows Scripture to do the talking. Two quotes from the prophecy of Jeremiah are offered. The Holy Spirit has been described as the speaker of Scripture (Hebrews 3:7) and also as Revealer, as found in Hebrews 9:8. Up to and including that stage of its unfolding, the Hebrews sermon made it clear that a new covenant is evident and believers are brought into this relationship. Now the preacher reminds the listeners that the Holy Spirit is the witness of the words of Jeremiah. The Holy Spirit does not simply prove something, but testifies to the words of God's Word. Based on the fact that the Spirit knows God's Word, the Spirit is also able to testify about it. It is therefore important to acknowledge that preaching has to speak about what God's Word is saying. The commitment of preachers to testify while preaching enjoys as its profound foundation that the Holy Spirit testifies that it is indeed God's Word.

2.2 The multitude of voices of preaching intertwined with the listeners' attitudes (the notion of the intrinsic voice)

Various concepts for preaching have been identified in this chapter. Interestingly, the concepts forming the polyphony are interrelated in a focused manner in relation to specific attitudes in the Hebrews sermon. Later in the present book, the connection between preaching and a change in attitude will briefly be discussed further. The present chapter focusses on the earnestness with which preachers and listeners should approach preaching. The Hebrews sermon reveals that this earnestness is based on the fact that the power of God's Word is such that no-one can hide any attitude. Therefore, once the materials in Hebrews 3-4 have been expounded with the command to appropriate God's Word, the preacher offers the deeper reason why listeners' attitudes are exposed.

Du Toit discusses the fact that the sermon starts with the reality of a communicative God (Hebrews 1:1-2). After completion of the first major part (1:1-4:13), it addresses God's dynamic, vivid and exposing voice. This idea is presented in the form of a ring-composition. The diagram below illustrates this notion:

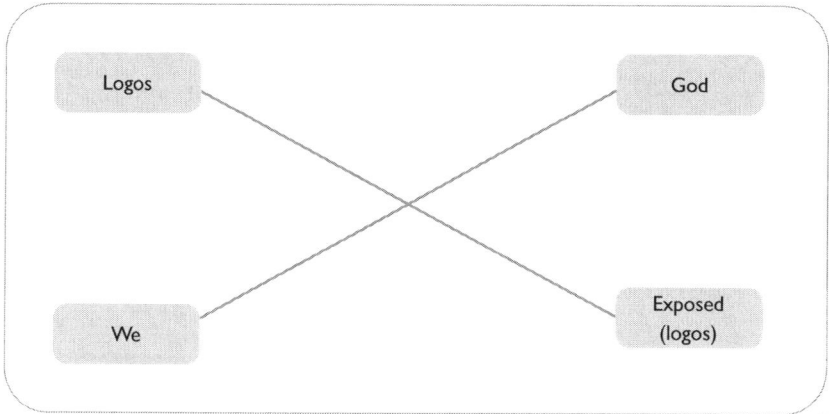

According to this, God's Word finds itself at the chiasmic intersection of the relation between the Word (logos) and exposure to the relationship between God and us/we *(marked 'We' in the diagram above)*. God communicates for listeners to realise something poignant, namely that they are listening to sermons that resonate with the words of He that speaks. It is striking that the Hebrews sermon tries to give space for the cognizance that God, Christ and the Holy Spirit in fact participate in speaking, while this interplay of voices cannot be ignored[34]. The word logos could also denote the idea of being addressed by someone who wants you to understand. God's living voice realise resounds within the interplay between his speaking and our response. In Hebrews 4:12-13, the imperative to listen to God's Word is accordingly emphasised as follows:

- God's Word is a living Word. God is a living God and therefore his voice is also a living voice. The expression 'Word of God' is closely related to God's spoken Word. It is furthermore striking that the attribute of *living* stands at the beginning of the Greek sentence. God's Word does not speak about him *in memoriam* but rather as the living God. This could be called the mystery of preaching, namely that God is present and speaks to us.
- If the Word of the living God is in itself living, it inevitably has the power to examine and to discern. The meaning of power in this context has to do with energy. God's Word is indeed active.

---

34 Du Toit, *Hebreërs*, 85.

Therefore, His Word is energising in its effect[35]. One can also describe it as effective and powerful[36]. The idea that God's Word is active, efficient and effectual cannot be ignored[37]. The power of His Word is also that no-one is beyond the reach of its energy. The Bible and preaching of the Word of God do not consist of dead letters according to the preacher of the Hebrews sermon. Preaching the Word of God has transformative power in the formation process.

- God's Word is sharper than any double-edged sword. The image of a sharp chirurgical knife, a scalpel, is central[38]. THE POWER OF GOD'S WORD, WHICH commends and rebukes, approves and disapproves, should be realised. The wrong attitude of taking God's Word for granted is an aspect that should be avoided according to the preacher of the Hebrews sermon. The scalpel cuts deep to discover the most delicate nerves of the human body, but for believing Christians the comfort is that it cuts to heal[39].
- God's Word is piercing and penetrative. It penetrates places where the human eye cannot follow[40]. The living Word of God penetrates listeners in such a manner that it will expose their deepest mysteries[41]. Preaching of God's Word is not done without purpose. It is purposeful and delivered to hit its target, the deepest existence of listeners' lives.
- God's Word is discerning. It can distinguish between thoughts and intents[42]. The living Word of God can judge every movement and feeling of listeners' hearts. It can even judge thoughts before they become words and human intentions before they become actions. Nothing remains untouched by God's Word[43]. The concept of discernment could also denote the idea of being a judge or critic[44].
- Eventually, Hebrews 4:13 underscores that God's Word uncovers everything: it is the result of the actuality that God is himself fully aware of all things. Listeners are limited to space and time, but God

---

35 Kistemaker, *Hebrews*, 116.
36 Ellingworth, *Commentary on Hebrews*, 261.
37 J.M. Flanigan, *Hebrews: What the Bible Teaches*, Ritchie New Testament Commentaries (Kilmarnock: John Ritchie, 1997), 7.
38 Flanigan, *Hebrews*, 79.
39 Flanigan, *Hebrews*, 112.
40 Kistemaker, *Hebrews*, 117.
41 Du Toit, *Hebreërs*, 87.
42 Flanigan, *Hebrews*, 79.
43 Kistemaker, *Hebrews*, 117.
44 Du Toit, *Hebreërs*, 87.

dwells in eternity and nothing is hidden from him. In realising that all things are open and exposed, the image of fruit that is peeled off until you see the core of it or a soldier that is stripped of his armour, is immanent[45]. In the core of this idea that everything is in open before God resides another important image that of a wrestler pinned down underneath his opponent[46]. The Hebrews sermon on the footprint of this idea makes it clear that preaching God's Word aims at placing listeners in the open in the presence of the living God to whom all people are accountable.

In Hebrews 5:11-6:20, the preacher highlights the attitude of the listeners. They became dull of hearing (νωθρος). The concept of laziness (tardiness to learn) is derived from the field of education of those days. Fully aware of the fact that depth in the conveyance of this message is not possible, the preacher has to interrupt it. The preacher, in this case also the author of the book, is now confronted by a dual problem. He or she is aware that preaching is important, while difficult aspects must be communicated, but the listeners are slow to listen to what he offers. The problematic praxis of laziness when it comes to listening to God's word, cannot be ignored. Such listening should inevitably lead to obedience, while laziness gives rise to a challenge around this. The listeners to whom formation is delivered have shot themselves in the foot. A relapse in the dynamics of formation activities has to reflect on flexibility of cognition. At this stage and on behalf of what the listeners have heard over the years, it is evident that they should have been teachers and lecturers.

The Greek word for *dull* refers to a kind of laziness and tardiness among listeners. This tardiness does not refer to the action of listening but rather to their reaction in response to what they have heard. They are like infants in choosing what they want to hear[47]. Difficulty consequently arises around listeners' growth in the truths of God's Word. Because of their lazy reaction to God's Word, they became like small children. Their growth in their faith-lives are endangered, as mentioned, and therefore they struggle to understand the mature truths of God's Word. This problem of attitude creates challenges for the preacher, because he or she has a considerable number of things to say but cannot, since the listeners cannot appropriate the essence of the preaching. The relationship between preaching and listening is then not healthy. All in all, the listeners' attitude of a limited reaction to God's Word limits growth in their faith-lives.

---

45 Du Toit, *Hebreërs*, 87.
46 Du Toit, *Hebreërs*, 87.
47 J. Vines, *The Believers Guide to Hebrews* (New Jersey: Loizeaux, 1993), 81-82.

2.3 A polyphony of voices in voicing voice- homiletical perspectives

The sermon utilises the use of a polyphony of words to indicate what preaching is about. One may glean the following aspects from this:

- Preaching is communicative in its essence. The communication of sermons should be directed to listeners' lives and therefore the main goal of the Hebrews sermon is to persuade listeners to respond to the message. Although persuasion is its main purpose, it could be said that the main rhetorical character is deliberative. Various concepts for preaching is utilised to renew the commitment of the listeners to the powerful Word of God.

- Preaching as encouragement of listeners' centres on the profound basis of what Christ has done once and for all. The various concepts for preaching indicate that the proclamation of the Word cannot be separated from what Christ has done. Preaching, as viewed from the Hebrews sermon, has to do with reminding listeners of what God has done for them in Christ.

- Although encouragement stands central in the sermon, the preacher is not afraid to provide helpful warnings. The relationship between preaching, listening and doing is hereby emphasised. This very idea is linked with the recognition that it is God who is speaking while listeners are listening to sermons. The preacher of the sermon takes time to persuade listeners in a logical manner that they are actually listening to God, who is speaking. They are placed in God's presence.

- Preaching in the Hebrews sermon is directed at a real-life situation and not a mere theoretical act. Therefore, listeners are reminded that God is speaking in current time.

- The preacher is well acquainted with the concrete circumstances of the listeners. In using familiar words for a sermon and in communicating the earnestness that should be evident in them, he or she connects with listeners. The preacher's concern for the listeners' attitudes is so important that a polyphony of concepts is utilised to enable them to understand the urgency of active listening within the here and now. Again, it is clear that the preacher is well aware of the concrete circumstances of the listeners. He or she is therefore able to use logic and various appeals to convince them of the message.

- Johnston[48] points to a very important aspect, namely that proper communication through preaching is dialogic and that it therefore takes time to flourish in local congregations. The approach followed

---
48 Johnston, *Epistle to the Hebrews*, 61.

by the preacher in the Hebrews sermon is more than a mere advertisement campaign: it carries the idea of a preacher taking time to carefully compile sermons that will influence listeners' attitudes.
- Preaching in its style can therefore not be done by means of a neutral communicative approach. Preaching does not merely provide information on an interesting topic, leaving the listener with a safe and comfortable option or choice to revert to the concealed and un-exposed depths of a sinful, self-justifying, self-pardoning existence. Preaching, according to the Hebrews sermon, reveals the true status and condition of the listeners and the world in which they live. For those who have been designated to live, preaching is a reinforcement of redemption. Exposure of their misery leads believers to seek and find their justification and holiness in Jesus Christ, outside themselves, and not within their own judgemental state and condition.
- Preaching ought to contain an element of urgency. Preaching takes place in the context of the last days: 'God, who at various times and in different ways spoke in time past to the fathers by the prophets, has in these last days spoken to us by His Son' (Hebrews 1:1 and 2; my emphasis).
- The multifaceted character of preaching should always be considered, namely:
  o Preaching as paraclesis underlines two sides of the same coin, namely preaching as intimate relationship between exhortation and encouragement. Without this interrelationship, preaching can be skewed as a legalistic framework of dos and don'ts from the side of the preacher.
  o Preaching as discourse/ conversation. This aspect of preaching underlines the importance of the fact that it should be genuine and simple to understand.
  o reaching as a proclamation of the Gospel emphasises that listening to it should lead to the appropriation of God's promises and his commands.
  o Preaching as witnessing means it offers the truth of God's Word. Preachers have to be convinced of the content they are giving witness to.
  o A sermon does not necessarily contain all the elements described above, but it is true that the contours of the various concepts should be evident. Preaching is the proclamation of God's Word via explication and application.

- o A crisis of faith, as in the case of the listeners to the Hebrews sermon, can manifest on the surface in a congregation in the form of different symptoms such as poor contributions, neglected family devotions and an unwillingness to be of any service in the congregation. One of the dangers that could follow in the wake of preaching that is focused on these surface manifestations only, is that people may be superficially inspired to bring about visible changes (on the surface) in their conduct to impress and please the church council and the minister of the congregation. Doing so may well be regarded as symptoms of an existing crisis and will do nothing to improve the remaining underlying crisis of faith. It may well happen that such believers fail to witness and experience Christ's work of redemption in its full scope, strength and life-giving qualities. This would be a crisis of faith related to holding on to the very beginning and source of a faith that is secure and steadfast and lasting. In such a case, the believers could easily lack the knowledge and equipment they need for protecting themselves against falling victim to the stagnating life of faith without a plan. This would be a crisis of faith related to issues that adversely affect their spiritual growth.
- It may also be that members of the congregation feel discouraged by many disappointments and much suffering or neglect of loving care and attention, and that they therefore may suffer from a lack of perseverance. This would amount to a crisis of faith related to the fullness of times, the eventual destination of a life of faith. More than the mere surface structure of the situation in which the listeners find themselves and the symptoms that manifest in their spiritual life should therefore be mentioned in the preaching. The underlying in-depth structure (see the reference to Hebrews 4:12-13) must be taken into account. When the Word is pointed in a direction and applied like a sword, it will be necessary to cut deeper than the surface. The cutting and opening up must reach the very root of the matter that is investigated and addressed.

2.4 Conclusion

The Hebrews sermon makes it clear that although a given *zeitgeist* may play a major role in the act of preaching, its essence of is not determined first of all by the spirit of the times. As indicated, God's purpose through the ages has not been to keep silent. He has spoken many times and in many ways. The various concepts utilised for preaching as found within Hebrews highlight that a sermon based on God's Word is a living voice. The tenses of the listeners' existence are directly at stake within the act of preaching. It means that the living God, who has spoken in the past, still speaks in the present amid the paradoxes of human life. He has spoken in the last days, therefore listening to preaching brings to the fore the responsibility to mix the hearing of the Word with faith. It is our interest to indicate that preaching in arduous times should emphasise that preaching of the Word is the opposite of the mere speaking of a preacher about God's Word. The multi-faceted character of preaching requires that preachers and listeners should have a relationship in which a profound process of strengthening and development according to preaching will be made optimal.

Preaching that focuses on the multi-coloured nature or, as we have described it, a polyphony of voices, is preaching that is concerned with the communicative God. Kolb[49] is correct in assuming that listeners are to hear God speaking in his saving power and his presence in the sermon. The aim of the sermon is therefore to help listeners understand the text and not merely a religious truth, but His living voice. Its goal is that God may speak a gracious word through a text so that people may be given faith or be strengthened in faith by the Holy Spirit. The power of God's proclaimed Word in a polyphony of voices is a power centred in the message of the living Christ. Kolb[50] reiterates Luther's words, namely that *'a person's word is a little sound that disappears into the air and quickly vanishes. God's Word is greater than heaven and earth, even death and hell, for it is the power of God and remains forever. If it is God's Word, a person should hold it fast and believe that God Himself is talking to us'* (emphasis mine).

This involves a quality of understanding that preaching deals with the field of tension of God's speaking within the last days. Preaching of God's Word therefore inevitably enjoys an eschatological outlook (see chapter 10). The eschatological dimension in preaching unites the facts of the advent (coming) of Christ in us, with us and through us, right to end of all things. This view of a new future in Christ also shapes a new look on present circumstances, therefore the Hebrews sermon does not hesitate to underline the importance of God who has spoken in the last days. Preaching of the living voice of God puts listeners in his living presence, of a God who was, who still is and ever will be. Preaching that engages the functioning of a polyphony of voices admits, as Maarten Luther once did, that God's voice is transformative. Meuser[51] quotes Luther as follows:

---

49 R. Kolb, *Martin Luther and the Enduring Word of God: The Wittenberg School and Its Scripture-Centered Proclamation* (Grand Rapids: Baker Academic, 2016), 73.
50 Kolb, *Martin Luther*, 48.
51 F.W. Meuser, *Luther the preacher* (Minneapolis: Augsburg Fortress, 1983), 52.

'*He speaks and things that never were come into existence while things that do exist are radically remade. Kingdoms fall. Battle bows are broken. Peace descends upon an unruly humankind*' (emphasis mine).This was the expectation when Luther stood up to preach. When God renames a thing in his Word we are not dealing in metaphors but with reality connects with the creative power of God's Word. We are confronted with the new creation in order that '*darkness becomes light. Death becomes sleep. Deserts bloom with life. The crooked becomes straight. The ungodly are justified. Weakness becomes a space for the power of sufficient grace. All these gifts are granted through the power of the one who promises*' (my emphasis).

Preaching is indeed a colourful picturing or painting act in which God's speaking in Christ within the last days is communicated. This involves a polyphony of interrelated voices, and the challenge will always be that a blending of voices has to materialise for the speaking of words to become true preaching of the Word of God. The pneumatological mystery of the unique blending of voices cannot be ignored. These various concepts for preaching enable the understanding that, after all, preaching is a creative act.

REFERENCES

Arndt, W., F.W. Gingrich, F.W. Danker, and W.A. Bauer. *Greek-English Lexicon of the New Testament and Other Early Christian Literature: A Translation and Adaption of the Fourth Revised and Augmented Edition of Walter Bauer's Griechisch-Deutsches Worterbuch zu den Schrift en des Neuen Testaments and der übrigen urchristlichen Literatur*. Chicago: University of Chicago Press, 2002.

Barton, B.B., D. Veerman, and L.K. Taylor. *Hebrews*. Life Application Bible Commentary. Wheaton: Tyndale House, 1997.

Brown, J. *Hebrews*. Geneva Series of Commentaries. Edinburg: The Bath Press, 1999.

Bruce, F.F. *The Epistle to the Hebrews*. The New International Commentary of the New Testament. Grand Rapids: Eerdmans, 1990.

Brueggemann, W. *The Word Militant: Preaching a Decentering Word*. Minneapolis: Fortress, 2010.

Buttrick, D.G. "A Reader on Preaching."
In *On Preaching a Parable: The Problem of Homiletic Method*, edited by D. Day, J.A. Astley, and L.J. Francis. Burlington: Ashgate, 2007.

Cilliers, Johan H. *Binne die kring-dans van die kuns: Die betekenis van estetika vir die gereformeerde liturgie*. Stellenbosch: Sun Press, 2007.

Coetsee, A.J. "The Unfolding of God's Revelation in Hebrews 1:1-2a." *HTS Teologiese Studies/Theological Studies* 72, no. 3 (2016): a3221. http://dx.doi.org/10.4102/hts.v72i3.3221.

Cromhout, M. "The 'Cloud of Witnesses' as Part of the Public Court of Reputation in Hebrews." *HTS Teologiese Studies/Theological Studies* 68, no. 1 (2012): Art. #1151, 6 pages. http:/ / dx.doi.org/ 10.4102/ hts.v68i1.1151.

De Wet, F.W., F.P. Kruger, and C. Stark. "Around Capes of Good Hope God's Wind Never Subsides."

In *Preaching Promise within the Paradoxes of Life*, Studia Homiletica 11, edited by J.H. Cilliers and L. Hansen. Stellenbosch: African Sun Media, 2019.

Du Toit, Anrie. *Hebreërs vir vandag [Hebrews for today]*. Vereeniging: CUM boeke, 2004.

Ellingworth, P. *Commentary on Hebrews*. New International Greek Testament Commentary. Grand Rapids: Eerdmans, 1993.

Flanigan, J.M. *Hebrews: What the Bible Teaches*. Ritchie New Testament Commentaries. Kilmarnock: John Ritchie, 1997.

Guthrie, Donald. *Hebrews*. Tyndale New Testament Commentaries. Grand Rapids: Eerdmans, 1996.

Hermelink, J. "Preaching as a Language of Hope."

In *Theological Understanding of Preaching Hope*, edited by C.J.A. Vos, L.L. Logan, and J.H. Cilliers. Pretoria: Protea Book House, 2015.

Hermelink, J. "The Theological Understand of Preaching Hope."

In *Preaching as a Language of Hope*, Studia Homiletica 6, edited by C. Vos, L.L. Hogan, and J.H. Cilliers. Zoetermeer: Boekencentrum, 2007.

Immink, Gerrit. *The Touch of the Sacred: The Practice, Theology, and Tradition of Christian Worship*. Grand Rapids: Wm. B. Eerdmans, 2014.

Johnston, W.B. *The Epistle to the Hebrews*. Calvin's Commentaries. Grand Rapids: Eerdmans, 1994.

Kistemaker, Simon J. *Hebrews*. New Testament Commentary. Grand Rapids: Baker Book House, 1994.

Kolb, R. *Martin Luther and the Enduring Word of God: The Wittenberg School and Its Scripture-Centered Proclamation*. Grand Rapids: Baker Academic, 2016.

Kruger, Ferdi P. "Prediking en gesindheidsverandering: 'n Prakties-teologiese studie in die lig van Hebreërs." ThD thesis. (Potchefstroom: North-West University, Dept. Practical Theology, 2002.

Lane, W.L. *Hebrews 1-8*. Dallas: World Books, 1991.

Long, Thomas G. *Hebrews*. Interpretation: A Bible Commentary for Teaching and Preaching. Louisville: John Knox Press, 1997.

Long, Thomas G. *Preaching from Memory to Hope*. Louisville: John Knox Press, 2009.
Long, Thomas G. *The Witness of Preaching*. Louisville: John Knox Press, 2005.
Louw, J.P. and E.A. Nida. *Greek English Lexicon of the New Testament (I)*. New York: United Bible Studies, 1989.
Louw, J.P. and E.A. Nida. *Greek English Lexicon of the New Testament (II)*. New York: United Bible Studies, 1989.
Meuser, F.W. *Luther the Preacher*. Minneapolis: Augsburg Fortress, 1983.
Mitchell, H.H. *Celebration and Experience in Preaching*. Nashville: Abingdon Press, 2008.
Ott, C. and S.J. Strauss. *Encountering Theology of Mission*. Grand Rapids: Baker House, 2010.
Pakpahan, B.J. *God Remembers: Towards a Theology of Remembrance as a Basis of Reconciliation in Communal Conflict*. Amsterdam: VU University Press, 2013.
Phillips, J. *Exploring Hebrews*. New Jersey: Loiszeaux Brothers, 1992.
Pieterse, Hennie J.C. *Verwoording en prediking*. Pretoria: N.G. Kerkboekhandel, 1985.
Pugh, J.C. *Religiousless Christianity: Dietrich Bonhoeffer in Troubled Times*. London: Clark, 2008.
Saliers, D.E. *Worship as Theology: Foretaste of Glory Divine*. Nashville: Abingdon Press, 2010.
Schlinger, M.A. "Transformative Learning: Educational Vision for the 21st Century." *Convergence* 33, no. 1 (2014).
Smit, D.J. *Geloof en openbare lewe*. Stellenbosch: Sun Press, 2008.
Stott, John R.W. *The Contemporary Christian*. Leicester: Inter-Varsity Press, 1992.
Tyagi, B. *Listening: An Important Skill and Its Various Aspects*. London: Longman, 2013.
Van Houwelingen, P.H.R. "The Epistle to the Hebrews: Faith Means Perseverance." *Journal of Early Christian History* 3, no. 1 (2013). DOI: 10.1080/ 2222582X.2013.11877278.
Venter, Cassie J.H. "Die Gees, die Woord en die bedienaar van die Woord." In *Koninkryk, Gees en Woord*, edited by J.C. Coetzee. Pretoria: N.G. Kerkboekhandel, 1988.
Vines, J. *The Believers Guide to Hebrews*. New Jersey: Loizeaux, 1993.
Vorster, Koos M. "Vernuwing in die prediking in die lig van hedendaagse lewensbeskoulike tendense." *In die Skriflig* 29, no. 3 (Maart 1995).
Williams, D.T. "After the Order of Melchizedek: Pre-Existence and Salvation in Hebrews." *The South African Baptist Journal of Theology* 5, no. 1 (1996).

CHAPTER 3

SERVANT OR MASTER?

Preaching and rhetoric

Maarten Kater

Preaching, as we seen yet as a polyphony of voices itself (cf. 2.1), is to use language in a proper way and speaking in an orderly fashion. At least, this should be a matter of fact in our preaching practices. Hardly a single homiletical handbook therefore exists that excludes rhetorical elements such as, for instance, sermon structures, effective and affective language, logical development of thoughts and using linguistic ornaments[1]. All this because of the intertwining with the listeners' attitudes (cf. 2.2.)

This chapter consists of three parts. It commences with a small phenomenological exploration from the first homiletical handbook we know, Augustine's *De doctrina christiana* [On Christian Teaching][2]. This handbook is explored to tap into his voice from the catholic tradition on the proper use of rhetorical elements. Subsequently, an overview is given of the rhetorical aspects of the Hebrews sermon. Lastly, a plea is offered from Hebrews as an impetus to use our imagination and imaginative language, once more while we are living in a so-called visual age[3]. It is astonishing to see how the author of Hebrews makes use of a picture that remains in the background while he speaks to this congregation living in the first century, which age could also be typified as visual.

---

1 A.o. Bert de Leede and Ciska Stark, *Ontvouwen: Protestantse prediking in de praktijk* (Zoetermeer: Boekencentrum, 2018), 141-232 on both narrative discourse (according to Aristotle's elements of *mythos*, *mimèsis*, and *catharsis*) and argumentative discourse (as in Quintillianus' famous handbook on rhetoric); Paul Scott Wilson, *The Practice of Preaching*, rev. ed. (Nashville: Abingdon Press, 2007), chapter 3 "Theology and Rhetoric". In sermon analysis there will be also always a rhetorical part, as shown in Wilfried Engemann, *Einführung in die Homiletik* (Tübingen: A. Francke Verlag, 2002), 439-443.

2 Augustine, *De Doctrina Christiana* [Oxford Early Christian Texts, ed. Henry Chadwick] (Oxford: Clarendon, 2001).

3 H. David Schuringa, *Hearing the Word in a Visual Age: A Practical-Theological Consideration of Preaching Within the Contemporary Urge of Visualization* (Kampen: TUK, 1995).

3.1 Phenomenological exploration - Augustine's voice

To start with a very broad question: 'what makes a speaker heard'? Nobody doubts that this is not only a matter of *what* he or she says, but certainly *how* he or she brings it to the floor. One has this experience many times in one's own life, sitting in a chair and listening to a speaker. There is a world of difference concerning *how* you express in words what you want to say or must speak and *what* is said, especially when presenting things in a way in accordance with what you want to demonstrate.

Book IV of Augustine's *Doctrina christiana* deals with the subject of presenting our thoughts to others. Why is rhetoric and oratorical ability so important for him in expounding the truth? Because, as he saw in his days, many people who tried to convince others of false opinions were masters in presenting what they would like people to believe in, although it was false:

> *Since rhetoric is used to give conviction to both truth and falsehood, who could dare maintain the truth, which depends on us for its defence, should stand unarmed in the fight against falsehood? This would mean that those who are trying to give conviction to their falsehoods would know how to use an introduction to make their listeners favourable, interested, and receptive, while we would not; that they would expound falsehoods in descriptions that are succinct, lucid, and convincing, while we expound the truth in such a way as to bore our listeners, cloud their understanding, and stifle their desire to believe, that they would assail the truth and advocate falsehood with fallacious argument, while we would be too feeble either to defend what is true or refute what is false[...]? (IV.4, 197).*

Surely, eloquence should go hand in hand with wisdom from Scripture. Augustine avers that divinely inspired writers enjoy 'a kind of eloquence appropriate to writers who enjoy the highest authority and a full measure of divine inspiration' (IV, 25, 207). His book on presentation gives many examples from Scripture to demonstrate how wisdom is attended by eloquence[4]. However, he continues to say that this does not mean that the writer was forced to do so by the rules of rhetoric. They observe the rules because they are eloquent, and they not use them to become eloquent. The goal obviously is not to use an excellent style as such but, by the effort of using all oratorical means to teach, delight and move listeners. Augustine exclaims:

---

4 A.o. Rom. 5:3-5 (climax, *gradatio*, using commata, cola and periods, Quintilianus, 9.3.54-7); 2 Cor. 11:16-30 moving by its rhythm caused by the divisions in two, three or four colas; a literal analysis of Amos 6:1-6.

What use is a golden key, if it cannot unlock what we want to be unlocked, and what is wrong with a wooden one, if it can, since our sole aim is to open doors? (IV, 73; 229).

Augustine spent much time on this classical (Aristotelian) rhetorical triad: instruct (*docere*), delight (*delectere*) and move (*movere*). He further suggests that this triplet corresponds with understanding pleasure and obedience on the side of the listeners. Nevertheless, the preacher

should be in no doubt that any ability he has and however much he has derives more from his devotion to prayer than his dedication to oratory; and so, by praying for himself and for those he is about to address, he must become a man of prayer before becoming a man of words. (IV, 87; 235)[5].

That classic triad is combined by Cicero with three styles as quoted by Augustine (IV, 96; 241): 'The eloquent speaker will be one who can treat small matters in a restrained style to instruct, intermediate matters in a mixed style to delight and important matters in a grand style to move an audience'[6]. There is another classic trio which is mentioned in almost all rhetorical handbooks and in many homiletical studies: *logos, ethos* and *pathos*. The grand style is not so much embellished with ornament - as often is the case when using the mixed style - but is inflamed by heartfelt emotion (*pathos*). One must be cautious not to think of the triad and three styles as having a one-to-one-relation to each other, but rather in the sense that a speaker should always have these three aims and pursue them to the best of his or her ability even when performing a particular style.

Characteristic	Verb	Purpose	Style
Logos	Docere	Understanding	Restrained
Ethos	Delectare	Pleasure	Mixed
Pathos	Movere	Obedience	Grand

---

5 Sit orator antequam dictor.
6 Augustine, *De Doctrina Christiana*, 241, quotes Cicero, *Orat.*, 101, already introduced in 69 where Cicero's descriptions are resp. *subtile, modicum, vehemens*.

In an *Encyclopedia of Rhetoric*, this special aspect and effect of *pathos* is stated as follows:

> *Of the three appeals of logos, ethos, and pathos, it is the last that impels an audience to act. Emotions range from mild to intense; some, such as well-being, are gentle attitudes and outlooks, while others, such as sudden fury, are so intense that they overwhelm rational thought. Images are particularly effective in arousing emotions, whether those images are visual and direct as sensations, or cognitive and indirect as memory or imagination, and part of a rhetor's task is to associate the subject with such images*[7].

It is important to highlight two things around this citation. The first is the relation between *pathos* and 'act'. There is a connection between using *pathos* and our will as the captain and steering wheel of our behaviour. Second, as far as our language is concerned, the use of our imagination by means of images and/ or metaphors or visual language.

Ultimately, the general function of eloquence in any of these three styles is to speak in a manner intended *to persuade*:

> *In the restrained style he persuades people that what he says is true, in the grand style he persuades them to do what they knew to be necessary, but were not doing; in the mixed style he persuades people that he is speaking attractively or elaborately* (IV, 143; 273).

For Augustine, then, preaching consists of sound teaching delivered in a clear and proper design, while it has its purpose as much in persuasion as information. His honouring of the use of rhetoric was not at all in conflict with his strong conviction of the necessity of the Inner Teacher in the heart as his *De doctrina Christiana* shows us[8].

3.2 Hebrews from rhetorical perspective

As has been argued, rhetoric is not simply a form of superfluous expression: its correct use sheds light on the meaning of what is said and can improve the eloquence of what is said. In the first chapter above, some signs of eloquence already surfaced, namely the use of the superlative (*kreiton*), the function of the *exempla* in Hebrews and what the connection

---

7 See '*pathos*' in: Thomas O. Sloane, ed., *Encyclopedia of Rhetoric* (Oxford: University Press, 2001).
8 See Peter T. Sanlon, *Augustine's Theology of Preaching* (Minneapolis: Fortress Press, 2014).

of these two phenomena should be in a well-thought-out speech such as a sermon.

Carefully considered, Hebrews actually appears to be deliberate in nature when it comes to its rhetorical elements. Why is Hebrews such a good specimen for delivering expressive and impressive sermons? I suggest one or two reasons below.

Hebrews enjoys an overall structure informed by its nature as a 'word of exhortation' (13:22). Consider one or two examples. Up to Hebrews 10:25, the homily alternates the expositions wherein two central themes of the Son and the High Priest are in the foreground with the corresponding exhortations five times (I: 2:1-4, II: 3:7-4:13, III: 5:11-6:12, IV: 10:19-39 and V: 12:14-29) before reaching its climax in Hebrews 12:25-20 as the closing part of the fifth one. The last chapter functions as a concise synthesis in which a climax is included, that is, the so-called *peroratio*.

Second, its structure relates to the opening verses, which is highly satisfactory. Much work has been done in textual analysis to explain the make-up and the meaning of this *exordium*. The start of a speech, referred to as the *exordium* in rhetoric, is an introduction that appears most often in argumentative texts. It consists of three purposes according to rhetorical rules: 1) *docere*, that is, informing the public on what you are to be about to say, 2) *placere*, that is, attracting attention and pleasing the public and 3) *persuadere*, that is, getting the audience on your side for your speech.

The *exordium* of Hebrews reads as follows (Hebr.1:1-4):

1-2a *Long ago, at many times and in many ways, God spoke to our fathers by the prophets, but in these last days he has spoken to us by his Son,*

2b-3 *whom he appointed the heir of all things, through whom also he created the world.*
He is the radiance of the glory of God and the exact imprint of his nature, and he upholds the universe by the word of his power. After making purification for sins, he sat down at the right hand of the Majesty on high,

4 *having become as much superior to angels as the name he has inherited is more excellent than theirs.*

The central theme (1-2a) appears to be that Gods has spoken 'eschatologicaly' ('in these last days') in one who is the Son! This does not merely function as information, but as a moving appeal to his addressees. Such an appeal is made very forcefully. How does the preacher amplify his appeal? By means of summarizing the awesomeness of the 'One who is Son' (2b-3) and his majestic and eminent position (4) as much superior to the angels, and even more excellent than that. In Him, God speaks absolutely, definitely and ultimately.

Furthermore, there is no doubt that Hebrews is a *sermon* written with the apparent intention of being *spoken*. Although in the scope of this study - which is not an exegetical study as such - it is not possible to discuss all the well-thought-out elements of this sermon, but it is worthwhile briefly to mention an instance or two of this. First of all, it is important that the author uses colloquial language and makes it clear that it is critical for the hearers to be able to remember what he has to say. Think, for example, of his exposition on Christ and his exhortations that remind Christians of the multifaceted work of Christ. In doing so, he makes use of all kinds of elements from rhetoric. The most important and/ or frequent are:

- the so-called *parallelismus membrorum* in the introduction (1-2a) to imprint the addressees and actualize the sermon for the hearers in the two lines of the God who speaks, then and now, as indicated formerly by mediators, the fathers and prophets, and now the Son. So, then, the second line always makes the first line stronger as a heightening of what has been said already. It sounds like a song, a poem!
- *alliterations* are of great help to ensconce the message in their memories: for instance, in the sentences right at the beginning, in Greek a fourfold 'p'-sound occurs, as found in *polumeroos, polutropoos, patrasin, profètais* in 1-2a as well as the ongoing 'e' and 'è' tones (2b-3).
- the *inclusion*, that is, inclusion of the thought of the 'You are the same' from Psalm 102 (Hebrews 1:10-12) and 'Jesus Christ is the same yesterday and today, and for ever' (Hebrews 13:8), connecting the beginning and end of the sermon; in the same way the inclusion of the central thought of the introduction (God is *speaking*, 1:1) and the end (*word* of exhortation; 13:22), which also joins exposition and exhortation as is done in the whole message.
- frequent use of the *anaphor*, the time and again repeated start of any example of the heroes of faith: 'by faith' (Hebrews 11). One can well imagine the impact it has while those past listeners engaged in sermon when reading aloud: by faith...., by faith, ... by faith..., by faith... and so forth. The repetition serves to imprint the message.
- the use of *paranomasia* as a rhetorical device that can be *defined* as a phrase intentionally used to exploit the confusion between words that enjoy homophonic similarities but enjoy different *meanings*. It

is word play, and is also known as a 'pun'. The citation of Psalm 40 in Hebrews 10:5-7, theologically understood, is admittedly more than a rhetorical issue (cf. chapter 1), but no less from the perspective of language.
- the sharp words of Hebrews 6:4-8 which are followed by the very kind words of the following verses, a rhetorical figure to underline the seriousness of the former in the amiable light of the latter. 'Though we speak in this way, yet in your case, beloved, we feel sure of better things — things that belong to salvation' (Hebr. 6:9). Consider also the context provided with the interruption that starts in Hebrews 5:11. Such an interruption, with its admonition, is rhetorically useful for regaining lost attention at that stage in the sermon, before entering into the body of the lengthiest expositional cycle.
- tying together two sections by means of a so-called 'hook-word', which was common practice in Greek rhetoric and was referred to as HUSTERON proteron, for instance, attaching letters to the word that has already been given, centring on the plural derived from a given singular, or repeating the same verb in another conjugation such as connecting lalounti (Hebr. 12:18-24) with lalounta (Hebr. 12:25-29).

Besides these rhetorical instruments, we must ponder very briefly another connected question, namely around logic and method. Within homiletics there has been much discussion of the method of preaching for instance in relation to a deductive or inductive approach and the use of propositions or narratives since the movement of the *New Homiletics* which started with Fred Craddock's booklet *As One Without Authority*[9]. This canonical Hebrew homily contains both aspects and we should bear in mind that many phenomena cannot be reduced to an either/ or status. All too often, proposition and narrative are dealt with as opposites. The proposition at the beginning of Hebrews, the phrase 'God has spoken', is however founded immediately on, connected with and illustrated by two narratives: the story of Israel evoked by the reference to fathers and prophets and the narrative of the Son Jesus Christ; both function throughout the sermon's development. So, we find all kinds of elements that belong at once to a deductive and inductive style of preaching:
- propositions as apodictic sentences proclaiming truth in all parts of this sermon: for instance, the propositions in 2:18-18 and 4:14-16;

---
9 Fred Craddock, *As One Without Authority*, rev. ed. (St. Louis: Chalice Press, 2001).

- narratives,, for instance the story of the exodus, chapters 3-4);
- abundant use of examples, for instance, the 'cloud' around us consisting of the many witnesses of faith, as found in chapter 11;
- use of an image such as the tabernacle that always serves as a means of imagining the unimaginable of the celestial sanctuary, entertained throughout the sermon.

It is of further interest to consider how *examples*, which function in one of the central arguments in Hebrews, are used according to the rules of rhetoric. After all, according to the rules of art, the *exemplum* is the most important form of speech in the *genus deliberativum*, that is, the genus used as a political device with the central question: shall we do it, or don't we? Aristotle then argues that in this way we receive clues for the future from what has happened in terms of the example from the past. Decisive, then, is the relationship between example and the future. Both aspects of an example, a relationship of analogy and the involvement with the future, occur in Hebrews. For instance, the eleventh chapter provide many *exempla* that do not look back to people who once lived, but gazes is forward! This is shown once again when we include the sequel in chapter 12 in these *exempla* (see chapter 7).

3.3 Imagination as an instrument

But what about the role of the imagination in homiletics? Is not our imagination a free tour through our mental kingdom, of free invention and therefore not governed by rules, wild and untamed, disconnected from what is real[10]? Paul Ricoeur has shown that we could speak of imagination from a different point of view, namely as a rule-governed invention and the power of re-description:

Through this first trait, the act of reading accords with the idea of a norm-governed productivity to the extent that it may be said to be guided by a productive imagination at work in the text itself. Beyond this, I would like to see in the reading of a text such as the Bible a creative operation unceasingly employed in decontextualizing its meaning and recontextualizing it in today's Sitz-im-Leben. Through this second trait, the act of reading realises the union of fiction and redescription that characterizes the imagination in the most pregnant sense of this term'[11].

---

10 Thomas H. Troeger, *Imagining a Sermon* (Nashville: Abingdon Press, 1980), 99-117 illustrates this line of thought.
11 Paul Ricoeur, *Figuring the Sacred. Religion, Narrative, and Imagination* (Minneapolis: Fortress Press, 1995), 144-145; Walter Brueggeman is another defender of the use of imagination as it belongs to the Scriptures itself. See his *Prophetic Imagination* (Minneapolis: Fortress Press, 2018) as a revised and updated revision of the

When we apply these thoughts to Hebrews 3:7-4:11, one experiences precisely that power of recontextualization from the productive imagination at work in the text itself as one listens to these very words: 'Today, when *you* hear [present tense!] His voice...' (Hebr. 3:7) (my emphasis).

Hebrews is attractive, not least because it stirs the imagination again and again by means of the stories told and even explicit *imaginative language*. This strikes one as an aspect that should be vital in today's sermons, as our culture is described and characterized by 'thinking by seeing', that is, as a visual age. Referring to our culture is just to plea for considering the importance of the use of our imagination in the field of homiletics for practical reasons. There is, however, a far more primary impetus for preaching as putting eyes in the ears of man. Cilliers (2016) has beautifully expressed this reality by showing the connection between sound and sight. Preaching is about voicing a vision[12]!

What kind of imaginative elements does Hebrews hand over to us? One can think of all kinds of 'loose' elements, such as the examples from the gallery of Hebrews 11. It almost resembles 'an imaginary journey and we take [it] along with us'. We experience the desert journey (Hebr.3-4), go on our way to the city that has foundations (Hebr.11-12), enter a stadium at the start of the twelfth chapter and stand at Sinai at that moment when it changes for us into the heavenly Jerusalem. Furthermore, Hebrews as the voicing of a vision reminds us of what is said about the tent sanctuary, the tabernacle, here introduced as a *parabola* and *paradigm*.

Last but not least, the sermon further suggests in terms of imagination the connection between a complex speech or lecture and the layout of a building. Cicero wrote in his *De oratore* that remembering consists of capturing a kind of 'background' and using images that find a place in that background. Having a visual background and making a point visually supports the memory of those who pass on or receive the message. In Hebrews, the visual background is that of the tabernacle as connected with the event of the Great Reconciliation Day, the Day of Atonement! Both images are engraved in the collective memory of the Jews. When we use a building as the layout of an image, it has the effect that the listener can move around in that building and give himself or herself a place in

---

2001-edition; *An Introduction to the Old Testament. The Canon and Christian Imagination* (Louisville/London: Westminster Press, 2003): 'The Bible is never simply reportage and description, but is always interpretive commentary that pushes upon the observable to the constructed, that is *imagination* beyond the 'given', 395.

12 Johan Cilliers, *A Space for Grace: Towards an Aesthetics of Preaching* (Stellenbosch: SUN Press, 2016).

that building. In the case of Hebrews, this is the temple. All this seems to me exemplary material towards modelling one's preaching in a concrete and visual way[13].

But how best to exploit profound imagistic functions in our preaching week in and week out? Richard Eslinger has elaborated the following considerations around the homiletic method[14]:

- Images allow us to recognize everyday objects as such:
- Using images is not a matter of depending overly much on narrative illustrations to achieve the recognition of the everyday world by the congregation. Illustrating cannot be reduced to to merely conveying some anecdote or other or appending " good stories' to 'points'. Two difficulties frequently arise around these considerations: first, overuse of stories in sermons ironically tends to diminish their impact. Second, when such stories are told, meaning tends to become more narrowly focused and less encompassing in scope. It is the hackneyed, indeed terrible 'I once met a man….' kind of sermonic anecdote that almost immediately works to *de*-generalize the issue at stake. In contrast to this, the homilitician often has a happy option at hand towards imaging the meaning at stake: images connect to narratives that are much more useful than providing a merely anecdotal illustration. It is not important that each and every person has the experience being imagined, since an effective image invites everyone to 'see' in the same way. Buttrick rightly says: 'Multiple illustrations will always weaken analogy, and thereby make understanding even more difficult'[15].
- Images allow us to focus on a particular aspect of what we experience:
- The converse of the insight that narratives evoke images is that the presentation of an image will invoke the narrative that gave birth to it. Of course, one image could be related to more than just one narrative, while the latter may not be compatible. E.g. the image of a high rock which could be used - and often is used - to tell the narrative of safety, but from this image could be ensued a narrative of great difficulties to overcome. One has to choose an image with

---

13 Paul David Landgraf, "The Structure of Hebrews: A Word of Exhortation in the Light of the Day of Atonement," in *A Cloud of Witnesses*, eds. Richard Bauckam et al. (London/New York: T&T Clark, 2008), 19-27.

14 R.L. Eslinger, *Narrative and Imagination: Preaching the Worlds that Shape Us* (Minneapolis: Fortress Press, 1995), 141-147.

15 D. Buttrick, *Homiletic: Moves and Structures* (Philadelphia: Fortress Press, 1987), 135-136.

precision around a well-focused point of view to bring into immediacy one particular facet of personal and communal experience with power.
- Images can provide new insights by invoking a shift in perspective:
- To say in a sermon which or whose perspective a narrative embodies can dramatically shift the assembly's experience and insight may well be knocking on a door that will be opened. This must therefore be kept in mind when preparing a sermon. When we look, for instance, to Judas is viewed in his aspect of being Jesus 'prophet, namely when he exclaims that Jesus really is innocent as indicated by the phrase 'I have sinned by betraying innocent blood' (Matthew 27:4), we really do gain a totally different perspective on him then seeing him just as Jesus' traitor.

3.4 Preaching with *pathos*

This Hebrew sermon as a 'word of exhortation' (*paraklèsis*) contains many elements that demonstrate the *pathos* of the character of the preacher. He reassures his addressees of God's trustworthiness when he demonstrates from the Old Testament that when God wants to make his intentions clear to his people, he uses emphatic forms of speech, such as promises and even oaths. With these emphatic forms come strong affections. Nevertheless, this is not preaching emotionally. Indeed, I would like to replace the word 'emotion' with another one, perhaps *pathos* since, even as it connotes an emotion, it is far more specific in character. This word is known - as we have seen already - as one of the three aspects of the art of persuasion that Aristotle mentions in his famous book *Rhethoric*. The book gives a systematic account of human psychology arranged on contrasting pairs such as anger versus calmness, friendship versus enmity and so on. He underscores the *cognitive* side of these *passions* or *affections*. Another famous rhetorician in the Latin tradition, Cicero, viewed the three elements of teaching, delighting and moving as the goals of an address. *Pathos* is related to the last two elements: to delight and to move. Surely, one has to choose *pathos* as the mode of persuasion to move the hearts and hands.

However, the power of *pathos* also poses a great danger[16]. To recognise this, one has to delve into the history of emotion, as described by Thomas

---

16 Quintilian in his *Institutio Oratoria* illustrates the (mis)use of that power: 'The man who can carry a judge with him, and put him in whatever frame of mind he wishes, whose words move men to tears and anger, has always been a rare creature. Yet this is what dominates the courts, this is the eloquence that reigns supreme (...). Where force has be brought to bear on judges' feelings and their minds distracted from truth there the orator's true work begins.'

Dixon, in his important book *From Passions to Emotions: The Creation of a Secular Psychology*[17]. He demonstrates that in the 19th century Charles Darwin and William James gave birth to 'emotion' as a *psychological* category. They cast off the Christian and inner connotations of *passions* and *affections*. Dixon shows that 'emotions' became confined to sensorial bodily expressions encapsulated in biological and measurable explanations. This became the fashionable way of thinking in many scientific circles and a great part of society. Think for example of the dogmatic view contained in the so-called *New Atheism* ironically 'preached' by Richard Dawkins and others. According to this movement, religion is reducible to a mere feeling, an emotional activity, and has nothing to do with rationality and science.

For these reasons, I suggest speaking of *affections* instead of emotions, because our *affections* stem from a deeper level than what, these days, people think about when they hear the word emotion. *Affections* are connected with our mind and heart, heart and will. *Pathos*, then, has to be in keeping with the two other components in preaching, namely *logos* and *ethos*. Theologically seen, this preference has to do with the *image of God* and the central biblical idea of our 'heart' as the centre of feelings and knowledge. Moreover, using *affections* corresponds to its current use in social science and theology.

In my mind, preaching without *pathos* is definitely and ultimately impossible. A preacher does not have a message: he or she *is* a messenger. The message becomes flesh and blood in the person of the messenger.

We all consider Christian preaching as a communicative form. Every communication is rhetorical, because it uses some technique to affect the beliefs, actions or emotions of an audience. The simplest verbal techniques are pitch, volume and repetition such as the cry 'help, Help, HELP!!' In this way we use affective language and, of course, many other rhetorical and expressive techniques.

But the most important reason for the argument made here has to do with communication itself. There is no communication without communion. Whoever wants to preach must have his audience in his or her heart. We are to open our hearts before we open our mouths. We have passion for others in heart and soul. Preaching is about '*Inter-esse/ Mit-Sein*', that is, *being among them*, being among the audience.

Bohren employs the German word *Sehnsucht*, of which the nuanced meaning and context are difficult to translate[18]. It involves a very deep

---

17 Thomas Dixon, *From Passions to Emotions: The Creation of a Secular Psychology* (Cambridge: University Press, 2003).
18 Rudolf Bohren, *Predigtlehre* (Gütersloh: Gütersloher Verlagshaus, 1993, 1971), 484-488.

longing. Without this *Sehnsucht* there never will be preaching as passion, that is, affectionate preaching. Our speech will be empty without this. *Sehnsucht* describes the mystery of love as the mystery of Christ's presence whereby preacher and listeners are brought together.

Or is this too much? At any rate, when our heart is involved in what we want to communicate it is impossible to speak without *pathos*, because it involves love deeper than the ocean and higher than the sky. It is, therefore, such a privilege that preaching is just part of the liturgy as a whole. Performative, formative, affective and imaginative words sound during the whole service

Most importantly: the gospel writers paint their portraits of Jesus using a kaleidoscope of brilliantly 'affectionate' colours. Jesus felt compassion; he was angry, indignant and consumed with zeal; he was troubled, greatly distressed, very sorrowful, depressed, deeply moved and grieved; he sighed, he wept and sobbed, he groaned, he was in agony, he was surprised and amazed; he rejoiced very greatly and was full of joy; he greatly desired and he loved.

From all this the following central remarks on preaching with *pathos* and the use of affectionate language arise:

- Use rhetorical devices freely.
- Prepare your heart by living attentively.
- The goal of our sermons is, besides teaching, to evoke passions to move heart and will. Love and reasonableness are connected.
- Remember Horace's proverb: *Artis etiam est celare Artem* ('It is the point of art to conceal art'). Too much explanation makes an image dead.

In sum, what is brought to the fore in this chapter is that rhetoric really functions in Hebrews as a good servant and not a master, for rhetoric as such cannot deliver the living God who speaks. If the human words of a sermon are to become God's Word, then only God could make them so and not by means of any technique. Hebrews shows us that it is God who speaks: so he wills and he does, actually today, when you hear his voice! However, God talk should be presented in gratitude with whatever rhetorical devices are useful and helpful for audiences to grasp the message, as a matter of life and death.

REFERENCES

Augustine, A. "De Doctrina Christiana." In *Oxford Early Christian Texts*, edited by H. Chadwick. Oxford: Clarendon, 2001.

Bauckam, Richard, Daniel Driver, Trevor Hart, and Nathan MacDonald, eds. *A Cloud of Witnesses: The Theology of Hebrews in Its Ancient Context*. London/New

Bohren, Rudolf. *Predigtlehre*. Gütersloh: Gütersloher Verlagshaus, 1993, 1971.

Brueggeman, W. *An Introduction to the Old Testament: The Canon and Christian Imagination*. Louisville/London: Westminster Press, 2003.

Brueggeman, W. *Prophetic Imagination*. Rev. ed. Minneapolis: Fortress Press, 2018.

Buttrick, D. *Homiletic: Moves and Structures*. Philadelphia: Fortress Press, 1987.

Cilliers, Johan. *A Space for Grace: Towards an Aesthetics of Preaching*. Stellenbosch: SUN Press, 2016.

Craddock, Fred. *As One Without Authority*. Rev. ed. St. Louis: Chalice Press, 2001.

Dixon, T. *From Passions to Emotions: The Creation of a Secular Psychology*. Cambridge: University Press, 2003.

Engemann, Wilfried. *Einführung in die Homiletik*. Tübingen: A. Francke Verlag, 2002.

Eslinger, R.L. *Narrative and Imagination: Preaching the Worlds that Shape Us*. Minneapolis: Fortress Press, 1995.

Landgraf, P.D. "The Structure of Hebrews: A Word of Exhortation in the Light of the Day of Atonement." In *A Cloud of Witnesses*, edited by Richard Bauckham, Daniel Driver, Trevor Hart, and Nathan MacDonald, 19-27. London/New York: T&T Clark, 2008.

Leede, B. and C. Stark. *Ontvouwen: Protestantse prediking in de praktijk*. Zoetermeer: Boekencentrum, 2018.

Ricoeur, P. *Figuring the Sacred: Religion, Narrative, and Imagination*. Minneapolis: Fortress Press, 1995.

Sanlon, P.T. *Augustine's Theology of Preaching*. Minneapolis: Fortress Press, 2014.

Schuringa, H.D. *Hearing the Word in a Visual Age: A Practical-Theological Consideration of Preaching Within the Contemporary Urge of Visualization*. Kampen: Theological University, 1995.

Sloane, Thomas O., ed. *Encyclopedia of Rhetoric*. Oxford: University Press, 2001.

Troeger, Thomas H. *Imagining a Sermon*. Nashville: Abingdon Press, 1980.
Wilson, P.S. *The Practice of Preaching*. Rev. ed. Nashville: Abingdon Press, 2007.

CHAPTER 4

THE INSEPARABLE INTERTWINING OF THE PREACHER'S AND THE LISTENERS' ATTITUDES IN THE ACT OF PREACHING

Ferdi Kruger

Preaching according to the Hebrews sermon spreads the Word of God and the Word of God is 'living and powerful, and sharper than any two-edged sword, piercing even to the division of soul and spirit, and of joints and marrow, and is a discerner of the thoughts and intents of the heart' (my emphasis). Not one thing or creature in all creation is unknown to God or hidden from his sight. Everything lies open and naked before his eyes. He is the God to whom we must give account, as indicated in Hebrews 4:12 and 13. This includes attitudes, of which a multitude is evident in the act of listening to preaching. The attitudes of people could be beneficial, but could also be so negative that they threaten the efficacy of preaching. The preacher of the Hebrews sermon is aware of this very insight, but does not address the listeners from the height that may go along with the insight. Instead, they are called *holy brothers*. The attitude of speaking to someone as one who is part of them and not addressing them as strangers or even as aliens is therefore of critical importance. The construction of the listeners through preaching will fall short of its deepest purpose if the relational aspect between preacher and listeners is not honoured. Construction through preaching cannot be functional if it is merely treated as a technical aspect of the sermon. The bond between preacher and listener within the framework of the Hebrews sermon has a deeper foundation, of people finding themselves in a relationship. With a view to the resultant zeal to speak words of exhortation, attitude is mentioned seven times, each time within the admonishing (paranetic) sections of this sermon, as found in Hebrews 3:6, 4:11, 4:16, 6:11, 10:19, 10:35 and 13:6. Three concepts are utilised to highlight the importance of attitudes, namely παρρησια [boldness], θαρουντθας [boldness] as well as σπουδαζω [diligence to carry something out].

Chapter 2 above has indicated that all the concepts for preaching have a close relationship with either the preacher's attitude or listeners' concrete attitudes. Within this chapter, the focus will be on the relationship between preaching and the need for a change in attitudes. All people, one should acknowledge, have attitudes towards life itself, worship services and preaching. Attitude-forming is a process that begins in childhood. It is therefore important to locate the issue of the functioning of attitudes and also to indicate the distinctive manner in which attitudes can be changed. Attitudes, one should further remember, determine the meaningfulness of facts in people's lives. Persons tend to protect their attitudes by rationalising facts that conflict with these attitudes[1]. Attitudes are, after all, orientations that locate objects of thought on dimensions of judgement[2]. With the help of their attitudes, people make favourable or unfavourable evaluations of the objects of their thought, even of preaching.

Cleary[3] regards persuasive communication as an effective manner in which to change attitudes. The process in which an attitude is influenced or changed is called persuasion[4]. Persuasive communication is highly effective when relationships between people are in good order[5]. To persuade people through communication is to help them gain consensus to cooperate according to God's will for their lives[6]. In preaching, the preacher does not gang up against the listeners of sermons. Persuasion is different from manipulation, which drives people away from the communicator. In using liturgical language, preachers must first of all have an understanding about the fact that they are guiding or accompanying people as responsible participants in liturgy, because he or she is also a participant in the liturgy. Preachers must become personally engaged in the acknowledgement that he or she acts as listener amongst listeners[7]. The preacher's engagement with God's Word and the humble way in

---

1 Ferdi P. Kruger, "The Preacher's Vulnerable Attitudes in Naming Reality in a Neglected Society," *Verbum et Ecclesia* 43, no. 1 (2015): 4, Art. #1383, 9 pages, from http://dx.doi.org/10.4102/ve.v36i1.1383.
2 W. Weiten, *Psychology: Themes and Variations* (California: Brooks and Cole, 1992), 593.
3 S. Cleary, *The Communication Handbook: A Student Guide to Effective Communication* (Cape Town: Juta, 2010), 164.
4 S. Tubbs and S. Moss, *Human Communication: Principles and Contexts* (New York: McGraw-Hill, 2008), 29.
5 Z. Berg and A. Theron, *Psychology in the Work Context* (Cape Town: Oxford University Press, 2006), 180.
6 T. Grant and R. Borcherds, *Communicating at Work* (Pretoria: Van Schaik, 2009).
7 G.D.J. Dingemans, *Als hoorder onder de hoorders: Hermeneutische homiletiek* (Kampen: Kok, 1991), 33.

which God's Word is directed to the attitudes in listeners' lives are important to the act of persuasion.

4.1 Speak-for-itself concepts in the Hebrews sermon related to attitudes

4.1.1 The attitude of the preacher in addressing the attitude of the listeners

Preaching is an act that exposes the attitudes of the preacher, who remains a vulnerable person[8][9]. Long[10] indicates that listeners listen faster than preachers preach, and quickly position themselves to decide whether they can believe the content of the sermon or not. In this process, preachers must never neglect the reality that, while they are preachers of their sermons, they are simultaneously listeners to their sermons[11][12]. Keller[13] expresses his concern about the vulnerable attitude of preachers if the spirit of their preaching is not right.

Hebrews strategically emphasises the idea of what the preacher should aim at. The concepts of building (Hebrews 3) and of growing (Hebrews 5) are emphasised. In this process of building and growing, the importance of preparing and equipping through preaching has to be underlined. The attitude of the preacher should be characterised by a willingness to serve as well as the commitment to be responsible in the act of preaching. Preaching should build up and should not be directed at breaking down. In the Hebrews sermon, five concepts for the preacher are utilised, namely:

- **The preacher as therapist.** The importance of the preacher's attitude of preaching in such a manner that it would promote healing, stands central, as found in Hebrews 3. Preaching as exhortation and encouragement has to provide perspectives that will allow listeners to experience profound healing of intrinsic destructive attitudes.
- **The preacher as leader.** The preacher has to guide listeners to be obedient to what God expects from them. The act of accompanying the congregation includes the attitude that preachers are not one-sidedly speaking from a great height. In this sense, the preacher

---

8 W. Brueggemann, *The Word Militant: Preaching a Decentering Word* (Minneapolis: Fortress Press, 2010), 2.
9 N. Geisler and D. Geisler, *Conversational Evangelism: How to Listen and Speak So That You Can Be Heard* (Minneapolis: Harvest House, 2009), 14.
10 Thomas G. Long, *The Witness of Preaching* (Louisville: John Knox Press, 2005), 177.
11 Dingemans, *Hoorder onder de hoorders*, 14.
12 Long, *Witness of Preaching*, 64.
13 T. Keller, "A New Kind of Urban Preacher," in *Prophetic Preaching*, ed. C.B. Larson (Massasuchets: Hendrikson, 2012), 86.

should enable listeners to understand God's Word as well as the importance of what is expected from them amid daily life's hardships.
- **The preacher as teacher** (instructor - as found in Hebrews 13). The preacher's responsibility is to offer new perspectives to listeners via explication and application of God's Word for them to grow spiritually. Creativity is needed in constructing and delivering sermons so that words could create a new seeing, a creative perspective in our outlook on life.
- **The preacher as shepherd.** The preacher should watch over his or her own life as well as the lives of listeners. The idea of discernment for what could be regarded as best practice for the listeners to grow, should be evident in the preacher's attitude. The importance of healthy relationships in ministry to direct God's Word cannot be underestimated or over-emphasised.

4.1.2 The listeners' attitudes in need of to be altered
Consider that the sermon to the Hebrews uniquely structures its contents[14]. As a consequence, persuasion through preaching surfaces, especially when one considers the fact that it mentions the theme of attitude seven times, each time within its admonishing (paranetic) sections, as found in Hebrews 3:6, 4:11, 4:16, 6:11, 10:19, 10:35 and 13:6. Challenges are prominent when it comes to persuading believers who have lost energy and the sense of the meaningfulness of duties or actions such as encouraging each other, communion with each other and meeting each other. The listeners in this congregation longed for the good old days, as has been mentioned. The writer of this sermon does not, however, communicate with emphasis on the good old days. On the contrary, the preacher underlines what it takes to live in the last days and the importance of the here and the now[15].

4.1.3 παρρησια -boldness (Hebrews 3:6, 4:16, 10:19 and 10:35)
Louw and Nida II[16] arrange this concept within the sub-domain of courage and boldness. It is important to realise that this boldness applies to one's attitude amid difficult circumstances. As a technical concept, it

---

14 C.R. Hume, *Reading through Hebrews* (Lymington: The Spartan, 1997), 9-13.
15 F.P. Kruger and C.J.H. Venter, "Die prediking van geloofsverantwoordelikheid: homiletiese perspektiewe vanuit Hebreërs [Preaching responsibility in faith: homiletical perspectives from Hebrews]," *Praktiese Teologie in Suid-Afrika* 21, no. 1 (2006): 65.
16 J.P. Louw and E.A. Nida, *Greek English Lexicon of the New Testament (II)* (New York: United Bible Studies, 1989), 306.

denotes the boldness of a Greek citizen to communicate in the open and with freedom of speech. The content of the communication is subjected to resistance. Brown[17] is therefore convinced that openness and fearlessness should be recognised in this concept. This kind of boldness enjoys a point of orientation in Hebrews 3:6, namely as the boldness to hold steadfastly to the truth. This opens the door to the idea of profound hope[18].

The intimate connection between one's understanding of being the house of God and one's attitude is highlighted in Hebrews 3:6. The concept of the attitude of παρρησιαν [courage] is used. This a key concept within Hebrews. In this context, it is the opposite of shyness. Among the Greeks, it was regarded as the biggest gift in life. For the Greeks and Romans, speech was also an indicator of one's character and place in society[19]. The concept implies *saying anything*. This kind of courage has the foundation of a solid legal basis. Greek citizens always had the courage to speak during public meetings. Within the context of Hebrews, it has to do with the courage to approach God and it offers a foundation for encouraging each other. Opposed to boldness in the sermon stands decay sermon[20]. The listeners previously experienced growth, but tends to experience a decline, and therefore the aim of the preacher becomes to develop and strengthen the listeners. The explicit warning not to turn away from the living God is notable, as expressed in Hebrews 3:12, and Hebrews 12:15 even encourages them to see that no one falls outside the grace of God.

Du Toit[21] describes the prominence of Hebrews 3:7-4:13. On this basis, the sermon could be regarded as typical of the first century. These typically started with an Old Testament pericope followed by the proclamation divided in a warning section as well as encouragement. A typical text from the Old Testament, namely Psalm 95:7-11, is announced in Hebrews 3:7-11. The sermon unfolds in two sub-headings, namely with a view to warning (Hebrews 3:12-19) and exhortation (Hebrews 4:1-11). Hebrews 4:12-13 offers an intriguing conclusion to the sermon. Within the framework which it creates, that today is a decisive day, the

---

17 J. Brown, *Hebrews*, Geneva Series of Commentaries (Edinburg: The Bath Press, 1999), 134.
18 F.F. Bruce, *The Epistle to the Hebrews*, New International Commentary of the New Testament (Grand Rapids, Michigan: Eerdmans, 1990), 94.
19 J.F. Hultin, *The Ethics of Obscene Speech in Early Christianity and Its Environment* (Leiden: Brill, 2008), 27.
20 W.A. Mack and D. Swavely, *Life in the Fathers House. A Member's Guide to the Local Church* (New Jersey: P&R Publishing, 1996), 10.
21 Anrie du Toit, *Hebreërs vir vandag [Hebrews for today]* (Vereeniging: CUM boeke, 2004), 74.

theme of boldness is announced in Hebrews 4:14-16. One is struck by the importance assigned to diligence and earnestness that must last until we enter rest[22]. On the fact that Christ is the merciful and faithful High Priest follows the idea that listeners receive their strength from him so as not to fall back on despondency[23]. Bruce[24] emphasises the importance of the mentioning of Christ as Great High Priest in Hebrews 4:14-10:31. It is mentioned fourteen times. Hebrews 1-3 describes how the message of salvation in Christ has come to listeners. In Hebrews 4:14-10:31 it is described how Jesus has enabled us to approach God with boldness, that is, confidence.

Hebrews 4:14-16 expresses the preacher's assurance that we do have a High Priest, the Son of God, who can sympathise with our infirmities[25]. Based on what our High Priest has achieved, we have the boldness to come to the throne of grace. We do not have to come to this throne with fear and dread. To come boldly implies freedom and liberty in speaking[26]. The boldness in coming to our High Priest has the foundation that He will listen and human sin will not cause Him not to listen when believers come to Him[27].

Hebrews 10:19, emphasises the theme of confidence to enter the sanctuary by the blood of Christ. The idea of parresia is utilised in a particular section of the Hebrews sermon: the application after very important doctrines are offered in Hebrews 9:1-10:18. It is as if the preacher wants to say that, since we have heard about the proclamation of Christ, let us have confidence to enter. Believers have access to the heavenly sanctuary[28]. Before the exhortation and the imperative for daily life are offered, the listeners should hear about what they have in Christ, namely confidence to come near. In Hebrews 10:35, the preacher even urges the listeners not to cast away their confidence[29]. This confidence should not be thrown away like an object that has no value. Ellingworth[30] goes as far as to highlight the use of the Aoristus imperative that underlines

---

22 J.M. Flanigan, *Hebrews: What the Bible Teaches*, Ritchie New Testament Commentaries (Kilmarnock: John Ritchie, 1997), 78.
23 Bruce, *Epistle*, 115.
24 Bruce, *Epistle*, 100.
25 Flanigan, *Hebrews*, 80.
26 J. Owen, *Epistle to the Hebrews* (Grand Rapids: Kregel, 1999), 77.
27 B.B. Barton, D. Veerman, and L.K. Taylor, *Hebrews*, Life Application Bible Commentary (Wheaton: Tyndale House, 1997), 61.
28 Barton, Veerman, and Taylor, *Hebrews*, 158.
29 Flanigan, *Hebrews*, 223.
30 P. Ellingworth, *Commentary on Hebrews*, New International Greek Testament Commentary (Grand Rapids: Eerdmans, 1993), 551.

the idea of meticulously paying attention to this confidence. Believers may come nearer to God with confidence even when they are in despair because of difficult circumstances. Preaching also communicates this kind of boldness and therefore boldness simultaneously acts as the sermon's indicative and imperative.

4.1.4 θαρουντθας (boldness) - Hebrews 13:6

The sermon communicates concern regarding important principles that were neglected in listeners' lives[31]. The importance of listeners putting in a diligence of effort regarding their relationship with God is further applied to the listeners' relationship with co-believers and people[32]. The sermon is aimed at enabling them to build on their attitude, making an effort around healthy inter-relationships[33]. Louw and Nida II[34] place this concept of θαρουντθας within the sub-domain of courage and boldness. A closer look shows that the concept denotes confidence and trust even in troublesome times. The liturgical overtone of Hebrews 12:28 and Hebrews 13 is striking[35]. Within the context of a commitment towards life in the spirit of being thankful, the practical implications of this are explained in Hebrews 13. Long[36] even notes the rapid change in the style of the sermon, a style that is so different that scholars have reflected on whether it could be the work of the same author[37].

The ethical dimension in this sermon and especially in the paranetic section of this sermon is notable. Since the life of a Christian is also practically oriented, the driving force is always love[38]. Smelik[39] remarks: *'Homiletics without ethics is empty and ethics without homiletics is blind'* (my emphasis). Without an integral reckoning with the ethical dimension with its strong imperative on doing what is right, preaching can become one-dimensional in the sense of only teaching sound doctrine isolated from reality or telling evocative stories aimed at making the Gospel attractive or accessible without necessarily making a call for change in the

---

31 Ferdi P. Kruger, "Prediking en gesindheidsverandering: 'n Prakties-teologiese studie in die lig van Hebreërs," ThD thesis (Potchefstroom: North-West University, Dept. Practical Theology, 2002), 69.
32 W.B. Johnston, *The Epistle to the Hebrews*, Calvin's Commentaries (Grand Rapids: Eerdmans, 1994), 204.
33 Owen, *Epistle to the Hebrews*, 268.
34 Louw and Nida, *Greek English Lexicon*, 306.
35 Owen, *Epistle to the Hebrews*, 272.
36 Long, *Witness of Preaching*, 142.
37 Bruce, *Epistle*, 367.
38 L.H. Evans, *Hebrews*, Communicator's Commentary (Washington: Macmillan, 1984), 239.
39 E.L. Smelik, *De ethiek in de verkondiging* (Nijkerk: Callenbach, 1967), 37.

world that we live in[40]. At its heart, the ethical dimension places preachers and their listeners in the presence of the living God and his will for their lives. The domains of homiletics and ethics complement each other regarding the message of obedience to God[41]. Burger[42] uses the German word *Anspruch* [claim] to explain that the Word of God requests a deed of obedience from hearers. He understands the word 'obedience' to mean the way in which hearers of the Word of God appropriate his grace for themselves[43].

Incorporation of the ethical dimension does not prove to be without its complexities, however. Cilliers[44] completed a research project on the state of preaching and found that only a few sermons contained an ethical dimension. His research results revealed the following reasons for this unassertiveness:

- The fear for moralistic preaching that regulates society.
- A lack of understanding of the relationship between grace and obedience.
- A fear that differences in understanding certain ethical questions could divide the congregation. Preachers do not want to complicate the sermons.
- Preachers get used to clichés and do not want to adapt to new situations.
- Preachers do not wholeheartedly believe in the power of sermons that can help to change people's lives.
- The danger of legalistic preaching that prevents ethical preaching.

Hebrews 13:1-6 addresses the following issues related to love: brotherly love and love to strangers and to sufferers. The issue of chastity in marriage and Christian contentment as well as courage are furthermore addressed. When perspectives are offered on ethical conduct and how it should be implemented, the role of attitude cannot be separated from it[45]. In Hebrews 13:6, a quotation from Psalm 118:6 is utilised to underline the importance of Christians' boldness in daily life. They have the privilege to say that God is their Helper. The fact that God helps even amid difficult circumstance creates the attitude of courage and boldness that is based on

---

40 Long, *Witness of Preaching*, 18.
41 Johan H. Cilliers, *Die genade van gehoorsaamheid* (Cape Town: Lux Verbi, 2000), 20.
42 C.W. Burger, "Riglyne vir prediking oor die Christelike deugde," in *Woord teen die lig*, eds. C.W. Burger, D.J. Smit, and B.J. Müller (Pretoria: N.G. Kerk-Uitgewers, 1996), 23.
43 Burger, "Riglyne vir prediking," 24.
44 Cilliers, *Genade van gehoorsaamheid*, 36.
45 Kruger, "Prediking en gesindheidsverandering," 70.

the firmness of what is doing on their behalf[46]. In the Hebrews sermon, preaching with an ethical dimension sees society with a sharp and wide optic lens, critically focusing on uprooting unrighteous praxis, but also providing a surprising and inspiring scope for a society destined to be renewed far beyond what we can imagine.

4.1.5 σπουδαζω [diligence to act]

This attitudinal concept denotes earnestness in what the listeners are committed to[47]. The idea of dedication is also evident. Flanigan[48] further makes clear that listeners' dedication to their acts is impossible without enthusiasm. Bruce[49] goes one step further when he argues whether this commitment is possible without any interest in what should be done. Brown[50] therefore underlines the notion of hurrying slowly. Hastiness rather than over-eagerness lies at the core of understanding this concept. In the Hebrews sermon obedience to what is heard as well as rest are prominent motives. Barton *et.al.*[51] make the interesting comment that the expression of '*Let us, therefore, make every effort to enter the rest*' (my emphasis) could be regarded as an intentional paradox, namely to labour in order that you can rest. Diligence in making what God has promised your own is pivotal. The attitude of diligence and labour rather than laziness is emphasised. It should be said again that the concept of σπουδαζω denotes eagerness and not speed[52]. This concept is utilised in close connection with holding fast to what is being proclaimed[53]. When it comes to attitude, the concept is often also closely interwoven with verbs that denote action and movement. In this instance the verb 'enter' is striking. The attitude of making an effort to appropriate God's promises and his demands cannot be ignored[54].

To illustrate the eagerness to concentrate on commitment towards their spiritual lives, an example of what has happened to the Israelites in the desert is utilised[55]. The danger of falling, as found in Hebrews 4:11, is a typical example of creative use of language that not only indicates the

---

46 Du Toit, *Hebreërs*, 227.
47 Louw and Nida, *Greek English Lexicon*, 298.
48 Flanigan, *Hebrews*, 78.
49 Bruce, *Epistle*, 11.
50 J. Brown, *Hebrews*, 1168.
51 Barton, Veerman, and Taylor, *Hebrews*, 55.
52 Ellingworth, *Commentary on Hebrews*, 258.
53 Du Toit, *Hebreërs*, 55.
54 Kruger, "Prediking en gesindheidsverandering," 71.
55 Simon J. Kistemaker, *Hebrews*, New Testament Commentary (Grand Rapids: Baker Book House, 1996), 113.

physical death of Israelites, but also falling away in the spiritual sense of the word. The encouragement of the Hebrews sermon is aimed at indicating the interdependence between eagerness and hope. In Hebrews 6:11, diligence of the listeners until the end is required[56]. The attitude of eagerness to hold fast until the end is emphasised[57]. The sermon opens windows to enable listeners that see that past, present and future cannot be separated from each other. Hebrews 6:11 underlines believers' inner zeal[58]. It is striking that this inner zeal is discussed within a broader context of this sermon, namely the exhortation to grow spiritually[59]. The attitude of diligence and inner zeal will be endangered when profound hope, that is, full assurance, is lacking[60]. The concept for full assurance is typical of ships that drop their anchors in the right place. One's attitude and eagerness to do this cannot be ignored.

Preaching as a nutritional process is one of the most important acts within ministry. Its value, of confronting listeners with their deepest attitudes regarding what is being heard, will ensure the relevance of sermons. Eagerness around one's faith-life and diligence towards full assurance cannot be separated from listeners' willingness to be nourished by God's Word. The eagerness to listen and to apply this to daily life are important. The attitude of eagerness should be cultivated through constant exposure to God's Word. When this is not upheld relaxation in one's faith-life will result[61]. Within a time of lock-down arrangements people are debating whether the Covid-19 pandemic stands between them and practising their faith-lives. What is clear around what is currently happening is that the attitude of eagerness to assist families and local communities within a time of uncertainty will definitely provide dynamic opportunities for listeners to engage in their immediate environment. Without providing listeners with opportunities to be exposed to the living voice of the Gospel relaxation in one's faith-life will create difficulties. This kind of danger will addressed in the next section.

4.2 Widening attitude dimensions in sermons illustrated from Hebrews

The following dimensions of the functioning of attitudes can be identified in the Hebrews sermon:

---

56 Ellingworth, *Commentary on Hebrews*, 261.
57 Kistemaker, *Hebrews*, 167.
58 Ellingworth, *Commentary on Hebrews*, 332.
59 G.B. Wilson, *Hebrews* (Edinburgh: BPC, 1996), 81.
60 Barton, Veerman, and Taylor, *Hebrews*, 121.
61 Kruger, "Prediking en gesindheidsverandering," 73.

Not to drift away	Hebrews 2:1
Slow to learn (listen)	Hebrews 5:11
Faith and patience	Hebrews 6:12
Patiently	Hebrews 6:15
Longing	Hebrews 11:16
Persevering like one seeing the invisible	Hebrews 11:27
Not growing weary and losing heart	Hebrews 12:3
Not making light the Lord's discipline	Hebrews 12:5
Strengthening feeble arms and weak knees	Hebrews 12:12
Being thankful and so worshipping	Hebrews 12:28

4.2.1 The attitudinal dimension of sermons

The polyphony of concepts to attitude illustrate that preaching as viewed in the Hebrews sermon is closely connected to an embroidered landscape of attitudes. Long[62] explains the difficult task of enabling listeners in the act of listening within liturgy, hence to translate a theological claim into everyday experience and help people see what this could look like in their own lives. It is an illusion to think that what is heard by listeners will necessarily bear resemblance to what preachers have said; this conviction should rather be avoided. Based on the footprint of this recognition, Cilliers[63] comprehensively indicates that listening can play an important role in adding colourful perspectives within the mind's eye. This art of the re-visioning of reality could also be called the reframing of perspective, according to Cilliers. Reframing is about revisiting existing things of the old and the past. It is articulated in the prefix 're', which enjoys the connotation of 'again and again'. It is both *re* and *creatio*[64].

4.2.1.1 Do not drift away (Hebrews 2:1)

In the Hebrews sermon, the organic relation between doctrine (teaching) and exhortation is always evident. The proclamation about Christ's eminence and greatness in Hebrews 1 emphasises the importance of listening to this message[65]. Bruce[66] makes the interesting point that the

---

62 Long, *Witness of Preaching*, 162.
63 Cilliers, *Genade van gehoorsaamheid*, 5-6.
64 Cilliers, *Genade van gehoorsaamheid*, 6.
65 J. Vines, *The Believers Guide to Hebrews* (New Jersey: Loizeaux, 1993), 19.
66 Bruce, *Epistle*, 66.

preacher is actually busy interrupting the sermon about Christ, the High Priest, to elucidate a particular concern. The rhetorical construction is striking. A command is given, namely: pay careful attention. Then an exhortation is given, namely that what we have heard could result in not drifting away. Based on the unique content of the Hebrews sermon about Christ as the High Priest, listeners should pay heed to what they have heard[67]. To seize and drift away are connected to each other. Du Toit[68] highlights that a specific crisis in the lives of the listeners is addressed. God's proclaimed Word functions as a lifebuoy, and when one does not hold on to this he or she will certainly drift away. The metaphor is striking. Drifting away could denote a ring that slides unnoticed from your finger or a ship that drifts away from the harbour, emphasising an attitude of vigilance[69].

4.2.1.2 Laziness to listen - Hebrews 5:11

Mental alertness around what preaching is about should be present in listeners' minds[70]. To achieve this outcome, an intermezzo between Hebrews 5:1-10 and Hebrews 6:20 is applied[71]. Before more complicated matters are explained further, a certain awareness should occur. To explain the importance of this, the preacher in the Hebrews sermon does not preach only the '*that*' but simultaneously the '*how*' of things to be undertaken. The negative attitude of laziness when it comes to listening to the preaching of God's Word, which leads to spiritual immaturity, is highlighted[72]. Listeners have to progress in their growth, a growth towards a deeper and fuller understanding of the content of God's Word. This is typical when it comes to dealing with a situation of spiritual decay, and laziness to listen to God's Word is a *symptom* of spiritual retardation. Learning inertia and thinking laziness are important aspects addressed in this sermon. Preaching has the purpose of enabling listeners to grow so that they could develop from pupils to teachers. The concept of *didaskalos* is utilised in an informal context to indicate what ordinary Christians should become. Hebrews 5:14 underscores that listeners who learn from God's Word have not only learned about theoretical ideas, but have also experienced life in a practical manner, that is, involving experiential learning. In becoming acquainted with the solid food aimed at formation activities of preaching, they will eventually be able to distinguish between

---

67 Hume, *Hebrews*, 24.
68 Du Toit, *Hebreërs*, 47.
69 Ellingworth, *Commentary on Hebrews*, 134.
70 Wilson, *Hebrews*, 72.
71 Du Toit, *Hebreërs*, 104.
72 Ellingworth, *Commentary on Hebrews*, 137.

good and evil in daily life. Growth and a committed effort to look into the fuller extent of God's Word should be evident among them. The profound attitude of dealing with God's Word to be able to assist other people is pivotal. Maturity in faith as a point of orientation entails that the difference between milk and solid food in one's growth should be acknowledged.

4.2.1.3 Through faith and perseverance/ endurance
The attitude regarding the preaching of the Word is summarised in a powerful manner in Hebrews 6:11-12. The emphasis on perseverance to the very end is striking. Perseverance until the end is anchored in these verses by the anchor of hope. An admonition to persevere in our service is further provided. The listeners to the sermon should become followers (imitators)[73]. The preacher's concern for the spiritual wellness of the listeners is evident. Imitating of the example of their predecessors should be evident in the lives of the listeners[74]. The lives of the predecessors are described as an example of faith and perseverance. Faith in God's promises and the realisation that all God's promises are real, is important. Through faith and perseverance, believers inherit what has been promised[75]. The persevering faith of their predecessors should be something that they imitate. The concept of perseverance actually denotes longsuffering. This very aspect is followed up in Hebrews 6:13-20 with the familiar example of Abraham. The attitude of faith and longsuffering is the antidote for laziness in listening God's Word.

4.2.1.4 Longing for - Hebrews 11:16
Hebrews 11 interrelates faith and hope[76]. Listeners are reminded of the power of longing for a better country, a heavenly one. A longing for the heavenly reality is something that preaching should also achieve[77]. Within the present, the eschatological realisation of our expectation that becomes reality as well as the tension embodied in yet-and-not-yet should also be acknowledged. The reference to biblical examples of faithful believers from the past (Hebrews 11) underlines that believers' horizon reckons with the here and now, but also with God's tomorrow[78]. The word *'eschatology'* indicates ultimate things and not just last things. Therefore, ultimate reality is not just what will transpire at the end of time, but what God has always sought to make a present reality. The expectation of the

---

73 Vines, *Believers Guide*, 97.
74 Du Toit, *Hebreërs*, 113.
75 Kistemaker, *Hebrews*, 167.
76 Du Toit, *Hebreërs*, 184.
77 Owen, *Epistle to the Hebrews*, 226.
78 Kruger, "Prediking en gesindheidsverandering," 212.

future stimulates and empowers human life in the present dispensation. Long[79] thinks that vibrant Christian preaching depends on the recovery of its eschatological voice. Preaching has the task to share and spread the hope in Christ to the world. In the resurrection of Christ, God already opened the future for his church. Believers share this hope in Christ and therefore they are a new reality and a new community. The eschatological dimension in preaching unites the facts of the advent, the coming, of Christ in us, with us and through us, right to end of all things. This view of a new future in Christ also shapes a new look on the present.

4.2.1.5 Persevere like one seeing the invisible
Hebrews 11:27 offers the example of Moses. His attitude is described as courage that was not primarily incarcerated in himself, but in the power of faith[80]. Listeners who have become disheartened should recognise the importance of faith that makes invisible things visible. The fact that Moses was able to renunciate all that Egypt has offered was due to the power of faith[81]. LONG[82] in fact indicates that faith sometimes induces a different view of reality. It is important to note that the Hebrews sermon does not proclaim the danger of mere escapism, but rather explores the possibilities that persevering faith offers to believers.

If a biblical view of eschatology falls away in preaching, sermons become legalistic[83]. That means that human potential replaces God's promises. In legalistic preaching, a distorted kind of apocalyptic is used to force people along the direction of fearing several concealed threats about the future. Changes in people's lives and in society that originate from fear however do not last. Threats around the future give rise to intense responses, but they do not console one[84]. Long[85] distinguishes between two kinds of eschatology: the first kind depends on a literalistic grip on biblical images and results in a Gospel that is intellectually implausible, stuck in the clouds of a pious and irrelevant heaven that never touches earth. If that is our only option, the retreat into a self-contained present tense is our only ethical choice. The second kind of eschatology, however, allows the eschatological affirmations that 'Christ is risen!' and 'Jesus is Lord!' to exercise tension upon the present tense,

---

79 Long, *Witness of Preaching*, 123.
80 Flanigan, *Hebrews*, 243.
81 Bruce, *Epistle*, 312.
82 Long, *Witness of Preaching*, 119.
83 Cilliers, *Genade van gehoorsaamheid*, 82.
84 Cilliers, *Genade van gehoorsaamheid*, 83.
85 Long, *Witness of Preaching*, 123.

generating both judgement and promise, creating the possibility of ethical action in the world sustained by hope.

Eschatological preaching promises a 'new heaven and a new earth', and invites people to participate in a coming future that, while it is not dependent upon their success, is open to the labours of their hands. This vision liberates the listener from a despondent attitude paralysed by the inability to make a difference in a society in which a destructive power like corruption seems to prevail unchallengeable. This eschatological perspective restores blurred vision so that the perceiver, through the work of the Holy Spirit, can become conscious of the distinct presence of the King calling his people to a blessed presence in this world and empowering them with his promise of restoration of an abundant life for all.

4.2.1.6 Not grow weary and lose heart
Hebrews 12:1-3 admonishes listeners to pay attention to the importance of perseverance in faith. After the proclamation of perseverance in doing God's will, the theme of perseverance in the race of faith, with focus on Christ, is announced[86]. The current contestants in the athletic race could look up and see the example of witnesses of the past to encourage them. The biblical voices of the past surround believers. In throwing away all that hinders them, believers should run with perseverance, eyes fixed on Christ. Hebrews 11:3 enriches the sense of this exhortation with the idea that the listeners should carefully consider Jesus Christ. In a careful consideration of what Christ has done lies the answer, and not in becoming weary and losing heart[87]. Weariness has a direct impact on relaxation in faith[88]. The danger of this kind of attitude for listeners is that they can easily lose their motivation for diligence in spiritual growth.

4.2.1.7 Not making light the Lord's discipline
Hebrews 12:4-11 takes the exhortation to persevere to a next level. Barton et al.[89] indeed indicate that the sermon takes the relevance of the current situation into account, mentioning understanding for listeners' struggle against sin. This struggle is personified as a force that confronts them. The preacher moves from one sport (athletics) to another, namely boxing[90]. In boxing, blood could flow from the boxers' faces due to vicious

---

86 Kistemaker, *Hebrews*, 365.
87 Kistemaker, *Hebrews*, 370.
88 R.C. Stedman, *Hebrews*, IVP New Testament Commentary Series (Illinois: InterVarsity Press, 1992), 138.
89 Barton, Veerman, and Taylor, *Hebrews*, 208.
90 Kistemaker, *Hebrews*, 72.

blows they receive[91]. Therefore, the preacher mentions bloodshed. Sin as mysterious opponent of the listeners, to be resisted, but the attitude of being aware of this formidable opponent should be present[92].

By describing the deeper-lying attitude that listeners should adhere to they are encouraged to see themselves within their relationship as sons of the Lord[93]. The idea of discipline to educate is subsequently announced[94], utilised ten times in seven verses. The concept of *paideia* denotes a pedagogue or pedagogy[95]. God is disciplining his children to educate and equip them. Listeners' positive attitude to persevere amid difficult circumstances and accept God's discipline should be seen as that God's discipline is not a nuisance, but a privilege[96]. By utilising a quotation from Proverbs 3:11-12, the preacher indicates understanding for the listeners' circumstances of hardship. It is clear that the Hebrews sermon does not over-simplify this and does not ignore its challenges. The attitude that listeners should look to deeper levels in seeking for answers is evident. The importance of the fact that listeners should not forget this lesson is emphasised.

4.2.1.8 Strengthen your feeble arms and weak knees
Hebrews 12:12 describes pastoral concern. The unique reasoning within the sermon indicates a kind of logic that does not allow the argument to float in the air. The preacher has raised the image of an athlete in Hebrews 12. The preacher then described the struggle of a boxer, as mentioned, as well as a wrestler, and he returns to the athlete[97], announcing the attitude of *strengthening yourself*. The danger of exhaustion and discouragement could possibly cause the reality of feeble hands and weak knees[98]. It is important to note that the attitude of strengthening or taking grip is aimed at all listeners. They should do it individually but also corporately[99]. Tired hands and weak knees could possibly cause a praxis of not working and persevering. The listeners are reminded of becoming involved in their challenges and not to become paralysed because of fear[100]. Through regular exercise in the effort with God's Word, they should strengthen

---

91 Du Toit, *Hebreërs*, 211.
92 Bruce, *Epistle*, 343.
93 Kistemaker, *Hebrews*, 373.
94 Du Toit, *Hebreërs*, 212.
95 Du Toit, *Hebreërs*, 211.
96 Kistemaker, *Hebrews*, 374.
97 Du Toit, *Hebreërs*, 213.
98 Kistemaker, *Hebrews*, 381.
99 Barton, Veerman, and Taylor, *Hebrews*, 214.
100 Kistemaker, *Hebrews*, 381.

themselves; the consequence should be to level the path for their feet. The attitude of carefully examining their track, the reality of life and awareness of vulnerability of the listeners are exposed[101]. When fatigue is manifest the danger of injury becomes a reality.

The sermon's logic is clear. Frequent exercises are needed. This should become a familiar habit. No listener should become stationary. Spiritual growth has to deal with a process-oriented commitment in moving towards solid food. The importance of listeners that need each other is striking in the sermon overall. Listeners should assist each other: the attitudes of interest and caring for each other is much needed. The awareness of the challenges of daily life should cultivate an attitude of strengthening yourself.

4.2.1.9 Let us be thankful and so worship
Hebrews 12:18-24 addresses the contrast between what was (Mount Sinai) and what is (Mount Zion), contrasting the two mountains. In contrast with the fear at Mount Sinai, there is a description of an important 'but', of the glory of God's Word and his coming to people, and the people coming to God[102]. Hebrews 12:25 emphasises that listeners should not refuse the God who is speaking. The preacher takes this idea one step further. The certainty about the Kingdom of God that cannot be shaken urges listeners to be truly thankful[103]. Around the concept of worship, du Toit[104] therefore rightly indicates that it is utilised in close connection to conducting a worship service. Hebrews 12:28 characterises this worship in daily life in terms of the attitude of thankfulness. Flanigan[105] further formulates the notion that worship is conducted in thankfulness. This service or worship to God should be done with reverence and awe. In living a life of thankfulness, listeners will worship God. Reverence has to do with dignity of demeanour, because of the acknowledgement of God's presence[106].

Applied to the act of preaching and of active listening, one should reckon with God's Word and listening to God's Word to appropriate its truths. Preaching of God's Word will always encourage listeners to be thankful for his grace and that his Kingdom cannot be shaken.

---

101 Barton, Veerman, and Taylor, *Hebrews*, 215.
102 Flanigan, *Hebrews*, 269.
103 Kistemaker, *Hebrews*, 400.
104 Du Toit, *Hebreërs*, 222.
105 Flanigan, *Hebrews*, 224.
106 Flanigan, *Hebrews*, 275.

4.2.2 The preacher's attitude in addressing the listeners' attitudes

Brueggemann[107] investigates the triangular relationship between the text, the preacher and hearers. A danger exists that the voice of the text could become silent and less authoritative. Preachers can easily become substitutes for the voice of the text, because their voices can become overly important. Brueggemann[108] states that this fact leaves preachers vulnerable and exposed, because their voice is now pitched against the voices of people in society. In extending these arguments, Pieterse[109] expresses concern about the attitude of preachers around their reluctance to deliver their sermons in such a way that the Word can perform true transformation. He identifies a possible reason for this, namely doubt about God's presence during the worship service and the act of sermon delivery.

Hansen[110] indicates that preachers' attitudes about the life and values of their hearers influence their shaping of sermons. The problem with this attitude is that it sets up the preacher against sinful society and sinful hearers. Preachers' attitudes influence their message of persuasion and the effectiveness of their message. The wrong attitude, namely exercising control over hearers, is destructive. Mohler[111] convincingly points out some of the negative attitudes of preachers, focusing on the following aspects:

- Preachers show ignorance and they neglect the attributes of God.
- They tend to show intellectual prejudice.
- Preachers often have a finite perspective on reality. This could be the reason why they neglect reality in society. How believers expect the day of the Lord is important for how they live.
- Preachers often draw the wrong conclusions and this determines their attitude. The reason for this is that people in general have a wilful denial of and blindness towards evidence.
- Preachers have problems with the stigmas attached to the outcasts in a society whose lifestyle is seen as deviant. Such lifestyles are

---

107 Brueggemann, *The Word Militant*, 36.
108 Brueggemann, *The Word Militant*, 37.
109 Hennie J.C. Pieterse, "Prophetic Preaching in the Contemporary Context of South Africa," *In die Skriflig/In Luce Verbi* 47, no. 1 (2009): 253, http://dx.doi.org/10.4102/ids.v47i1.114.
110 D. Hansen, "Who's Listening out There?," in *Preaching to a Shifting Culture*, eds. H. Robinson et al. (Grand Rapids: Baker Books, 2004), 131.
111 R.A. Mohler, "The Way the World Thinks: Meeting the Natural Mind in the Mirror and in the Marketplace," in *Thinking. Loving. Doing*, eds. J. Piper et al. (Illinois: Crossway, 2011), 56-57.

different from those of mainstream church members'. It often happens that a minister just wants to minister to obedient people, but has no eye for the vacuum where no-one is ministering. This requires a change of attitude in the preacher's mind and heart.

Preaching has the intention of naming the realities of listeners' lives. The issue at stake is that preachers should not dare to preach without a thorough examination of their vulnerable attitudes. Gibson[112], for example, is interested in the answer to the question of whether it is possible for preachers not to be influenced by their shifting culture. Hansen[113] highlights the fact that their decision about the life and values of the listeners in a shifting culture influence everything in the sermon. Preachers will not take the reality of their listeners seriously if they do not take their own lives seriously[114]. Firet[115] warns against the fact that preachers can live in a show-world with a particular view on reality in society and among their hearers. Preachers' attitudes can play a dominant role in this show-world. A few of these examples could be fear, the tendency to be too assertive, beliefs, perceptions, views and the danger of not being in touch with reality in society; these are traits of the typical study preacher. For Firet[116] the problem is that sermons very often become phenomena dominated by the likes and dislikes of preachers.

In naming reality in society, it is important for preachers not to neglect a careful examination of their attitudes. In the previous discussion, attention was paid to the attitudes regarding the manner of preaching. It became evident that preachers must have pastoral sensitivity for their listeners because of the ambivalence of the listeners' lives[117]. God the Holy Spirit is working in his children, and therefore the pastoral attitude of individualisation must be part of the preacher's attitude. The preacher always has to be a person of relationships. To be tender in rebuking has nothing to do with neglecting the reality in listeners' lives, but it opens the way for the right manner to do it[118]. To preach with all purity has to do with the intentions of preachers. Preachers must always be aware of wrong ideas about reality and wrong ideas about their listeners[119].

---

112 S.M. Gibson, *Preaching with a Plan* (Grand Rapids: Baker House, 2012), 12-13.
113 Hansen, "Who's Listening," 131.
114 Hansen, "Who's Listening," 131.
115 J. Firet, *Het agogisch moment in het pastoraal optreden* (Kampen: Kok, 1988), 285-287.
116 Firet, *Agogisch moment*, 285.
117 Kruger and Venter, "Prediking van geloofsverantwoordelikheid," 179.
118 Kruger and Venter, "Prediking van geloofsverantwoordelikheid," 180.
119 Kruger and Venter, "Prediking van geloofsverantwoordelikheid," 181.

4.3 Homiletical perspectives on the functioning of attitudes

The functioning of attitudes and its influence on listeners' lives cannot be underestimated. In the Hebrews sermon, this idea stands central, because negative attitudes of listeners also distort their attitude towards God's Word and its preaching. Ballard and Pritchard[120] add that at least six modes or spheres are directly influenced by the functioning of attitudes:

- **The cognitive sphere.** People constantly receive information that influences their lives. Attitudes are strengthened by information they receive daily[121]. Communication via preaching, catechetics, pastoral care, liturgy and mission are therefore imperative building blocks in forming attitudes, because they provide information about God's plan for this world and the importance of the workplace. It is important to understand that attitudes are learned. People therefore have to learn the right attitudes regarding corruption.
- **The affective sphere.** People have attitudes based on their daily experiences. They tend to have a specific positive or negative feeling for someone or towards something that makes them react in a certain way.
- **The behavioural sphere.** When people are exposed to individuals who suffer because of the effects of certain phenomena, it can lead to a change in behaviour. People's attitudes normally lead to intentions or even resolutions on how to handle certain situations.
- **The interpersonal sphere.** People are exposed to other people. They should learn daily how to manage themselves in their workplaces, in society or in corruptive situations. Christians are often challenged with difficult choices. They can become escapists of reality or can even become cynical because of their daily interactions with corrupt people. They can go as far as to withdraw from society. This withdrawal from society can create an even deeper chasm between the world and the church of today. Language such as 'them' against 'us' cannot be part of the communication used by Christians.
- **The social and political sphere.** People often tend to regard themselves as mere observers of societal and political tendencies.

---

120 P. Ballard and J. Pritchard, *Practical Theology in Action: Christian Thinking in the Service of Church and Society* (London: Ashford Colour Press, 2006), 166-167.
121 Kruger, "Prediking en gesindheidsverandering," 115.

The realisation that they are part of a community with societal and political responsibilities can lead to a change in attitude. Christians often tend to withdraw themselves from societal and political issues. Stott[122] expresses his concern about the possibility that believers dare to wonder whether they have a social responsibility or not. On the contrary, in all aspects of ministry that includes the prophetic voice of the church, there should always be a clear vision of what to do in social and political spheres.
- **The spiritual sphere**. Spiritual maturity empowers people to live with vision and propels them towards reformation of all things that contaminate human life. Spiritual maturity helps people engage in human lives to fulfil the mission of God in this world and believers should actively participate in this.

When speaking about people's attitudes, it is important to realise that the topic of the functioning of attitudes is more problematic than the naked eye can see. Woolfolk[123] indicates that attitudes can distance people from each other while they can also bring people together. With the help of attitudes, people make favourable or unfavourable evaluations of the objects of their thought[124]. Attitudes develop through interaction between parent and child, periods in development, ways of learning, social- and cultural influences, information transmitted through mass-media and personal experiences[125]. The triangular compilation of attitudes is important in visualising the essence of attitudes. Kruger[126] indicates that scholars are unanimous that attitudes consist of three components:

- A cognitive component: thoughts and beliefs.
- An affective component: evaluation of phenomena and emotions.
- A conative or behavioural component: motives and intentions as ways in which attitudes are expressed.

The nature of the functioning of attitudes can differ according to the extent to which it is more cognitive or more emotional[127]. Changes in one of the components also influence the functioning of the others. A different way of thinking will influence people's feelings and also their behaviour and vice versa. Applied to preaching and liturgy, it means that a distorted

---

122 John R.W. Stott, *The Contemporary Christian* (Leicester: Inter-Varsity Press, 1992), 4.
123 A. Woolfolk, *Educational Psychology* (Boston: Pearson, 2007), 89.
124 Kruger, "Vulnerable Attitudes," 3.
125 Berg and Theron, *Psychology*, 174.
126 Kruger, "Prediking en gesindheidsverandering," 137.
127 Berg and Theron, *Psychology*, 173.

way of thinking about God's Word could have a negative influence on people's feelings and actions. When the components of attitudes are inconsistent, one of them may be more closely related to specific forms of behaviour than the other[128]. It is important to note that certain attitudes are more difficult to change and can be regarded as central. Other attitudes are regarded as peripheral, since they are subject to change[129]. This fact underlines that liturgists must carefully reflect on the use of language. It is important to distinguish what the outcome of employing the language must entail.

The issue of the interrelatedness of the three components of attitudes leads to considering the matter of attitude-strength. Without over-simplifying the matter, it is important to note that stronger attitudes are better at predicting behaviour than the other way around[130]. Baron and Byrne[131] emphasise that direct experience, vested interest and self-awareness play an important role in the strength of attitudes. Attitudes that are formed through direct and personal experiences are normally stronger than attitudes that are formed through observation. A vested interest in the object of the attitude also plays a major role. Self-awareness refers to the extent to which persons focus on their attitudes and action. If people can bring their attitudes to mind through cognition, the possibility is greater that it will affect behaviour[132].

This chapter indicates that the concepts for preaching have to do with challenges in the listeners' lives, demonstrating that the challenges of the listeners to the Hebrews sermon included their attitudes around the following:

- Faithfulness to hold fast to their hope in Christ. Therefore the listeners are admonished to care for each other to make sure that encouragement to hold fast will occur.
- The negative attitude of neglecting God's Word and not paying careful attention to the proclamation of the Word.
- Listeners to sermons should realise that they enjoy the boldness to approach God. Therefore the importance of an earnest attitude and taking God's Word seriously have to be evident to respond in obedience to God's Word.

---

128 S. Steinberg, *An Introduction to Communication Studies* (Cape Town: Juta, 2011), 130.
129 Berg and Theron, *Psychology*, 174.
130 Tubbs and Moss, *Human Communication*, 104.
131 R.A. Baron and D. Byrne, *Social Psychology* (Massachusetts: Mass, Allyn and Bycan, 1994), 139.
132 L. Schwartz and C. de la Rey, *Introduction to Psychology* (Oxford: University Press, 2007), 178.

- The listeners' attitude towards the preaching of God's Word simultaneously has implications for their attitude towards life.

4.4 Conclusion

This chapter has elucidated that preachers as well as listeners have functional attitudes. All aspects of life are subjected to the functioning of attitudes that could be positive or negative. It should be said that attitudes are important because they enable people to make sense of events in their lives. Attitudes help them to come to terms with an array of ambiguous stimuli they face on a daily basis. In arduous times, people's attitudes could help them to cope with challenges, therefore it is pivotal for preachers to show insight into the complex process of the forming and functioning of attitudes. Under these kinds of circumstances, listeners and preachers could listen to the preaching of God's Word with an attitude that is not receptive to what is heard, which renders active listening even more problematic. Preaching and daily life experiences cannot be separated. The preacher's engagement with listeners has to enable the "him" or "her" to have clarity on the attitudes of listeners, and these should be addressed within sermon delivery. The preacher's responsibility in the act of preaching is to help listeners to become aware of their attitudes, and communicate the radiant light of God's Word on the contours of those attitudes. In this process, cognitive harmony has been created where the radiant light of God's Word could penetrate the thoughts, feelings and listeners' acts. No-one could ever hide the functioning of attitudes, because God's Word always exposes preachers' as well as listeners' attitudes.

People's attitudes are currently integrally influenced by what could be called the *trolley-problem*[133], namely to take a decision on the coronavirus-pandemic and social distancing to prevent harm in other people's lives. They are suddenly separated from their families, sustainability of jobs

---

133 M.K. Koerner, "Death, Time, Soup: A Conversation with William Kentridge and Peter Galison," *The New York Review of Books* 1, no. 1 (June 20, 2012): http://www.nybooks.com/blogs/nyrblog/2012/jun/30/kentridge-galison-refusal-of-time/.
(accessed March 24, 2020). Foundation for economic education. 'The class of trolley problems, which seek to reveal whether you'd take a deliberate, positive action that you know will harm someone in order to reduce harm to others. The purpose of these thought experiments is to shed light on morality and moral intuition. The classic exemplar considers whether you'd flip the points on a train track to send a trolley loose from a train that was going to kill three people on its current course down another track where it will kill only one. If you flip the points, then the moral upside is that you saved three-minus-one-equals-two lives net; the moral downside is that you were directly responsible for killing a man.'

and businesses is under threat, fears about a sustainable increase and attitudes about the future are inevitably influenced. This is exactly why it is important for preachers to take note of forming and functioning of attitudes. Within the heart of people's attitudes is the increase of anxiety and of emerging uncertainty while facing a phase of quarantine. Perhaps further reflection on the dangers of societal collapse should realise be engaged. Eventually, people's attitudes will cascade into each other and one has to admit that a revised praxis of preaching within challenging circumstances has to deal with people's attitudes. Homiletical praxis has to enable listeners around their adaptive capacity to adjust to possible harm or embrace new dynamic opportunities, or respond to the consequences people are facing. The Hebrews sermon helps us realise that no human being can really change challenging circumstances on their own. The other side of the coin is also legitimate, namely that all listeners are in need of anchors when their attitudes are influenced by communication via the media. Eventually, people's attitudes will be influenced by constant exposure to reports on the internet, and it will pose a challenge to preachers to preach dynamically to develop and strengthen listeners in a profound manner so that their attitudes are scrutinised by the illuminating light of God's speaking in Christ.

Significant geographic and social changes in listeners' living environments will produce a substantial impact on their average hope levels. De Gruchy[134] perceives hope that should participate in actions and attitudes that anticipate a transformed world. This involves preaching hope that simultaneously serves as an antidote to despair, because of distorted attitudes will cause inability among listeners to seek meaningulness. Simultaneously, a sensitivity for not participating from the point of view of a falsely utopian ideology that is imperialist in character has to emerge. The imperialist knows that giving false hope to people can potentially mislead them into opening up themselves and their resources for one's own self-serving interests. When hope is called upon, it should never be done with the motive of misleading, but with the eye on releasing the distinct energy of the life humanity is destined for already in this broken present. Preaching amidst life's paradoxes also reckons with the surprising act of hope against hope for the citizens of God's Kingdom. To name the reality of hopelessness in preaching should have the starting point of God's speaking in Christ in the last days, which entails the victory of Jesus Christ and of the living faith in him. This living faith is powerful because it offers the perspective of God's supremacy above anything. The

---

134 J. de Gruchy, *"Real Presence" and Sacramental Praxis: Reformed Reflections on the Eucharist* (Stellenbosch: Sun Media, 2013), 196.

proclamation of the new life in Christ offers a framework enabling listeners to deal with their attitudes to experience real hope.

REFERENCES
Ballard, P. and J. Pritchard. *Practical Theology in Action: Christian Thinking in the Service of Church and Society*. London: Ashford Colour Press, 2006.
Baron, R.A. and D. Byrne. *Social Psychology*. Massachusetts: Mass, Allyn and Bycan, 1994.
Barton, B.B., D. Veerman, and L.K. Taylor. *Hebrews*. Life Application Bible Commentary. Wheaton: Tyndale House, 1997.
Berg, Z. and A. Theron. *Psychology in the Work Context*. Cape Town: Oxford University Press, 2006.
Brown, J. *Hebrews*. Geneva Series of Commentaries. Edinburgh: The Bath Press, 1999.
Bruce, F.F. *The Epistle to the Hebrews*. The New International Commentary of the New Testament. Grand Rapids: Eerdmans, 1990.
Brueggemann, W. *The Word Militant: Preaching a Decentering Word*. Minneapolis: Fortress, 2010.
Burger, C.W. "Riglyne vir prediking oor die Christelike deugde." In *Woord teen die lig*, edited by C.W. Burger, D.J. Smit, and B.J. Müller. Pretoria: N.G. Kerk-Uitgewers, 1996.
Cilliers, Johan H. *Die genade van gehoorsaamheid*. Cape Town: Lux Verbi, 2000.
Cleary, S. *The Communication Handbook: A Student Guide to Effective Communication*. Cape Town: Juta, 2010.
De Gruchy, J. *"Real Presence" and Sacramental Praxis: Reformed Reflections on the Eucharist*. Stellenbosch: Sun Media, 2013.
Dingemans, G.D.J. *Als hoorder onder de hoorders: Hermeneutische homiletiek*. Kampen: Kok, 1991.
Du Toit, Anrie. *Hebreërs vir vandag [Hebrews for today]*. Vereeniging: CUM boeke, 2004.
Ellingworth, P. *Commentary on Hebrews*. New International Greek Testament Commentary. Grand Rapids: Eerdmans, 1993.
Evans, L.H. *Hebrews*. The Communicator's Commentary. Washington: Macmillan, 1984.
Firet, J. *Het agogisch moment in het pastoraal optreden*. Kampen: Kok, 1988.
Flanigan, J.M. *Hebrews: What the Bible Teaches*. Ritchie New Testament Commentaries. Kilmarnock: John Ritchie, 1997.

Geisler, N. and D. Geisler. *Conversational Evangelism: How to Listen and Speak So That You Can Be Heard*. Minneapolis: Harvest House, 2009.
Gibson, S.M. *Preaching With a Plan*. Grand Rapids: Baker House, 2012.
Grant, T. and R. Borcherds. *Communicating at Work*. Pretoria: Van Schaik, 2009.
Hansen, D. "Who's Listening out There?"
In *Preaching to a Shifting Culture*, edited by H. Robinson, R. Chappel, D. Sunukijian, and S.M. Gibson. Grand Rapids: Baker Books, 2004.
Hultin, J.F. *The Ethics of Obscene Speech in Early Christianity and Its Environment*. Leiden: Brill, 2008.
Hume, C.R. *Reading through Hebrews*. Lymington: The Spartan, 1997.
Johnston, W.B. *The Epistle to the Hebrews*. Calvin's Commentaries. Grand Rapids: Eerdmans, 1994.
Keller, T. "A New Kind of Urban Preacher."
In *Prophetic Preaching*, edited by C.B. Larson. Massachusetts: Hendrikson, 2012.
Kistemaker, Simon J. *Hebrews*. New Testament Commentary. Grand Rapids: Baker Book House, 1994.
Koerner, M.K. "Death, Time, Soup: A Conversation with William Kentridge and Peter Galison." *The New York Review of Books* 1, no. 1 (June 20, 2012). http://www.nybooks.com/blogs/nyrblog/2012/jun/30/kentridge-galison-refusal-of-time/.
Kruger, F.P. and C.J.H. Venter. "Die prediking van geloofsverantwoordelijkheid: homiletiese perspektiewe vanuit Hebreërs [Preaching responsibility in faith: homiletical perspectives from Hebrews]." *Praktiese Teologie in Suid-Afrika* 21, no. 1 (2006).
Kruger, Ferdi P. "The Preacher's Vulnerable Attitudes in Naming Reality in a Neglected Society." *Verbum et Ecclesia* 43, no. 1 (2015): Art. #1383, 9 pages. from http:/ / dx.doi. org/ 10.4102/ ve.v36i1.1383.
Kruger, Ferdi P. "Prediking en gesindheidsverandering: 'n Prakties-teologiese studie in die lig van Hebreërs." ThD thesis. (Potchefstroom: North-West University, Dept. Practical Theology, 2002.
Long, Thomas G. *The Witness of Preaching*. Louisville: John Knox Press, 2005.
Louw, J.P. and E.A. Nida. *Greek English Lexicon of the New Testament (II)*. New York: United Bible Studies, 1989).
Mack, W.A. and D. Swavely. *Life in the Fathers House: A Member's Guide to the Local Church*. New Jersey: P&R Publishing, 1996.
Mohler, R.A. "The Way the World Thinks: Meeting the Natural Mind in the Mirror and in the Marketplace."

In *Thinking. Loving. Doing*, edited by J. Piper, D. Mathis, R. Warren, F. Chan, R.A. Mohler, R.C. Sproul, T. Anyabwile. Illinois: Crossway, 2011.

Owen, J. *Epistle to the Hebrews*. Grand Rapids: Kregel, 1999.

Pieterse, Hennie J.C. "Prophetic Preaching in the Contemporary Context of South Africa." *In die Skriflig/In Luce Verbi* 47, no. 1 (2009): 1-6. http://dx.doi.org/10.4102/ids.v47i1.114.

Schwartz, L. and C. de la Rey. *Introduction to Psychology*. Oxford: University Press, 2007.

Smelik, E.L. *De ethiek in de verkondiging*. Nijkerk: Callenbach, 1967.

Stedman, R.C. *Hebrews*. The IVP New Testament Commentary Series. Illinois: InterVarsity Press, 1992.

Steinberg, S. *An Introduction to Communication Studies*. Cape Town: Juta, 2011.

Stott, John R.W. *The Contemporary Christian*. Leicester: Inter-Varsity Press, 1992.

Tubbs, S. and S. Moss. *Human Communication: Principles and Contexts*. New York: McGraw-Hill, 2008.

Vines, J. *The Believers Guide to Hebrews*. New Jersey: Loizeaux, 1993.

Weiten, W. *Psychology: Themes and Variations*. California: Brooks and Cole, 1992.

Wilson, G.B. *Hebrews*. Edinburgh: BPC, 1996.

Woolfolk, A. *Educational Psychology*. Boston: Pearson, 2007.

CHAPTER 5

PREACH AS YOU TEACH

The lex orandi - lex credend' -rule (LOLC) as viewed from the perspective of Hebrews

Maarten Kater

In the former chapter attention has been given to several attitudes and the vices and virtues of them. The Hebrews sermon deals with a spiritual decline in the congregation. Practical theology 'is dedicated to enabling the faithful performance of the gospel and so exploring and taking seriously the complex dynamics of the human encounter with God'[1]. Hebrews offers a specific perspective on this encounter. It deals addresses the topic of spiritual decline in a congregation. In a certain sense, they get senseless - they are in danger of losing their senses - concerning the ultimate reality, the reality of their living King and Priest in heaven. And why? Because they suffer from several social and economic injuries, but perhaps the biggest loss, spiritually, is a 'dull hearing' (cf. 4.2.1.2).

What is occurring in the congregation? To answer this question I first explore the phenomenon of listening, because within homiletics we have to deal very much with communication as a two-sided phenomenon in preaching the Word of God (Otto, 1987)[2]. This exploration will be given from a general point of view as well as more specifically as concerns Hebrews.

Now, theology is about the art of living towards Gods (*vivendum Deo*), and practical theology underscores how practice and doctrine are interwoven in this respect. After Calvin has shown us how praxis and *pietas* are interwoven with the *doctrina christianae* as a doxology, the Princeton theologian Charles Hodge (1797-1878) made the same connections between life and theology. Talking to an audience of theological students,

---

1 John Swinton and Harriet Mowat, *Practical Theology and Qualitative Research* (London: SCM Press, 2006), 4.
2 Cf. Gert Otto, *Predigt als rhetorischen Aufgabe: Homiletische Perspektiven* (Neukirchen: Neukirchener Verlag, 1987) has given a strong impetus to keep this two-sidedness in mind within homiletical reflections.

he tied piety to theology, arguing that bad theology often grows out of dying religious feelings or affections: 'if a man's religious opinions are the result and expression of his religious feelings, if *heterodoxy be the consequence rather than the cause of the loss of piety*, then "keep your hearts with all diligence, for out of them are the issues of life"' (Prov. 4:23). This relation between theology and worship is formulated in the well-known and very often cited *lex orandi - lex credendi* rule (LOLC): what we believe is what we pray and this means, for instance, that our life of prayer is the hermeneutical key to our doctrine of God.

So, then, my second purpose here will be to show how this rule is misunderstood when we put the cart before the horse. Lastly, some remedies from Hebrews are considered to find the medicine against the disease of spiritual decline. This chapter will therefore have the character of a triptych: the middle part will be the main scene - on the *lex orandi, lex credenda* - rule - with the left and right panels illustrating the most important value of this main scene.

5.1 Short phenomenological exploration on listening

One of the great purposes of preaching is the call for change, to inform the head to move the heart and so the hands. When things go wrong in church or society, behavioural scientists and brain researchers offer all kinds of interesting insights into mental processes, which of course must receive consideration and possibly implementation within the field of homiletics. Thus, when we think about communicating the Gospel in the 21first century, we have the luxury of knowing more about how we make decisions. These often turn out to be taken just intuitively and are less rational than is often thought, as has been demonstrated by the Nobel Prize winner Daniel Kahneman, who distinguishes between fast and slow thinking[3]. By describing mental life with the metaphor of two characters in our mind, called System 1 and System 2, he gives us insight into how we form an opinion about something and the choices we make. Intuitive System 1 has more influence than we are aware of and is the secret author of many of our choices and decisions. That system is also highly associative and constantly tries to give a coherent interpretation of what is happening in the world for every moment. It cannot think about many aspects in one moment. System 2, on the other hand, requires attention and as soon as this attentiveness is gone, this System 2 is disturbed. System 2 aims at overcoming the impulsive signals of System 1. It controls a person's thoughts and behaviour: it has the function of monitoring. Only System 2 is suitable for well-considered essential decisions, and that kind of

---

3 D. Kahnemann, *Thinking, Fast and Slow* (New York: Farrar, Straus and Giroux, 2011).

decisions requires slow thinking. What is also characteristic of System 2 is that it does not work on autopilot, but requires effort. However, System 2 turns out to be rather lazy and needs to be continuously activated and cultivated, otherwise cognitive languor will quickly occur.

The use of (flashing) images leads to a different way of knowing, and to a decision made at first sight. Words need to go a longer route to lead to a more responsible choice and insight into a certain situation, along the path of slow thinking. It is therefore advisable to listen longer. The processes of System 1 and System 2 seem to me to be homiletically important with a view to the communication of the Word as far as the use of our senses is concerned, especially when it comes to listening. The notorious saying, 'a picture paints a thousand words' is much too easily used for a plea to use images in worship services. As we follow Kahnemann findings, this could lead to a laziness in the church and superficial decision making because there only is an appeal on System 1. Homiletics have to make clear and to stimulate the power of words: a single word should say more than a thousand pictures.

The *New York Times* contributor Kate Murphey offers another aspect worthy of discussion around this phenomenological exploration. In her book *You Are Not Listening. What You're Missing & Why It Matters* (2020)[4], she focusses phenomena related to our habit of (non)-listening to each other. To listen may be hard, but mainly it seems that people listen to their own heart, their own inner voice, their own deep emotions and their own gut feelings. Moreover, due to many other possibilities for communication such as the social media, listening is more and more seen as a superfluous activity. True listening, however, will elevate a person, as they hear the other out.

As we turn to the congregation of the Hebrews, time and again the question arises as to why the author of this sermon places so much emphasis on listening. There is more to this question than just the logical answer that listening has to do with words that sound in our ears. As we know, the whole of Hebrews is referred to by the author as 'words of admonition' (Hebrews 13:22). Earlier in this volume we have illustrated that the word used here for 'exhortation' (*paraklèsis*) can also mean 'revival' or 'admonition'. Within the Hebrew congregation there appears to have been a crisis of faith, as has been mentioned. The greatest danger does not come from outside - not from wandering teachers or even from robbing their goods with perhaps coarse or sophisticated violence - but enters from within.

---

4 K. Murphey, *You're Not Listening: What You're Missing and Why It Matters* (New York: Celadon Books, 2020).

The writer of Hebrews therefore wants to strengthen and deepen the weakened faith of those who are addressed, for they suffer from an inner chronic illness that could be called *acedia*. In the *New York Times* bestseller Kathleen Norris writes about this condition in the soul of men and women. She describes many aspects of it, and summarizes these as follows:

Acedia may be an unfamiliar term to those not well-versed in monastic history or medieval literature. But that does not mean it has no relevance for contemporary readers [...]. I believe that such standard dictionary definitions of *acedia* as 'apathy', 'boredom', or 'torpor' do not begin to cover it, and while we may find it convenient to regard it as a more primitive word for what we now term depression, the truth is much more complex. Having experienced both conditions, I think it likely that much of the restless boredom, frantic escapism, commitment phobia, and enervating despair that plagues us today is the ancient demon of acedia in modern dress[5].

As a result of chronic mental *anemia* - a condition in which you lack enough healthy red blood cells to carry adequate oxygen to your body's tissues - *acedia*, leads to a sluggishness of hearing (see Hebr. 5:11), and symptoms such as limp hands and nodding knees (see Hebr.12:12). They cannot or do not want to keep pace with their fellow believers (Hebr. 3:1, 14; 4:11, 6:4), and gradually they stay away from church meetings. In this way the distance between them and the fellowship of faith grows. These signs of weariness reveal a 'limp' Christian life, and for this reason all kinds of very practical exhortations for the practice of faith are given in this sermon as the 'red blood cells' that will transport to the hearts and souls 'oxygen' from our heavenly Christ.

In his famous allegory *The Christian Journey* John Bunyan gives a (visual) description of what may be happening in the congregation of the Hebrews when he writes about the Enchanted Ground where pilgrims have a constant tendency to become sleepy. Precisely by continuing to talk to each other ('let us fall into good discourse') about who the Lord is and about his guidance in their lives, Christian and Hopeful remain awake[6]. Similarly, there is much 'Christ talk' in the Hebrew sermon and an ongoing plea for and endeavour to evoke and strengthen one another by looking on Christ as the active, heavenly High Priest and King (3:1).

Are there any specific causes to be pointed out that shed light on their

---

5 K. Norris, *Acedia & Me: A Marriage, Monks, and a Writer's Life* (New York: Riverhead Books, 2008), 2-3.
6 J. Bunyan, *The Pilgrim's Progress: An Allegory; One Man's Search for Eternal Life* (Grand Rapids: Baker Book House, 1999), 127.

spiritual decline? One possible cause is the influence of the spiritual climate of Platonism in the third generation of Christians (ca. 80-100). The common view of God at that time can be typified with words such as transcendent, distant, strange, unattainable, unrecognizable, unapproachable and so on. Such an image of God soon leads to existential loneliness and spiritual paralysis, especially in times of crisis.

Was this sad image of God the only (possible) cause? There hardly ever is just one cause, but it is twisted much like the deistic thinking that has taken hold of many Christians in our western countries. God is not present, or hardly so, in our ordinary lives, and we don't even miss his presence. This view of God can also develop in the direction of moral self-assertion, of a God who should keep his hands at home and neither demand nor give anything: surely, then, not his own Son! This brings men and women to a feel-good belief, a so-called Moralistic Therapeutic Deism, which becomes shipwrecked in no time when a storm wind ravages us or a panepidemic surrounds us, such as Covid-19 in present days.

But surely there were also several other possible causes for the spiritual laziness of the Hebrews. Perhaps this laziness is 'just' the result of habituation, rut, with all the attendant symptoms of fatigue. In any case, Hebrews creates this impression by means of the imagery we have already heard, which leads to falling away, resulting in the deadly danger of 'not being able to enter into rest' (Hebr. 3:19) and thus being left behind (Hebr. 4:1), while the promise of rest is still open. Decisive, then, is the question of whether we believe, and if not, what we should pray or sing? One could equally put it the other way round: if we do not worship, what do we really believe?

5.2 The lex orandi - lex credendi- rule (LOLC)

This topic requires a brief introduction. What does this saying mean: *lex orandi lex credendi* rule? Very often this rule is put in this way: what we pray is, ought *to be* and/ or *is, decisive* for the way we believe. A rule that seems to derive from the *lex orandi* follows the *lex credendi*, and not the other way round. But where is the verb? We'll see that originally there was no verb in this sentence at all. Who has invented or given us this rule? It seems important to know this, because our faith practices are involved, our theologies are involved, and the complete formation by means of education in preaching and catechism classes and by means of pastoral care, are involved in our churches. Fortunately, this rule did not appear out of the blue although, sometimes, it seems to be used in that way, as though it belongs to the *regula fidei* itself.

You could almost hear a Catholic defend this rule by saying: of course we must keep our liturgy in an iron form, otherwise our faith will be diminished. On the other hand, a Protestant embraces the rule in quite another sense: of course we subscribe to this rule (we love), because the congregation is the source for real theology for us; there's no other theology than that occurring from the lived or espoused theology in the church[7]. So this seems to be a rule one can interpret in the way one likes, and that would actually be to say the same as this is no rule at all. And at the end - as we will see in this chapter - it is actually true: there is not a LOLC- rule at all in the sense it is very often used, while the abbreviated version turns out to be just a short-cut of the original intention. Nevertheless, I keep writing about this rule because it is that short version which is in the mind of most people and has obtained a place in many practical theological studies. To put it very briefly, although this rule is historically seen appears to be a monster, from a theological perspective nevertheless it could be useful. Nevertheless, everything depends on how we use it, from which direction we read it as will be shown.

Therefore, after we have explored the current use, as found in section 3.2.1 below, we will take a brief historical detour in 3.2.2 because, if we miss the historical information, the formation of this often used rule, we have to be aware of the great danger of 'education, *de*formation and the church'. Once we have thus visited the background, we will briefly consider this rule as it is used from the perspective of Hebrews (3.2.3). Why from the perspective of the letter to the Hebrews? Because this is a biblical text - after all a homily or sermon in itself - that has played a formative role in Christian theology throughout the centuries and more than any other part of the New Testament is connected with aspects of the worship of God. I will then close the chapter with some remarks about the use and misuse of this rule considering such practical-theological phenomena as education and formation in relation to the church.

5.2.1 State of the art - 'what's going on'?
One of the maxims of contemporary liturgical theology has remained the slogan introduced above: *lex orandi, lex credenda* (LOLC). Recently and increasingly scholars have argued that liturgy itself is theology, indeed, primary theology (*theologia prima*) from which is derived all secondary theology (*theologia secunda*), namely subsequent theological reflection on the liturgy[8]. Thus, the liturgy is primary and formulated doctrines are

---

7 H. Cameron et al., eds., *Talking about God in Practice: Theological Action Research and Practical Theology* (London: SCM Press, 2010), esp. 49-60 on 'Four Voices': normative, formal, operant and espoused theology.

8 D.W. Fagerberg, *Theologia Prima: What is Liturgical Theology?* (Chicago/Mundelein: Hillenbrand Books, 2004), 36-39.

secondary, derivative and subordinate. This notion 'challenges the common Reformed view that liturgy follows theology'[9]. For several decades now, there has been a 'tug-of-war' between liturgical scholars 'over whether liturgy should exercise control over doctrine or doctrine should exercise control over liturgy'[10].

A very short exploration shows us the two main streams in the use of the expression LOLC. This saying is interpreted as *orandi* == > *credendi* by Aidan Kavanagh and David Fagerberg to mean that 'the law of praying (*lex supplicandi* or *lex orandi*) establishes (*statuat*) the law of believing (*legem credendi*)'[11]. Thus, in their view, what is meant by *lex orandi* exists prior to and determines the *lex credendi*, and the latter, therefore, cannot be the foundation of the former. The 'relationship of praying and believing is unidirectional; we do not believe and then worship, but we encounter God in worship, and therefore we believe' (ibid.). The liturgy, then, is primary and establishes theology: the order cannot be reversed. 'Secondary theology, then, as a presentation of belief, follows from worship'[12].

This interpretation of *credenda* LOLC has been challenged by several scholars, including Geoffrey Wainwright (1980), Kevin Irwin (1990) and Bryan Spinks (2013). For example, Spinks remarks that 'the idea that doctrine only flowed from liturgy and that doctrine never impacted and changed liturgical practice is pious humbug and wishful thinking'[13]. Similarly, Wainwright and Irwin demonstrate that the Latin epigram does not presume liturgical fixity, nor does it mean that the church should draw on liturgical practice as the sole or chief norm for doctrine. Rather, the liturgy expresses the church's faith and may only serve as a source for establishing theology to the degree that it is founded on Holy Scripture. Wainwright argues that LOLC may be construed in two ways. The more usual way makes the rule of prayer a norm for belief: what is prayed indicates what may and must be believed. But from the grammatical point of view, it is equally possible to reverse subject and predicate and so take the tag as meaning that the rule of faith is the norm for prayer: what must be believed governs what may and should be prayed. The linguistic ambiguity of the Latin tag corresponds to a material interplay which in fact takes place between worship and doctrine in Christian practice:

---

9 M.L. Moore-Keish, *Do This in Remembrance of Me: A Ritual Approach to Reformed Eucharistic Theology* (Grand Rapids: Wm. B. Eerdmans, 2008), 12.
10 F.C. Senn, *The People's Work: A Social History of the Liturgy* (Minneapolis: Fortress Press, 2006), 227.
11 Moore-Keish, *Remembrance*, 63.
12 Moore-Keish, *Remembrance*, 63.
13 B.D. Spinks, *Do This in Remembrance of Me: The Eucharist from the Early Church to the Present Day* (London: SCM Press, 2013), xii.

worship influences doctrine and doctrine, worship[14]. Thus, the relationship between theology and liturgy is dialectical: it is a two-way relationship. Wainwright underscores that LOLC is a two-directional principle: theology and liturgy are mutually formative, they are correlative norms[15].

Another theologian who has weighed in on the issue is Paul Marshall. Marshall delivers a stinging critique of the interpretation of LOLC by Kavanagh and Fagerberg[16]. They present, says Marshall, the liturgy as simply a given that 'the people receive passively, rather than actively participating in the formation and critique of that liturgy'[17].

To claim that there is 'a one-way street, from the divinely given liturgy to the human response of believing' is to perpetuate 'a view of the liturgy that is fixed, authoritarian, and hierarchical'[18]. Contrary to this interpretation, Marshall claims that Prosper 'never intended to posit liturgical action as the single norm that establishes Christian believing'[19]. Rather, 'Prosper's overall point, arguing against semi-Pelagianism, is that believing is a gift from God, not a human achievement'[20].

5.2.2 Historical background

The expression LOLC appears to be derived from a fifth century brief work ascribed to Prosper of Aquitaine, a monk in the region of Marseille and secretary to Leo the Great, and fierce adherent to Augustine's theology. That work is known by various titles, including *Indiculus de gratia Dei* and *Epistolae* or *Capitulae Caelestini*. In this writing, Prosper does not mention a LOLC as such but does write *ut legem credendi lex statuat supplicandi*. In chapter eight of his *Indiculus* one finds the following passage:

    Besides the inviolable sanctions of the most blessed and apostolic see, with which the most pious fathers, having cast down the pride of the pestilential novel teaching, taught us to ascribe to the grace of Christ the origins of good will, the growth of commendable efforts, and perseverance in them to the end, let us consider the sacraments of priestly prayers that, having been handed down by the apostles, are uniformly practiced

---

14 G. Wainwright, *Doxology: the Praise of God in Worship, Doctrine and Life; A Systematic Theology* (New York: Oxford University Press, 1980), 218.
15 Wainwright, *Doxology*, 161.
16 Moore-Keish, *Remembrance*, 129-151.
17 P.V. Marshall, "Reconsidering 'Liturgical Theology': Is There a *Lex Orandi* for All Christians?," *Studia Liturgica* 25 (1995): 129-151, 134.
18 Moore-Keish, *Remembrance*, 82.
19 Marshall, "Reconsidering," 145.
20 Marshall, "Reconsidering," 145.

throughout the world in every Catholic church, ut legem credendi lex statuat supplicandi[21]. (emphasis mine)

This last expression reads: so that the law [or rule or pattern] of supplicating [not the more general *orandi*, 'praying'] may establish [or confirm] the law [or rule or pattern] of believing [not 'the faith']. Thus, Prosper appeals to the universal liturgical practice of praying for the salvation of all people, 'not because it is the only source, or even the first source, for theological reflection, but because it is a reliable source that demonstrates the broad apostolic Christian faith'[22]. Moreover, he coined it while his controversy with the semi-Pelagians was in the background! Especially when this passage in the *Indiculus* is juxtaposed with a parallel passage in *De vocatione omnium gentium*, one can see that Prosper's referent is very precise. His *lex supplicandi* refers to 1 Timothy 2:1-4. That prayer, those supplications, underscore the Christian belief that grace comes from God through Jesus Christ by the Holy Spirit. Prosper's referent again turns out to be very precise. His *lex supplicandi* refers to Pauls' exhortation in 1 Timothy 2:1-4. This is even more clear when the *Indiculus* is juxtaposed with a parallel passage in *De vocatione omnium gentium*[23]. Prosper's argument is based on Christian prayers of intercession, beseeching God for the conversion of sinners according to the precept of 1 Timothy 2.

Besides this, not all early Christian prayer was liturgical. A direct connection between *lex orandi* and liturgy therefore begs the question. Prosper himself does not give any indication that he was talking about officially sanctioned and corporate prayer within the Roman Mass[24].

Whatever Prosper may have intended by his maxim, however, it has provided the occasion for a modern debate about the relationship between theology (*lex credendi*) and liturgy (*lex orandi*). In which way? Historical research has shown that there was another man, named Dom Guéranger (1805-1875), who was also called Prosper. How ironic history sometimes is! He introduced the much-discussed abbreviated version in his *Institutions liturgiques* - he called it an axiom - and that variant has become popular in discussions about liturgical theology. And indeed Hebrews offers us in a sermon the various aspects of liturgy, and even Jesus Christ is referred to as the Liturgist *par excellance* (Hebr. 8:1).

---

21 Wainwright, *Doxology*, 225-226.
22 Moore-Keish, *Remembrance*, 66.
23 D.G. van Slycke, "*Lex orandi lex credendi*: Liturgy as *Locus Theologicus* in the Fifth Century?," *Josephinum Journal of Theology* 11, no. 2 (2004): 130-151, 131.
24 Cf. Study Van Slycke, "*Lex orandi lex credendi*," 130-151, and P. de Clerck, "'Lex orandi, lex credendi': The Original Sense and Historical Avatars of an Equivocal Adage," *Studia Liturgica* 24 (1994): 178-200.

So, it is appropriate to give some attention within the context of this volume to the debate about the connection between theology and liturgy that has divided Protestants and Catholics since the time of the Reformation. The Reformers' Catholic opponents usually conceded that, while the substance of their eucharistic theology had its foundation in scripture, there were aspects of the Mass (such as the Roman Canon) that had developed over time. Like their medieval forebears, 16th century Catholic apologists assumed that the *lex orandi* should determine the *lex credendi*. Scripture was a source of Catholic doctrine but so were the liturgical practice of the church and the testimony of the fathers. Thus the fact that many Catholic liturgical practices had no explicit scriptural warrant was not necessarily problematic for Catholic apologists (Thompson, 2005:4-5)[25].

On the other hand, the Reformers believed that certain biblical doctrines were incompatible with various liturgical practices in the Roman church. For example, the Roman Mass—particularly the sacrificial language of the Latin canon—was hardly compatible with the doctrines of the perfection of Christ's atonement and of justification by faith alone. Like the gift of justification, Protestants saw the Lord's Supper as a gift (*beneficium*) received from God and not a sacrifice (*sacrificium*) offered to God. Protestant theology, therefore, inevitably led to changes in liturgy. Hence, the Reformers believed that *lex credendi* could exercise control over *lex orandi* 'when it came to forms of existing worship that needed correction'[26]. Theology can critique worship and improve it wherever and whenever necessary.

The Latin maxim LOLC thus offers a helpful corrective to the common tendency in modern Protestant circles to bifurcate theology and liturgy as two independent branches of ecclesial life. Theology and liturgy are, in fact, interrelated and mutually formative. True doctrine forms the foundation of true worship, and true worship is an expression of true doctrine. Theology shapes the church's liturgy but, over time, the worship of the church will inevitably influence its theology.

5.2.3 Perspective from Hebrews
How on Earth Did Jesus Become a God? This is the provocative title of Larry Hurtado's thought provoking study of 2005. He examines the keen devotion to Jesus that emerged with surprising speed soon after his death. Reverence for Jesus among early Christians, notes Hurtado, included

---
25 N. Thompson, *Eucharistic Sacrifice and Patristic Tradition in the Theology of Martin Bucer, 1534-1546* (Leiden: Brill, 2005), 4-5.
26 K. Irwin, *Liturgical Theology: A Primer* (Collegeville, MN: Liturgical Press, 1990), 16.

grand claims about Jesus' significance and a pattern of devotional practices that effectively treated him as divine. In a previous publication, *One God, One Lord* (1988), he mentions six specific devotional practices:

- Hymns about Jesus as part of early Christian worship;
- Prayer to God 'through' Jesus and 'in Jesus' name', and even direct prayer to Jesus himself, especially the invocation of Jesus in the setting of corporate worship;
- Calling upon Jesus: baptism, healing and exorcism;
- A common Christian meal enacted as sacred where the risen Jesus presides as 'Lord';
- Confessing Jesus in the context of Christian worship;
- Christian prophecy as oracles of the risen Jesus and the Holy Spirit understood as the Spirit of Jesus. (Hurtado, 2005, 27-28; see 1998: 100-114).

This theology stems from early Christian worship, and could be named a kind of liturgical theology. So, then, Jesus became a God in the lives of so many people, but for what reasons? This is exactly where Hebrews offers a wonderful answer. Let this sermon inform us of its answer by connecting the exposition in Hebr.1:1-4 with its application in 2:1-4:

1. Long ago, at many times and in many ways, God spoke to our fathers by the prophets,
2. but in these last days he has spoken to us by his Son, whom he appointed the heir of all things, through whom also he created the world.
3. He is the radiance of the glory of God and the exact imprint of his nature, and he upholds the universe by the word of his power. After making purification for sins, he sat down at the right hand of the Majesty on high,
4. having become as much superior to angels as the name he has inherited is more excellent than theirs.
 (Hebr. 1:1-4)

First and foremost, there is no *lex credendi* that existed already here, but God 'exists' - He *is* - and *God has spoken* (*ho lalèsas*) or even in the present tense, He is 'The One Who is Speaking' (Hebr. 12:25).

1. Therefore we must pay much closer attention to what we have heard, lest we drift away from it.

> 2 For since the message declared by angels proved to be reliable, and every transgression or disobedience received a just retribution,
> 3 how shall we escape if we neglect such a great salvation? It was declared at first by the Lord, and it was attested to us by those who heard,
> 4 while God also bore witness by signs and wonders and various miracles and by gifts of the Holy Spirit distributed according to his will.
> (Hebr. 2:1-4)

By God's grace the Hebrews started to pray to Jesus, sing their songs, make their confession of faith - due to the fact that God has spoken in the Son. A *lex audiendi*, then, precedes both *lex credendi* and *lex orandi*. However, what is the situation in this congregation according to the text of this sermon?

> 1 Therefore, while the promise of entering his rest still stands, let us fear lest any of you should seem to have failed to reach it.
> 2 For good news came to us just as to them, but the message they heard did not benefit them, because they were *not united by faith* with those who *listened*.
> (Hebr. 4:1-2, my emphasis)

To understand this, we turn to what we have already seen in the 'phenomenological exploration of listening' offered at the beginning of this chapter. The Hebrews were dull of hearing (5:10), unskilled in the word of righteousness (5:13), and had not gained the power of discernment by means of constantly practicing distinguishing good from evil. All this leads to the great danger of falling away (6:12). What happens in the Hebrew congregation according to the transmogrified LOLC-rule? What was their method of prayer at that very moment in history? There was no living practice of the *lex orandi* left, because their faith had diminished. Sound theology does not come from their worship any longer.

Therefore, time and again they must be admonished 'let us draw near', 'let us hold fast' and so forth. They did not realise themselves what it meant to come to the church (12:22-24) and they disregarded the worship service, refrained from it and, in this way, there was no education or formation of the Christian life at all. What did this preacher to the Hebrews therefore do? He started right from the beginning: God speaks. And, this whole sermon is a great song of love and of knowledge of our great High Priest whom we confess. That *lex credendi* could inspire and enliven the *lex orandi*, of which the practice had diminished.

5.3 Remedies leading to recovering

The history of the LOLC-rule shows us the real danger of parroting as a threat to real education and formation and the initial words have been changed, as though the rule is classical, stemming from the Early Church. The abbreviated rule does remind us of the great importance of holding doctrine and faith together.

If we allow the 'rule of praying' to determine the 'rule of belief' one-sidedly, Hebrews can show us that we ultimately will believe everything and so we will believe nothing at all. Hebrews emphasises the great importance of listening to the *verbum externum* as the *viva vox dei*, considering true formation as practical education in church, at schools and at home. The German theologian Bernd Wannenwetsch therefore rightly emphasises the necessity of starting with and thinking from *the verbum externum* and not from 'felt needs', 'religious experiences' or some such. 'From a theological point of view, the choice to take the religious market as a starting point has an even more problematic consequence. By offering the gospel in a market of competing religious players, the church has ceased to consider and receive this gospel as God's own Word'[27].

In sum: listening according to Hebrews is an exercise in practical theology to revive the living faith, an exposition of truth directed to the correction of that congregational practice suffering *acedia*. This 'word of exhortation' (13:22) appears to be an admonition: acting as a warning as well as an encouragement.

One could argue that the *lex orandi* is a prerequisite for the *lex credendi*, at least in the sense that, without prayer, we will not understand what we believe at all. A theological discussion is not a substitute for knowing God. If you are a theologian, you pray truly. And if you pray truly, you are a theologian (Evagrios Pontus). An active life of prayer before God sits at the centre of a disciple's existence. Prayer is the core spiritual discipline indeed. Prayer pursues and blossoms in knowledge of God through dialogue and listening, silence and speech. Surely, the way of praying does influence what we believe. How many prayers of mothers are a great blessing in the faith formation of our children and youngsters! They hear how we appeal to God, and even in our voices our deepest convictions of love and fear, hope and distress, and so forth, are heard. The teaching ministry of the congregation could not function as a real blessing without these practices. But, how do we address God? Is there not the great danger that we might pray to an idol because we project our ideas on a 'God' who

---

27 B. Wannenwetsch, "Inwardness and Commodification: How Romantic Hermeneutics Prepared the Way for the Culture of Managerialism; A Theological Analysis," *Studies in Christian Ethics* 21, no. 1 (2008): 28-46, 37.

is *not there*? Therefore, the *lex credendi* is definitely important for the well-being of the *lex orandi*.

From this mutual reciprocal relation between the *orandi* and the *credendi* in the life of the church as a whole, I turn for a moment to our theological training institutes, theological departments of a university or whatever. Just three remarks, which may be seen as a bucket list for the field of homiletics and liturgy:

- In our theological education the interrelatedness of *meditatio* and *disputatio* is paramount. The Middle Ages reflects a separation between them, due to the fact that *meditation* seems to be at home in cloisters and *disputations* in universities. This division still has great consequences, even in the field of practical (!) theology. For instance, too often, using so-called scientific (exegetical) methods and personal meditation are separated in the homiletical processes of preparation of the sermons. The suggestion behind this divide is the distinction between 'objective' and 'subjective' truth, which division has been introduced by René Descartes in the 17th century and has influenced so much scientific and ecclesial practice[28].
- Singing and saying are both necessary for a sound theology. '*Theologein*' ultimately is *doxologein* or it is nothing at all. In Hebrews, sayings about Jesus Christ function as songs. In the Early Church, *theologien* and *hymnein* are intertwined. Accordingly, theology
- 'as a concept in Christianity was first understood in the sense of a hymnal "calling God", in which the pronouncing of God's name aimed at the presence of God himself and did not make him for instance the "object" of a *logos, about* which one thinks or speaks'[29].
- The importance of combining liturgical 'poetry' and theological/doctrinal 'prose'. Worship is the main vehicle of Christian theology, because there are quite a few people who do not read any theological books on a regular basis. In our worship, there should be room for imagination to stir up the life indicated by *lex orandi* as well as the teaching ministry marked by *lex credendi*. To create room for a life of listening there should be, in our services, more room for silence, for preparing hearts and moving our thoughts.

---

28 Charles Taylor, *A Secular Age* (Harvard: University Press, 2007).
29 B. Wannenwetsch, "Singen und Sagen. Zur musisch-musikalischen Dimension der Theologie," *Neue Zeitschrift für Systematische Theologie und Religionsphilosophie* 46, no. 3 (2004): 330-347, 335.

All in all, from the perspective of Hebrews the LOLC-rule should be extended as follows:

lex audiendi <-> *lex orandi* <-> *lex credendi* <-> *lex vivendi*.

That is, the rule states: from listening to living via liturgy and love, and the other way round. All parts are interconnected as a four-leaf clover. The heart of this clover is our heavenly High Priest in heaven whose service is 24/7/365.

It is all about the formation of faith, in classrooms as much as in sanctuaries. To hold these four in a creative tension by means of a critical conversation is the task of practical theology.

REFERENCES

Bunyan, J. *The Pilgrim's Progress: An Allegory; One Man's Search for Eternal Life*. Grand Rapids: Baker Book House, 1999.

Cameron, H., D. Bhatti, C. Duce, J. Sweeney, and C. Watkins. *Talking about God in Practice: Theological Action Research and Practical Theology*. London: SCM Press, 2004.

De Clerck, P. "'Lex orandi, lex credendi': The Original Sense and Historical Avatars of an Equivocal Adage." *Studia Liturgica* 24 (1994): 178-200.

Fagerberg, D.W. *Theologia Prima: What is Liturgical Theology?* Chicago/Mundelein: Hillenbrand Books, 2004.

Hurtado, L.W. *How on Earth Did Jesus Become a God? Historical Questions about Earliest Devotion to Jesus*. Grand Rapids: Wm. B. Eerdmans, 2005.

Hurtado, L.W. *One God, One Lord: Early Christian Devotion and Ancient Jewish Monotheism*. Minneapolis: Fortress Press, 1988.

Irwin, K. *Liturgical Theology: A Primer*. Collegeville, MN: Liturgical Press, 1990.

Kahnemann, D. *Thinking, Fast and Slow*. New York: Farrar, Straus and Giroux, 2011.

Marshall, P.V. "Reconsidering 'Liturgical Theology': Is There a Lex Orandi for All Christians?" *Studia Liturgica* 25 (1995): 129-51.

Moore-Keish, M.L. *Do This in Remembrance of Me: A Ritual Approach to Reformed Eucharistic Theology*. Grand Rapids: Wm. B. Eerdmans, 2008.

Murphey, K. *You're Not Listening: What You're Missing and Why It Matters*. New York: Celadon Books, 2020.

Norris, K. *Acedia & Me: A Marriage, Monks, and a Writer's Life*. New York: Riverhead Books, 2008.

Otto, Gert. *Predigt als rhetorischen Aufgabe: Homiletische Perspektiven.* Neukirchen: Neukirchener Verlag, 1987.

Senn, F.C. *The People's Work: A Social History of the Liturgy.* Minneapolis: Fortress Press, 2006.

Spinks, B.D. *Do This in Remembrance of Me: The Eucharist from the Early Church to the Present Day.* London: SCM Press, 2013.

Swinton, John and Harriet Mowat. *Practical Theology and Qualitative Research.* London: SCM Press, 2006.

Taylor, C. *A Secular Age.* Harvard: University Press, 2007.

Thompson, N. *Eucharistic Sacrifice and Patristic Tradition in the Theology of Martin Bucer, 1534-1546.* Leiden: Brill, 2005.

Van Slycke, D.G. "Lex orandi lex credendi: Liturgy as Locus Theologicus in the Fifth century?" *Josephinum Journal of Theology* 11, no. 2 (2004): 130-151.

Wainwright, G. *Doxology: The Praise of God in Worship, Doctrine and Life; A Systematic Theology.* New York: Oxford University Press, 1980.

Wannenwetsch, B. "Inwardness and Commodification: How Romantic Hermeneutics Prepared the Way for the Culture of Managerialism; A Theological Analysis." *Studies in Christian Ethics* 21, no. 1 (2008): 28-46.

Wannenwetsch, B. "Singen und Sagen: Zur musisch-musikalischen Dimension der Theologie." *Neue Zeitschrift für Systematische Theologie und Religionsphilosophie* 46, no. 3 (2004): 330-347.

CHAPTER 6

PERSUASIVE PREACHING'S PERTINENT FOCUS ON THE CHANGING OF ATTITUDES THAT IMPEDE THE INTERRELATIONSHIP BETWEEN LISTENING AND DOING

Ferdi Kruger

The preacher's pastoral concern finds full expression in Hebrews. The sermon is delivered in the spirit of a friend speaking to friends[1], therefore with compassion[2]. Its nature is urgent, because the situation of the listeners required urgent attention. It could not wait for a later time when the preacher might visit them and strengthen them in person. He wrote the sermon to encourage Christians (Hebrews 13:22) to stand firm in their faith and to warn them of the danger if they remained immature[3]. The strongest encouragement is to remind the listeners of the character of the Lord who cares for them. The Greek word for encouragement literally means *to stir up, to provoke, to incite people in a given direction*. Verbal encouragement embodies the idea of one person accompanying another on a journey, with emphasis on *come on, let us do it*. The companion speaks words that encourage people to keep pressing on despite obstacles and fatigue[4]. It seems as though the expression that is applicable in this context is that *a word of encouragement during a failure is worth more than an hour of praise after success*. Preaching to encourage therefore amounts to the sharing of comforting words, words of life that soothe. It re-routes a human life to experience meaningfulness.

---

1 W.L. Lane, *Hebrews 1-8* (Dallas: World Books, 1991), 25.
2 Donald Guthrie, *Hebrews*, Tyndale New Testament Commentaries (Grand Rapids: Eerdmans, 1996), 47.
3 Lane, *Hebrews*, 6.
4 Y.J. Wong, "The Psychology of Encouragement: Theory, Research, and Applications," *Counselling Psychologist* 43, no. 2 (2015): 180.

One of the important lessons we can learn from this sermon is the value of preaching with pastoral intent. From beginning to end, this is a message to real people with real problems, temptations, needs and burdens. It is designed to minister to them, to strengthen, rebuke, encourage and challenge them. Real issues from daily life are addressed. The listeners are tired of serving the world, tired of worship, tired of being whispered about in society, tired of the spiritual struggle and tired of trying to keep their prayer-life going[5]. The preacher does not only speak about the biblical text but also about the lives of the people who are listening to this sermon. The urgent encouragement to stand firm in faith has to deal with the functioning of attitudes. Attitudes, one should acknowledge, are formed because they are useful in helping people to master their environment and also to express themselves[6]. Attitudes are, after all, functional in helping persons to understand life (see the previous chapter). People's attitudes are not only influential for the act of listening to sermons, but also for daily life.

In the Hebrews sermon, it becomes clear that preaching inevitably has to deal with the functioning of attitudes as well as the persuasive power of preaching[7]. Preaching could also be regarded as an important manifestation of persuasive communication. Firet[8] emphasises the idea of *agogie* [change] to denote the patience preachers should have in preaching to listeners. To assist listeners to change their attitude, an understanding of the underlying aspects of their attitudes is needed. This word, namely *agogie*, suggests a framework of change and the importance of understanding of exactly what is in need of change. This kind of guidance to change from the preacher's side has to do with enabling listeners to live according to the clear theological principle of God's image. Within a homiletical view, one could say that preaching has to with the mediation (proclamation) of God's Word through explication and its application, for listeners thus to understand their calling within daily life to live congruent to the idea of *Imago Dei*[9]. Persuasive preaching deals with change, but a kind of change that engages with the concreteness of attitudes and also in aligning them to God's purpose with a liveable life based on the values of his Kingdom.

---

5 Thomas G. Long, *Hebrews*, Interpretation: A Bible Commentary for Teaching and Preaching (Louisville: John Knox Press, 1997), 3.
6 E.R. Smith and D.M. Mackie, *Social Psychology* (New York: Psychology Press, 2007), 231.
7 F.P. Kruger and C.J.H. Venter, "Die prediking van geloofsverantwoordelikheid: homiletiese perspektiewe vanuit Hebreërs [Preaching responsibility in faith: homiletical perspectives from Hebrews]" *Praktiese Teologie in Suid-Afrika* 21, no. 1 (2006): 55.
8 J. Firet, *Het agogisch moment in het pastoraal optreden* (Kampen: Kok, 1978), 249.
9 Kruger and Venter, "Prediking van geloofsverantwoordelikheid", 56.

To achieve this, one should remember that persuasive communication aims intentionally at changing a person's attitudes and behaviour[10]. Preachers have to keep in mind that people have a natural tendency to oppose persuasion. Lord[11], for example, highlights the following aspects in this regard:

- If listeners are aware of the content of persuasive communication, they will have the natural tendency to ignore the message of persuasion and transformation. Listeners would not want to let other persons know that their heads have been swayed by the message.
- There must be time for cognitive closure. If listeners receive the opportunity to reach closure about certain things, they feel secure. Cognitive closure opens the way for attitudes to change. Communicators (preachers) have to keep in mind the tendency of listeners to use self-defence strategies.

Fiske[12] has pointed out that persuasion inherently has to do with the deliberate attempt to change another person's attitude. When people receive a persuasive message, they think about the arguments that are made and, in some instances, they also think about the information that has been left out[13]. These thoughts about the message influence a change in attitude[14]. When persuasive messages deal with issues that are relevant to people's lives, they are likely to devote their attention to the message and its arguments.

Brown[15], as well as Evans[16], have indicated that the Hebrews sermon is directed in the fashion described above towards being persuasive. Various formulations are found that underline this idea. In preaching persuasively, the preacher of the Hebrews sermon is not interested in artificial techniques, but rather in preaching about the nature and essence of what it means that God has spoken in and through his Son in the last days.

---

10 D. Louw and D. Edwards, *Sielkunde: 'n Inleiding vir studente in Suider-Afrika* (Sandton: Heinemann Voortgesette onderwys, 1998), 711.
11 C.G. Lord, *Social Psychology* (Orlando: Harcourt Brace, 1997), 266-270.
12 S.T. Fiske, *Social Beings: A Core Motives Approach to Social Psychology* (Princeton: Wiley, 2004), 243.
13 R.H. Gass and J.S. Seiter, *Persuasion, Social Influence and Compliance Gaining* (New York: Harper Collins, 2003), 159.
14 Fiske, *Social Beings*, 238.
15 J. Brown, *Hebrews*, Geneva Series of Commentaries (Edinburg: The Bath Press, 1999), 5.
16 L.H. Evans, *Hebrews*, Communicator's Commentary (Washington: Macmillan, 1984), 21.

Lloyd-Jones[17] has rightfully referred to logic on fire and eloquent reasoning to indicate what preaching is all about. The preacher of the Hebrews sermon takes these words even further in proclaiming the message about Jesus Christ eloquently.

This chapter will further scrutinise, the essence of preaching directed at persuading change in listeners' lives. One should remember that this sermon is preached to listeners who were disheartened. They no longer had the energy to stand firm in their faith. Therefore, the Hebrews sermon opens truth to make a relevant point. It emphasises the reciprocal relationship between life and the Gospel, which is interactive, and should be lived as such.

6.1 Persuasive communication and the importance of the use of language

Change is always difficult to achieve in people's lives, unless they can see the resulting benefits. In the Hebrews sermon, the preacher is trying to help listeners understand the difficulty of their circumstances as well as the urgent need to stand firm in their faith. In the present section, a few comments will be made on the importance of the use of language, while section 3 will subsequently elaborate on how the preacher in the Hebrews sermon applies this principle. Swets[18] indicates the importance of five concepts that should function in the use of persuasive language, namely attention, comprehension, belief, repetition and action. He further elaborates on the five words and indicates the following aspects[19]:

- To be influential, preaching should evoke the interest and the positive attitude of participants. In the Hebrews sermon, the preacher skilfully blends encouragement and comfort with warning, rebuke and challenge for the listeners to realise why they should listen attentively. In this instance, the preacher has to be aware of the kind of information needed best to understand the participants in liturgy. This process requires active listening and knowledge about different viewpoints. Persuasive preaching in the Hebrews sermon leaves the listeners not just willing to listen, but also with a commitment of wanting to walk God's way. Each person's attitude on liturgy in the narrow sense of the word as well as in the expanded sense of the word, on life itself or aspects of life,

---

17 M. Lloyd-Jones, *Preaching and Preachers* (Grand Rapids: Zondervan, 1971), 97.
18 J. Swets, "On the Literary Genre of the 'Epistle' to the Hebrews," *Novum Testamentum* 11 (2003): 159-172.
19 Swets, "Literary Genre," 162.

includes cognitive but also affective elements. That is what the preacher of Hebrews intends to do. By warning, rebuking, encouraging and comforting, by speaking of the majesty and humility and suffering of Christ, by laying out the examples of old covenant saints who have gone before them, by warning of the judgement of God and the danger of apostasy and by depicting the glory of Mount Zion and the reward of Christian pilgrimage, the preacher seeks to persuade them that it would be folly to give up when, by persevering, they would receive the richest reward[20].

- In shaping the persuasive language of preaching, it should be born in mind that preachers have to help participants understand the message of persuasive language. Persuasive language in the Hebrews sermon addresses willingness via understanding, giving reasons, incentives and motivations for the appropriate action. The kind of language that is familiar to participants and words that have a definite meaning to participants must be used for an optimal outcome. What kind of words are considered to be persuasive? Words that are clearly understood and language that is direct and vigorous aided by an imagination that can paint word-pictures. Cilliers[21] has performed extensive research on the topic of aesthetics in liturgy. This entails that concrete examples are very helpful. Without understanding the meaning or intent of the preacher's style of language, nobody can really act according to the sermon.
- The preacher should believe what he or she is communicating effectively. The issue at stake is that the preacher's own attitude must be correct for addressing listeners' attitudes. It is true that aspects such as appearance, fluency, rate of speech and others could influence the communication process, but it must be highlighted that no liturgical language will ever contribute towards a change in attitude unless participants notice enthusiasm from the liturgist and also receive enough information to understand what is expected of them. Enthusiasm intrigues people. On noticing enthusiasm, participants will look for clues as to why the liturgist is so enthusiastic. Participants may change their attitudes because of the information they explore themselves. Enthusiasm could help hearers in the exploration process. Language must help participants understand why the persuasive message of liturgy is the solution to wrong and sinful attitudes.

---

20 S. Olyott, *Preaching: Pure and Simple* (Bryntirion: Bryntirion Press, 2005), 24.
21 Johan H. Cilliers, *Binne die kring-dans van die kuns: Die betekenis van estetika vir die gereformeerde liturgie* (Stellenbosch: Sun Press, 2007), 80.

- For language to be persuasive, preachers should be aware of the fact that listeners have to be enabled to remember the essence of the sermon. They must be able to recall what they were persuaded to do. The influence of liturgical language has to with important messages that are spaced during the act of preaching. Spaced repetition of important messages will ensure increased retention. Therefore, coherence between preaching and the other elements of liturgy is also needed.

Action and the change of attitude that affect the liturgy of life and the liturgy of the streets are the deepest purpose of persuasion, and has to do with a kind of understanding to act according to God's will. Preaching and ethics cannot be separated. Preaching without the outlook of ethics will become blind and short-sighted. Through the use of language in liturgy, Christ is presented in such a manner that everybody will realise that God is present, but liturgy also cultivates the discovery that God is present in daily life. Cilliers[22] highlights the importance of this kind of encounter with God and the transforming power of this encounter. He underlines rapprochement or affection. Four key components are distinguished, namely people's affection towards God, God's affection towards people through his promises, the sacraments and his Word and people's affection towards the world.

6.2 Deliberateness in preaching enables listeners to stand firm in their faith.

Guthrie[23] underlines the line of argumentation in the Hebrews sermon that utilises explication and application to persuade listeners. It begins by focussing attention on the God who has spoken to his people in the past, and who is speaking to his people in the present (Hebrews 1:1-2a). Hume[24] indicates the purposefulness of this sermon towards changing listeners' attitudes. The emphasis on persuasion functions within the paraenetic and hortatory sections of the Hebrews sermon[25]. It is striking that the preacher does not utilise a preaching method that is manipulated by a scheme of dos and don'ts. Along the contours of what the listeners should do or do not do, clear motivation of the importance of listening and obedience is offered. One could say that regular alternation between the doctrinal (kerugma) and paraenesis is evident. The utilisation of a

---

22 Cilliers, *Kring-dans van die kuns*, 80.
23 Guthrie, *Hebrews*, 117.
24 C.R. Hume, *Reading through Hebrews* (Lymington: The Spartan, 1997), 9-13.
25 Kruger and Venter, "Prediking van geloofsverantwoordelikheid," 57.

balanced relationship between the indicative and the imperative is striking[26]. The construction of the listeners through the certainty of what God has done is augmented by the relevance of the implication of what it means that God has indeed spoken through his Son. It is evident that the imperatives in this sermon emanate from this indicative stance.

Cleary[27] regards persuasive communication as an effective manner in which to change attitudes. The process in which an attitude is influenced (changed) is called persuasion[28]. The essence of persuasive messages is a definite attempt not simply to evoke negative emotions regarding the content of the message, but to evoke positive emotions towards God that break through into this world[29]. The goal of persuasive messages is to equip listeners to live the message of hope in their daily lives and to convey this message to others. De Wet and Kruger[30] indicate that persuasion and manipulation should not be confused. Cilliers[31] is correct to indicate that it is not just mere proclaiming of the Word of God that can contribute towards a change in attitude. Any proclaimer or preacher who does not believe that the Word of God came to change people's lives (*sermo Dei venit mutaturus*) will experience trouble with his or her attitudes. To proclaim persuasively entails an awareness that changes in attitude will not necessarily occur overnight and the preacher's attitude will always be exposed.

The purposefulness of the Hebrews sermon is also illustrated in the following aspects[32]:

- Preaching has to connect God's Word with the concrete circumstances of the listeners.
- Persuasive preaching has the purpose to illustrate what God has done in and through his Son with the exhortation of appropriation of the truths.
- Profound preaching should proclaim the implication of the passage for listeners' daily life.

---

26 Kruger and Venter, "Prediking van geloofsverantwoordelikheid," 57.
27 S. Cleary, *The Communication Handbook: A Student Guide to Effective Communication* (Cape Town: Juta, 2010), 164.
28 S. Tubbs and S. Moss, *Human Communication: Principles and Contexts* (New York: McGraw-Hill, 2008), 29.
29 Tubbs and Moss, *Human Communication*, 480.
30 F.W. de Wet and F.P. Kruger, "Blessed are Those that Hunger and Thirst for Righteousness: Shaping the Ethical Dimension of Prophetic Preaching in a Context of Corruption," *Verbum et Ecclesia* 43, no. 1 (2013): 13, Art. #722, 10 pages, DOI: 10.4102/ ve.v34i1.722.
31 Johan H. Cilliers, *Die genade van gehoorsaamheid* (Cape Town: Lux Verbi, 2000), 17.
32 G.E. Sweazy, *Preaching the Good News* (New Jersey: Prentice Hall, 2003), 16-24.

- Preaching has to provide perspectives on standing firm in your faith-life via exhortation and encouragement.

Hebrews, also described as a three-dimensional sermon, reminds believers to honour their responsibilities of faith[33]. Consider that the sermon to the Hebrews structures its contents in a unique manner[34]. This structure induces persuasion through preaching, especially when one considers the fact that it mentions the theme of attitude seven times, each time within its admonishing (paraenetic) sections, as found in Hebrews 3:6, 4:11, 4:16, 6:11, 10:19, 10:35 and 13:6. Challenges are prominent in this sermon when it comes to persuading believers who have lost energy and the sense of the meaningfulness of duties or actions such as encouraging each other, communion with each other and meeting each other. The listeners in this congregation longed for the so-called good old days. The writer of this sermon does not, however, communicate with emphasis on these supposed phenomena. On the contrary, he underlines what it takes to live in the last days and the importance of here and now[35].

The book contrasts two dispensations, namely the past and the present (Hebrews 1:1-3). God has communicated *polumeros kai polutropos* that is, through fathers and prophets in the past, but in the last days, he speaks through his Son. The purposefulness of God's communication is striking. He did not say all things at once, but said it purposefully over years. Thorough planning in sermon making and - delivery cannot be over-emphasised. This involves an important lesson for preachers and liturgists, namely to plan deliberately in formulating something that Olyott[36] calls pointed preaching. As part of the manner of introducing an important focal point gradually and in a structured way, the preacher in the Hebrews sermon utilises Old Testament quotations at least on 35 occasions[37], utilising vivid memories of the past to provide dynamic perspectives for the present. For instance, he enumerates various figures from the Israelite tradition to encourage first listeners or readers to remain loyal themselves[38]. Hebrews 2:1 emphasises that listeners should take heed of things they have heard, since these are linked to salvation in Christ.

---

33 Kruger and Venter, "Prediking van geloofsverantwoordelikheid," 54.
34 Hume, *Hebrews*, 9-13.
35 Kruger and Venter, "Prediking van geloofsverantwoordelikheid," 65.
36 Olyott, *Preaching*, 3.
37 P. Ellingworth, *Commentary on Hebrews*, New International Greek Testament Commentary (Grand Rapids: Eerdmans, 1993), 37.
38 M. Cromhout, "The 'Cloud of Witnesses' as Part of the Public Court of Reputation in Hebrews," *HTS Teologiese Studies/Theological Studies* 68, no. 1 (2012): 1, Art. #1151, 6 pages. http://dx.doi.org/10.4102/hts.v68i1.1151.

6.3 Persuasion to change attitudes

6.3.1 Rhetorical devices underlining the essence of persuasion

Van Houwelingen[39] underlines that the book of Hebrews has often been characterised as highly rhetorical. A considerable number of literary devices that could be associated with persuasive oratory or urgent debate can be identified in this sermon. One rhetorical device, called *synkrisis*, is a detailed comparison between two or more things designed to convince audiences to affirm the speaker's point of view. A typical example of *synkrisis* appears in Hebrews in 7:11-28. The preacher argues that Jesus is a royal priest like Melchizedek, a priest and king mentioned in the book of Genesis. But, rather than simply asserting this belief, the author of Hebrews gives the listeners a compelling, eight-point comparison between the two: parentage, genealogy, birth, death, office, actions, status and achievements. These detailed comparisons are designed to settle doubts about the claim that Jesus is the great, royal High Priest. The preacher aims to proclaim four reasons why Jesus' as royal Priest exceeds humans: he frees us from sin, God has confirmed his priesthood with an oath, his priesthood is eternal and he is a perfect Priest[40].

Another rhetorical device used to address the attitude of the listeners in the Hebrews sermon is known as *exempla*. *Exempla* are lists of illustrations or examples that follow one after the other to build a persuasive argument for a particular point of view[41]. This oratorical technique appears in the familiar list of the faithful in Hebrews 11. There the preacher lists by name Abel, Enoch, Noah, Abraham, Sarah, Isaac, Jacob, Joseph, Moses, the Israelites, Rahab, Gideon, Barak, Samson, Jephthah, David, Samuel and the prophets. This long list is designed to persuade the audience that servants of God should remain faithful throughout their persecution.

A third device used is known by the Hebrew expression *qol wahomer*. This expression is well-known in Greco-Roman and rabbinical traditions and may be translated to read *'light to heavy,'* less to great, or *'simple to complex'*. This type of argumentation begins with a simple premise that is not disputed by the listeners. It then builds to a more complex conclusion that the listeners initially doubt, but can now more easily accept[42]. Simply

---

39 P.H.R. van Houwelingen, "The Epistle to the Hebrews: Faith Means Perseverance," *Journal of Early Christian History* 3, no. 1 (2013): 99, DOI: 10.1080/ 2222582X. 2013.11877278.
40 Anrie du Toit, *Hebreërs vir vandag [Hebrews for today]* (Vereeniging: CUM boeke, 2004), 122-125.
41 C.E.B. Cranefield, *A Critical and Exegetical on the Epistle of Romans* (New York: Bloomsbury, 2004), 599.
42 Lee S. Bond, "Renewing the Mind: The Role of Cognition Language in Pauline Theology and Ethics," *Tyndale Bulletin* 58, no. 2 (2007): 302.

put, this line of argumentation says that, because the premise is true, surely the more difficult conclusion must also be true. Therefore the attitude of rejecting God's Word is similar to a trampling under the foot of the Son of God[43].

Further rhetorical devices are inclusion, repetition, anaphora as well as hook-words[44]. In Hebrews 2:5-9, the citation from Psalm 8 is used to complement the words in Hebrews 1:5-13. In Hebrews 11:3-31, the repetition of the same word (known as anaphora), namely faith, is audible eighteen times. The preacher hammers this idea of faith into the ears and hearts of the listeners[45]. The use of inclusion or the envelope technique to arrange similar material at the beginning or end of the argument is also striking[46]. Guthrie actually identifies eighteen examples of inclusion throughout the Hebrews sermon. The use of hook-words at the end of one section and its continuation at the beginning of the next section is also a clear indication of a well thought-through act of communication woven into the sermon. The preacher is making sure that the sermon makes sense to the listeners[47]. Transition and logical movement among sections are used. Deliberative rhetoric to persuade the listeners to change their attitude is furthermore important. One infers that preachers should be aware of appropriate manners by which to arrange material in their sermons.

In conjunction with this recognition, Guthrie[48] identifies two prominent elements in arranging the material in the Hebrews sermon to persuade listeners: the expository and the hortatory.

- Regarding the expository element of this sermon, Guthrie[49], underlines that after the purposeful introduction, two important movements are evident. Hebrews 1:5- Hebrews 2:18 announce the first movement, which discusses the position of the Son in relation to the angels. Hebrews 4:14 right to Hebrews 10:25 introduce the second movement, which examines the position of the Son in relation to the earthly sacrificial system. The spatial orientation of the expository material is notable, that is, spatial movement

---

43 P.S. Wilson, *The Practice of Preaching*, rev. ed. (Nashville: Abingdon Press, 2007), 140.
44 J.Y. Yang, "Communicative Preaching: A Homiletical Study in the Light of Hebrews," ThD thesis (Potchefstroom: Department of Practical Theology, PU for CHE, 2007), 63.
45 Yang, "Communicative Preaching," 63.
46 Guthrie, *Hebrews*, 15.
47 Yang, "Communicative Preaching," 64.
48 Guthrie, *Hebrews*, 117.
49 Guthrie, *Hebrews*, 118.

between heaven and earth, humiliation and glory and suffering exaltation. The purposeful or step-by-step development of explication for the listeners to understand their High Priest, Jesus Christ, is striking in this regard.
- In contrast with the expository arrangement of material, the hortatory material does not follow this step-by-step arrangement of arguments. Instead, a chiastic arrangement of hortatory material is notable:

3:1-6 Jesus, the supreme example of a faithful son
  3:7-19 The negative example of those who fell
    4:3-11 The promise of rest
      4:12-13 **Warning**
        4:14-16 Hold fast and draw near
          5:11-6:3 The present problem with listeners
            6:4-8 **Warning**
          6:12-19 The preacher's desire for the listeners
        10:19-25 Draw near and hold fast
      10:26-31 **Warning**
      10:32-39 Admonition to endure and examples from the past
  11:1-40 Faithful examples from the Old Testament
12:1-2 Fix your eyes on Jesus

Preachers utilise encouragement and warning to induce changes in attiude. In this instance, it is not merely limited to knowledge, but rather serves to urge listeners to make the right decision. Guthrie[50] goes as far as to indicate that the hortatory material is affectionally rather than educationally directed. The preachers aim to elicit an affectional response. Exposition and exhortation function like two powerful horses in this sermon. One should also admit that the expository and hortatory sections do not function in waterproof compartments but rather in an intertwined fashion.

Buttrick[51] emphasises that part of the preacher's responsibility in preparing and delivering sermons is to decide on appropriate use of language. Yang[52] indicates that the Hebrews sermon was meant to be read

---

50 Guthrie, *Hebrews*, 139.
51 D. Buttrick, *Homiletic: Moves and Structures* (Philadelphia, Fortress Press, 1987), 40.
52 Yang, "Communicative Preaching," 51.

aloud and therefore the style and pattern of argumentation underline the essence of rhetorical discourse. Lindars[53] highlights that, because the preacher of the Hebrews sermon is acquainted with the concrete challenges of the listeners, every available rhetorical skill is utilised to communicate persuasively. The preacher's concern that the listeners do not necessarily understand the danger they are facing is important for how the communication is offered. Yang[54] puts the finger on the root of the danger and in the heart of the problem around attitude. The listeners have lost confidence in the power of the sacrifice of Christ. As time passed, the listeners slowly but surely began to reflect on this very matter. The Hebrews sermon makes it clear that Christ's offer also has meaning for the present and that it could be maintained for the future[55]. Pfitzner[56] addresses the attitudinal challenges experienced by listeners by underlining their struggles to remain faithful to their confession (Hebrews 10:23), not drift away (Hebrews 2:1-3) and not lose confidence in God's promises (Hebrews 3:1-6). The preacher was afraid that the attitude of sluggishness could lead to something worse, namely apostasy (Hebrews 10:26).

De Silva[57] indicates that the rhetorical challenge described above is addressed by the preacher by utilising familiar passages from the Old Testament, though in a Christocentric manner. The preacher utilises the sermon to provide a salvation-historical perspective on the listeners' situation. One could say it offers a profound outlook on contemporary dilemmas. It is important that listeners understand that they are even more privileged than believers in 'good old times'[58]. The Hebrews sermon makes it clear that preachers should be able to understand the rhetorical situation of the listeners to prepare and deliver their sermons effectively. The importance of preachers that are in touch with the concrete circumstance of listeners cannot be over-emphasised.

6.3.2 Persuasiveness in the light of the serious crisis experienced by listeners

The interplay between the three aspects of *ethos, pathos* and *logos* can fruitfully be applied to the Hebrews sermon[59]. In chapter 3 the authors

---

53 B.L. Lindars, *The Theology of the Letter to the Hebrews* (Cambridge: University Press, 1991), 7.
54 Yang, "Communicative Preaching," 54.
55 Yang, "Communicative Preaching," 56.
56 V.C. Pfitzner, "The Rhetoric of Hebrews: Paradigm for Preaching," *Lutheran Theological Journal* 27, no. 5 (1997): 19.
57 A. de Silva, *Persevere in Gratitude* (Grand Rapids: Eerdmans, 2000), 1-7.
58 Yang, "Communicative Preaching," 61.
59 Yang, "Communicative Preaching," 74.

has indicated the outline of the three aspects and now we want to elucidate these aspects within the context of persuasion. It entertains a distinctive foundation, namely that God is a communicative God (Hebrews 1:1-3). His audible communication (his voice) is regarded as important, and that is why this is mentioned as an introduction to the sermon. The listeners' attitudes should be aligned according to this insight, but the challenge lies in how this could be achieved. De Leede and Stark[60] highlight the importance of three instruments that preachers have at their disposal to persuade their listeners.

6.3.2.1 Logos or logical argumentation
The importance of the argument built by a sermon cannot be underestimated[61]. The preacher of the Hebrews sermon has a clear purpose, namely to persuade the listeners[62]. In the preceding section, we discussed the logical argumentation around this purpose. Pfitzner[63] makes the interesting point that the Hebrews sermon operates with an inferential kind of logic, which entails that further meaning is adduced from propositions that are assumed to be true. One could also formulate it differently: the sermon often provides reasons or motivations for previously mentioned premises. Certain particles such as *gar* (used 93 times) and *oun* (used thirteen times) demonstrate that the preacher wants to draw important conclusions for listeners' lives. Koester[64] affirms this when he indicates that the relationship between proposition and argumentation cannot be overlooked.

Three statements are made in the proposition phase of this sermon, and later on the preacher elaborates on this according to Koester[65]. The three statements are:

- The listeners have to look to Jesus, who was exalted after suffering faithfully, opening the way for others. In the *exordium* in Hebrews 1:1-2:4 this idea is discussed.
- Through suffering, Jesus offers complete sacrifice for sins, so that they may draw near to God with confidence (Hebrews 2:10-10:25).
- Like previous generations who endured disappointment, the

---

60 Bert de Leede and Ciska Stark, *Ontvouwen: Protestantse prediking in de praktijk* (Zoetermeer: Boekencentrum, 2016), 152.
61 De Leede and Stark, *Ontvouwen*, 152.
62 Yang, "Communicative Preaching," 71.
63 Pfitzner, "Rhetoric of Hebrews," 7.
64 C.R. Koester, "Hebrews, Rhetoric and the Future of Humanity," *The Catholic Biblical Quarterly* 64, no. 1 (2001): 87.
65 Koester, "Hebrews," 87.

listeners are called to persevere their faith in God's promises (Hebrews 11:1-12:24).

To persuade listeners, the preacher utilises transitional digressions at the end of each major section (Hebrews 2:1-4, Hebrews 5:11-6:20, Hebrews 10:26-39 and Hebrews 12:25-27). Yang[66] indicates that the preacher wants to appeal to the attention of the listeners for them to understand that they should not neglect the Word of God. It is striking around the unfolding of the logical argument that the preacher does not stand outside the message, but uses instead the inclusive noun '*we*'.

6.3.2.2 Ethos (character)

One of the most important prerequisites of communications aimed at persuasion is that the communicator should be trustworthy[67]. Preaching can therefore not be separated from the character of the preacher. The life and example of the preacher outside the pulpit really matters[68]. In the Hebrews sermon, the preacher starts with the emphasis that God himself is the communicator. It is made clear that the preacher's identification with the listeners is central[69]. The preacher's credibility does not speak down to the listeners: profound concern for the responsibility for listeners' faith is highlighted. Pfitzner[70] intriguingly underlines that the preacher of the Hebrews sermon utilises three figures for his responsibility: teacher, expositor and worship-leader.

The experience of an attentive and authentic preacher indeed activates an honest and authentic response within the listener. While the listeners' concrete response is beyond the preacher's control, it seems that the preacher's passion enables a reciprocal and dynamic relationship of the listeners with the preacher and the sermon content[71]. As teacher of the listeners, the preacher is well acquainted with the content of God's Word and can deliver the message on a level that listeners could understand[72]. The preacher of the Hebrews sermon knows how to interpret and apply truths from God's Word to the listeners' lives. This is manifest in the manner in which the preacher use Old Testament citations such as from

---

66 Yang, "Communicative Preaching," 86.
67 Yang, "Communicative Preaching," 87.
68 Silva, *Persevere*, 84.
69 Koester, "Hebrews," 176.
70 Pfitzner, "Rhetoric of Hebrews," 6.
71 M.L. Gaarden, "The Emerging Sermon: The Encounter between the Words of the Preacher and the Listeners' Experience," (paper presented at Aarhus University, Denmark, 2014), 3.
72 Yang, "Communicative Preaching," 87.

Psalm 8, Psalm 95 and Psalm 110[73]. The preacher maintains the concern that the attitude of the listeners regarding God's Word could influence their worship (Hebrews 10:25), emphasising that listeners should hold fast and also that they should encourage each other. Cultic or liturgical figures are integrated into the argument, including images of approaching the throne of grace, drawing near to God, coming to God and offering to God a sacrifice of praise. The preacher can be described as an interlocutor, a theological reflector stimulating the internal dialogue. The inner dialogue can best be described as a polyphony of voices circling around themes from the listener's personal life[74].

6.3.2.3 Pathos (emotion)
The starting point in the act of preaching should be the concreteness of listeners' lives in order that the heard sermon could merge with life experiences[75]. Consequently, the words of the sermon are not attributed meaning until they are used in relation to the listener's personal experience. The listeners' experiences or feelings within a congregation obviously vary widely, and thus sermon-reception within a single congregation also varies[76].

The preacher of the Hebrews sermon successfully arouses listeners' emotions[77]. This sermon utilises positive and negative feelings in a masterful manner. The manner in which the preacher speaks about the eschatological reality is striking because, by emphasising expectations, he enables the listeners not only to look at their current circumstances[78]. He is aware of the fact that the listeners and he live in the last days[79]. It is important for the preacher that the listeners should comprehend what it means to be in Christ during the last days within which they live. Awareness of the fact that God has spoken in Christ will prevent them from losing focus on Jesus Christ, the Perfecter of faith (Hebrews 12:1-2). The preacher does not threaten the listeners with the eschatological reality. The notion of promise (*epangelia*) within the Hebrews sermon can in fact not be ignored (see Hebrews 2:12-13 and 10:7, 9). Worley[80]

---

73 Silva, *Persevere*, 32.
74 Gaarden, "Emerging Sermon," 4.
75 Gaarden, "Emerging Sermon," 5.
76 Gaarden, "Emerging Sermon," 5.
77 Yang, "Communicative Preaching," 89.
78 B.B. Barton, D. Veerman, and L.K. Taylor, *Hebrews*, Life Application Bible Commentary (Wheaton: Tyndale House, 1997), 3.
79 Kruger and Venter, "Prediking van geloofsverantwoordelikheid," 65.
80 D.R. Woley, *God's Faithfulness to Promise: The Hortatory of Commissive Language in Hebrews* (New York: Abilene University, 2019), 71.

indicates that God alone is the promiser within this sermon. In Hebrews, ἐπαγγελία may refer to the concreteness of a promised object, namely to inherit it (Hebrews 6:12), to be heirs of it (Hebrews 6:17; 11:9b), to obtain it (Hebrews 6:15; 11:33) and to receive it (Hebrews 10:36; 11:13, 39;[81]). It is clear that listeners should take action around the promises God offers. To remember God's promises, the preacher encourages listeners in a persuasive manner in order for them to realise the importance of listening within the last days.

What is nonetheless clear, is that the Hebrews sermon does not shy away from the reality of what the consequences would be if the listeners would continue to neglect God's Word[82] [83]. The manner in which the preacher utilises shame is striking. By comparing the listeners with small children, he creates shame to indicate the problem, namely that they should have been teachers by this time. The metaphors of milk and solid food are functional in creating a feeling of shame. There is a notable contrast between listeners who should disdain the shame of society on the one hand and, on the other, become aware that God is not ashamed of them[84]. It is clear that the preacher wants to evoke an emotional response from the listeners. Persuasion rather than coercion is evident. Based on the listeners' personal experiences, they are in fact to generate a new meaning in dialogue with the words of the sermon.

6.4 Persuasive preaching to promote a change in attitude

This section brings into focus two striking passages regarding a necessary change in listeners' attitude. The two passages are Hebrews 10:19-25 and Hebrews 13. The purpose of this selection has to with the interrelatedness of preaching and liturgy, a relationship that cannot be neglected.

6.4.1 *The importance of the construction of the community of faith - Hebrews 10:19-25*

The present book has been addressing the idea that God has spoken many times and in numerous manners but that, in the last days, he has spoken in and through his Son. Preaching has to do with voicing God's voice, but preaching is often confronted by the recalcitrance of attitudes among listeners. It is also clear that preaching should be purposeful for the interaction between preaching and active listening to materialise. The aim of this is to guide listeners to become mature in their faith,

---

81 Woley, *God's Faithfulness*, 17.
82 Yang, "Communicative Preaching," 92.
83 Koester, "Hebrews," 97.
84 Yang, "Communicative Preaching," 94.

consequently to enjoy discernment between good and bad. In Hebrews 10:19-13:19, an extensive application is offered[85]. It connects the work of the High Priest, Jesus Christ, with the importance of constructing (building up) God's house. The idea of community (*communitas*) figures prominently. The contents found in Hebrews 3:12-19 is further expounded in Hebrews 10:19-25.

The confession of *'whose house we are, if we hold fast our boldness and the glorifying of our hope'* is important (my emphasis). Christ's functioning as the High Priest of God's house is the binding factor here[86]. In acknowledging this very fact, listeners should become aware of their responsibility to each other. The use of the three cohortatives in Hebrews 10:22-24 followed by to two participials in Hebrews 10:25 cannot be ignored. This passage commences with the idea that the listeners enjoy the boldness or confidence necessary to enter the holy place by the blood of Jesus. Literally, it means that the listeners have confidence to enter the holy place[87]. The listeners can now entertain the attitude of standing with boldness in God's presence. In Hebrews 10:20, the way in which the listeners can proceed in their boldness is described as follows:

- It is new. The word in Greek has the meaning of just slaughtered[88]. The way on which the listeners proceed with daily life is new and fresh similar to animals that have just been slaughtered. The religious or liturgical context of this concept is notable.
- It is living. This denotes that this road is everything but a dead-end way. This road after all leads to the entrance of the presence of God[89].
- It is inaugurated by Christ's sacrifice. Jesus Christ has opened the curtain to God through the curtain of his body. The veil between God and the listeners has been removed.

This wonderful indicative is proclaimed to the listeners who, proverbially speaking, become lame in the knees for them to become aware of God's presence. The essence of preaching as communicating the living voice of

---

85 Ferdi P. Kruger, "Prediking en gesindheidsverandering: 'n Prakties-teologiese studie in die lig van Hebreërs," ThD thesis (Potchefstroom: North-West University, Dept. Practical Theology, 2002), 79.
86 Cassie J.H. Venter, "Die Gees, die Woord en die bedienaar van die Woord," in *Koninkryk, Gees en Woord*, red. J.C. Coetzee (Pretoria: N.G. Kerkboekhandel, 1988), 18.
87 Du Toit, *Hebreërs*, 168.
88 Simon J. Kistemaker, *Hebrews*, New Testament Commentary (Grand Rapids: Baker Book House, 1996), 287.
89 Kistemaker, *Hebrews*, 288.

God's Word is after all not proclaiming a God who is held captive in history. It is remarkable that the preacher tries to persuade the listeners to become throne-oriented in their daily lives. They are invited to do so because of the fullness of faith (Hebrews 10:22). The emphasis on continuous boldness is important. Within this context of the confidence to come near based on what God has done for us, listeners should observe or see each other as family within God's house[90]. The responsibility of the believers for each other's construction could be described in the following manner[91]:

- They should edify the community of faith in caring for each other. Attentiveness for what Jesus did also indicates the importance of renewed and committed paying of attention to and consideration of each other's life in faith. According to Hebrews 10:24, this consideration for each other should provoke love and good works. The attitude of caring for other people amid the despair of the listeners is highlighted.
- Not forsaking each other in not exhorting each other. The encounter with the living God on a frequent basis should not be forsaken. The attitude of being shepherds for each other in encouraging each other to come to regular appointments with God and edifying one another is notable.
- The intimate relationship between individual and corporative growth in Hebrews 10:19-25 cannot be ignored. In taking care of your own growth, the listener should also learn to have discernment for other listeners. The need of taking care for other listeners who may be getting tired and disheartened should be taken in account. Encouragement and exhortation cannot be neglected.

6.4. The importance of the liturgy of daily life

In Hebrews 12:28, the preacher has announced the importance of offering service to God with reverence and awe so that it will be well-pleasing to him. Du Toit [92] mentions that one could also speak about the worship of gratitude. The Hebrews sermon is well constructed, and now the preacher aims to persuade listeners to change their attitude and have understanding of what God is expecting from them even amid challenging circumstances. Hebrews 13:1-4 discusses the concreteness of brotherly love. Hospitality (*filoxenia*) is something that should not be regarded as of lesser

---

90 Du Toit, *Hebreërs*, 171.
91 Venter, "Gees," 18-20.
92 Du Toit, *Hebreërs*, 225.

importance[93]. Other aspects addressed include indicating that listeners should take care of society, for instance showing love for prisoners as well as love within the sphere of marriage.

Long[94] indicates that a shift in the preacher's argumentation is conspicuous within Hebrews 13. Normal and daily life experiences are now addressed. One could say that the ministry of hospitality, the prison ministry and stewardship in general are highlighted. Long[95] also makes the interesting comment that the *amen* at the end of the sermon is not really the sermon's end. Phillips[96] maintains that Hebrews 13 should be seen as the covering letter to the Hebrews sermon. Therefore, the purpose of this sermon is practical and shows awareness of the ethical implication of the functioning of attitudes, which are scrutinised. Typical ethical themes are addressed such as compassion, chastity, Christian contentment and courage. Stedman[97] underlines the pastoral attitude of the preacher around enabling the listeners to understand that the message of the sermon should be integrated within the liturgy of life. It is clear that the application of this sermon is not aimed at being estranged from reality. The listeners should look at how they have to engage with reality in daily life.

The benediction in Hebrews 13:20-21 comprises one long sentence of 53 words[98]. The preacher of the Hebrews sermon anchors the listeners' lives in the almighty deeds of God that provide peace and was in fact able to bring Jesus back from the dead. This God provides peace to listeners for them to effect peace among people[99]. This is the assurance that this God will also equip the listeners with everything in doing his will[100]. The sermon admonishes listeners towards a change in attitude where listening to the Word becomes obedience. Now the preacher assures the same listeners of the God who will equip them to be obedient. The preacher is clear about how God will equip them. The work done within listeners through Jesus Christ pleases God[101]. The word for 'equip' denotes to make something *complete*. They are assured that the God who works in them

---

[93] Du Toit, *Hebreërs*, 226.
[94] Long, *Hebrews*, 142.
[95] Long, *Hebrews*, 142.
[96] J. Phillips, *Exploring Hebrews* (New Jersey: Loiszeaux Brothers, 1992), 191.
[97] R.C. Stedman, *Hebrews*, IVP New Testament Commentary Series (Illinois: Inter Varsity Press, 1992), 149.
[98] Du Toit, *Hebreërs*, 234.
[99] Kistemaker, *Hebrews*, 429.
[100] Du Toit, *Hebreërs*, 234.
[101] Kistemaker, *Hebrews*, 429.

through his Spirit makes them suited for their calling in daily life[102]. Therefore, doing his will in the liturgy of daily life brings pleasure to God.

The preacher preaches the Hebrews sermon in absentia; it was sent in the manner of an epistle[103]. The attitude of the preacher becomes evident in Hebrews 13:22-25, namely to ask listeners to bear with his words of exhortation. It makes sense, because this was a long sermon and simultaneously a difficult one to preach[104]. The preacher asks for endurance and patience and therefore he prays for the positive outcome of a change in attitude[105]. It is clear that he is convinced that preaching this sermon should be regarded as urgent. He utilises every possible technique and style to persuade the listeners of his message[106].

6.5 Persuasive preaching and a change in attitude - homiletical perspectives

The way in which an attitude functions will differ depending on the extent to which it becomes perceptible either cognitively or emotionally[107]. Changes in one of the components also influence the functioning of the others. A different way of thinking will influence people's feelings and their behaviour and vice versa. Applied to preaching, this means that a distorted way of thinking about God's Word and preaching could also have a negative influence on people's feelings and actions. When the components of attitudes are inconsistent, one of them may be more closely related to specific forms of behaviour than the others[108]. This fact underlines that preachers should carefully reflect on the use of language. In the Hebrews sermon, listeners' understanding of God's communication in the past is important and they had indeed forgotten that God was still speaking. Consequently, the sermon challenges the emotional and conative dimensions of their belief.

When listeners experience preaching as meaningful, while the typical language that conveys persuasion regarding the meaningfulness of the preaching are integrated, preaching will be experienced as relevant. Preaching should not create fear for daily life or any avoidance of reality. To persuade people through communication is to help them gain

---

102 J.M. Flanigan, *Hebrews: What the Bible Teaches*, Ritchie New Testament Commentaries (Kilmarnock: John Ritchie, 1997), 292.
103 Long, *Hebrews*, 148.
104 Du Toit, *Hebreërs*, 235.
105 Du Toit, *Hebreërs*, 235.
106 Du Toit, *Hebreërs*, 235.
107 Z. Berg and A. Theron, *Psychology in the Work Context* (Cape Town: Oxford University Press, 2006), 173.
108 S. Steinberg, *An Introduction to Communication Studies* (Cape Town: Juta, 2011), 30.

consensus and to cooperate according to God's will when it comes to their attitudes regarding their lives[109]. In sermons, it is not a case of preachers that gang up against the participants in liturgy. Therefore, persuasion is different from manipulation, which drives people away from the communicator. It is pivotal that preachers have to become personally engaged in the act of preaching, as a hearer amongst hearers. It is important to note that persuasion has to do with concrete changes in listeners' lives.

Cleary[110] further elaborates the following aspects related to the functioning of attitudes:

- To be influential, preaching has to evoke the interest and the positive attitude of listeners. In this instance, the preacher must be aware of the kind of information needed to best communicate with them. Understanding of the listeners' language and thoughts is necessary to promote a situation in which they can operate on the same wavelength. This process also requires active listening and knowledge of differing viewpoints.
- In shaping the persuasive language of preaching, one should bear in mind that preachers have to help listeners understand the message of persuasive language. What kind of words are considered to be persuasive? Words that are clearly understood and language that is direct and vigorous, aided by an imagination that can paint word-pictures, are very persuasive. As mentioned, Cilliers[111] has performed extensive research on the topic of aesthetics in liturgy. This entails that concrete examples are especially helpful. Liturgical language must make sense to participants. Language has to be intentional to help them worship meaningfully[112].
- The preacher should believe in what he or she is communicating. The issue at stake is that the preacher's own attitude must be correct. It is true that aspects such as appearance, fluency, rate of speech and others could influence the communication process, but it must be underlined that no liturgical language will ever contribute towards a change in attitude unless listeners notice enthusiasm and urgency from the preacher and receive enough information to understand what is expected of them. This centres on the matter

---

109 T. Grant and R. Borcherds, *Communicating at Work* (Pretoria: Van Schaik, 2009), 3.
110 Cleary, *Communication Handbook*, 162.
111 Cilliers, *Kring-dans van die kuns*, 80.
112 G. Hughes, *Worship as Meaning: A Liturgical Theology for Late Modernity* (Cambridge: University Press, 2003), 127.

that preachers have to show that the content of their language is also a living voice within themselves. Enthusiasm intrigues people. On noticing enthusiasm, listeners will look for clues as to why the liturgist is so enthusiastic. It is possible that listeners will change their attitudes because of the information they explore themselves. Enthusiasm could help listeners, as they are listening to sermons, in the exploration process. It could be described as the expository essence of the act of listening to sermons that requires a receptive heart and focussed attitude.

- For language to be persuasive, preachers have to be aware that listeners must be able to recall what he or she is persuaded to do. Preaching takes place within the space of liturgy. Persuasive preaching does not end in the worship service, but has the function of an arrow aimed at daily life.
- Action and a change of attitude that affect the liturgy of life and the liturgy of the streets are the deepest purpose of persuasion; it relates to a form of cognition to act according to God's will. Influential sermons emphasise the urge for a change in attitude. Preaching and ethics cannot be separated. Preaching without the outlook of ethics will become blind and short-sighted, as has been mentioned. Through the the use of language in preaching Christ is presented in such a manner that everybody will realise that God is present, but also cultivate the discovery that God is present in daily life.

6.6 Conclusion

This chapter has demonstrated that the Hebrews sermon is a reminder not to overlook an important aspect, namely that people persuade themselves to change attitudes. Communicative preaching provides the arguments and motivation for the change, but preaching provides the deeper-lying reason why it should occur. This makes preaching unique, in the sense that the sermon places listeners in God's presence and within a field of tension around God's dynamic Word. It is important to realise that persuasion through preaching normally takes time, especially if one acknowledges that it takes time for attitudes to become a reality in listeners' lives[113]. It is nonetheless clear that preaching should always be intentional but, in being intentional, one should be aware of the danger of manipulation. After all, people are persuaded by the living God who is utilising the living voice of his Word to change listeners' attitudes.

---

113 R.M. Perloff, *The Dynamics of Persuasion: Communication and Attitudes in the 21st Century*, 2nd ed. (Mahwah, New Jersey: Lawrence Erlbaum Associates, 2003), 3.

One powerful emotion that often affects attitudes and behaviour is fear[114]. It can be such a powerful tool that campaigns have been developed focussing on the ironic and even disturbing reality that *fear appeals*, involving messages that try to persuade people about the potential harm that may happen to them if they do not accept the messenger's recommendations, for example at a time of extreme measures to decrease the effects of Covid-19. It is clear, though, that the evoking of fear alone does not change people's behaviour. Certain behaviours that people engage in are potentially harmful for them and other people; yet, people still do engage in these[115]. It is clear that society is in need of more than this. Preaching to persuade listeners to engage in attitude change regarding daily life and faith acts has to deal with providing a message of hope that is anchored in God's voice, indeed within the last days that the Hebrews sermon focusses on.

Young[116] makes the convincing argument that listeners are not passive collectors or even decoders of information. Based on preaching that was delivered to them numerous times before, listeners are accustomed to decision-making. Listeners are in search, though, for certain characteristics within a sermon that will persuade them to make a particular decision. Eventually, one has to acknowledge that it is not the preacher who persuades the listeners, but it is the living voice of the Gospel and the powerful work of the Holy Spirit that enable listeners to change their attitudes regarding various aspects in their lives. The manner in which the preacher compiles a sermon is after all influential around providing seed for listeners to make this kind of decision. Persuasion is indeed an act of communication and preachers have to be aware that daily life is packed with messages that want to persuade. News via the online environment and newspapers will eventually shape people's attitudes[117]. Within a time of extreme lockdowns and of self-isolation people are dependent on the online environment and their attitudes are shaped regarding uncertainty in daily life. It is clear that, while preaching is a communicative act, while persuasion also involves a communicative act, that preaching in arduous times has to deal with providing new perspectives on reality for listeners to realise the importance of decision-making within the *today* that the Hebrews sermon emphasises.

---

114 M.B. Tannenbaum et al., "Appealing to Fear: A Meta-Analysis of Fear Appeal Effectiveness and Theories," *Psychological Bulletin* 141, no. 6 (2015): 4, http://dx.doi.org/10.1037/a0039729.
115 Tannenbaum et al., "Appealing to Fear," 5.
116 R.O. Young, *Persuasive Communication: How Do Audiences Decide?* (New York: Taylor and Francis, 2017), 11.
117 Perloff, *Dynamics of Persuasion*, 5.

REFERENCES

Barton, B.B., D. Veerman, and L.K. Taylor. *Hebrews*. Life Application Bible Commentary. Wheaton: Tyndale House, 1997.

Berg, Z. and A. Theron. *Psychology in the Work Context*. Cape Town: Oxford University Press, 2006.

Bond, Lee S. "Renewing the Mind: The Role of Cognition Language in Pauline Theology and Ethics." *Tyndale Bulletin* 58, no. 2 (2007).

Brown, J. *Hebrews*. Geneva Series of Commentaries. Edinburg: The Bath Press, 1999.

Buttrick, D. *Homiletic: Moves and Structures*. Philadelphia: Fortress Press, 1987.

Cilliers, Johan H. *Binne die kring-dans van die kuns: Die betekenis van estetika vir die gereformeerde liturgie*. Stellenbosch: Sun Press, 2007.

Cilliers, Johan H. *Die genade van gehoorsaamheid*. Cape Town: Lux Verbi, 2000.

Cleary, S. *The Communication Handbook: A Student Guide to Effective Communication*. Cape Town: Juta, 2010.

Cranefield, C.E.B. *A Critical and Exegetical on the Epistle of Romans*. New York: Bloomsbury, 2004.

Cromhout, M. "The 'Cloud of Witnesses' as Part of the Public Court of Reputation in Hebrews." *HTS Teologiese Studies/Theological Studies* 68, no. 1 (2012): Art. #1151, 6 pages. http:/ / dx.doi.org/ 10.4102/ hts.v68i1.1151.

De Leede, Bert and Ciska Stark. *Ontvouwen: Protestantse prediking in de praktijk*. Zoetermeer: Boekencentrum, 2016.

De Silva, A. *Persevere in Gratitude*. Grand Rapids: Eerdmans, 2000.

De Wet, F.W. and F.P. Kruger. "Blessed Are Those That Hunger and Thirst for Righteousness: Shaping the Ethical Dimension of Prophetic Preaching in a Context of Corruption." *Verbum et Ecclesia* 43, no. 1 (2013): Art. #722, 10 pages. DOI: 10.4102/ ve.v34i1.722.

Du Toit, Anrie. *Hebreërs vir vandag [Hebrews for today]*. Vereeniging: CUM boeke, 2004.

Ellingworth, P. *Commentary on Hebrews*. New International Greek Testament Commentary. Grand Rapids: Eerdmans, 1993.

Evans, L.H. *Hebrews*. The Communicator's Commentary. Washington: Macmillan, 1984.

Firet, J. *Het agogisch moment in het pastoraal optreden*. Kampen: Kok, 1978.

Fiske, S.T. *Social Beings: A Core Motives Approach to Social Psychology*. Princeton: Wiley, 2004.

Flanigan, J.M. *Hebrews: What the Bible Teaches*. Ritchie New Testament Commentaries. Kilmarnock: John Ritchie, 1997.

Gaarden, M.L. *Listeners as Authors in Preaching.* Copenhagen: Aarhus University Press, 2014.

Gass, R.H. and J.S. Seiter. *Persuasion, Social Influence and Compliance Gaining.* New York: Harper Collins, 2003.

Grant, T. and R. Borcherds. *Communicating at Work.* Pretoria: Van Schaik, 2009.

Guthrie, Donald. *Hebrews.* Tyndale New Testament Commentaries. Grand Rapids: Eerdmans, 1996.

Hughes, G. *Worship as Meaning: A Liturgical Theology for Late Modernity.* Cambridge: University Press, 2003.

Hume, C.R. *Reading through Hebrews.* Lymington: The Spartan, 1997.

Kistemaker, Simon J. *Hebrews.* New Testament Commentary. Grand Rapids: Baker Book House, 1994.

Koester, C.R. "Hebrews, Rhetoric and the Future of Humanity." *The Catholic Biblical Quarterly* 64, no. 1 (2001).

Kruger, F.P. and C.J.H. Venter. "Die prediking van geloofsverantwoordelikheid: homiletiese perspektiewe vanuit Hebreërs [Preaching responsibility in faith: homiletical perspectives from Hebrews]." *Praktiese Teologie in Suid-Afrika* 21, no. 1 (2006).

Kruger, Ferdi P. "Prediking en gesindheidsverandering: 'n Praktiesteologiese studie in die lig van Hebreërs." ThD thesis. Potchefstroom: North-West University, Dept. Practical Theology, 2002.

Lane, W.L. *Hebrews 1-8.* Dallas: World Books, 1991.

Lindars, B.L. *The Theology of the Letter to the Hebrews.* Cambridge: University Press, 1991.

Lloyd-Jones, M. *Preaching and Preachers.* Grand Rapids: Zondervan, 1971.

Long, Thomas G. *Hebrews.* Interpretation: A Bible Commentary for Teaching and Preaching. Louisville: John Knox Press, 1997.

Lord, C.G. *Social Psychology.* Orlando: Harcourt Brace, 1997.

Louw, D. and D. Edwards. *Sielkunde: 'n Inleiding vir studente in Suider-Afrika.* Sandton: Heinemann Voortgesette onderwys, 1998.

Olyott, S. *Preaching: Pure and Simple.* Bryntirion: Bryntirion Press, 2005.

Perloff, R.M. *The Dynamics of Persuasion: Communication and Attitudes in the 21st Century.* 2nd ed. Mahwah, New Jersey: Lawrence Erlbaum Associates, 2003.

Pfitzner, V.C. "The Rhetoric of Hebrews: Paradigm for Preaching." *Lutheran Theological Journal* 27, no. 5 (1997).

Phillips, J. *Exploring Hebrews.* New Jersey: Loiszeaux Brothers, 1992.

Smith, E.R. and D.M. Mackie. *Social Psychology.* New York: Psychology Press, 2007.

Stedman, R.C. *Hebrews*. The IVP New Testament Commentary Series. Illinois: InterVarsity Press, 1992.

Steinberg, S. *An Introduction to Communication Studies*. Cape Town: Juta, 2011.

Sweazy, G.E. *Preaching the Good News*. New Jersey: Prentice Hall, 2003.

Swets, J. "On the Literary Genre of the 'Epistle' to the Hebrews." *Novum Testamentum* 11 (2003).

Tannenbaum, M.B., J. Hepler, R.S. Zimmerman, L. Saul, S. Jacobs, K. Wilson, and D. Albarracin. "Appealing to Fear: A Meta-Analysis of Fear Appeal Effectiveness and Theories." *Psychological Bulletin* 141, no. 6 (2015). http://dx.doi.org/10.1037/a0039729.

Tubbs, S. and S. Moss. *Human Communication: Principles and Contexts*. New York: McGraw-Hill, 2008.

Van Houwelingen, P.H.R. "The Epistle to the Hebrews: Faith Means Perseverance." *Journal of Early Christian History* 3, no. 1 (2013). DOI: 10.1080/ 2222582X.2013.11877278.

Venter, Cassie J.H. *Die Gees, die Woord en die bedienaar van die Woord*. In *Koninkryk, Gees en Woord*, edited by J.C. Coetzee. Pretoria: N.G. Kerkboekhandel, 1988.

Wilson, P.S. *The Practice of Preaching*. Rev. ed. Nashville: Abingdon Press, 2007.

Woley, D.R. *God's Faithfulness to Promise: The Hortatory of Commissive Language in Hebrews*. New York: Abilene University, 2019.

Wong, Y.J. "The Psychology of Encouragement: Theory, Research, and Applications." *Counselling Psychologist* 43, no. 2 (2015).

Yang, J.Y. "Communicative Preaching: A Homiletical Study in the Light of Hebrews." ThD thesis. Potchefstroom: Department of Practical Theology, PU for CHE, 2007.

Young, R.O. *Persuasive Communication: How Do Audiences Decide?* New York: Taylor and Francis, 2017.

CHAPTER 7

PREACHING ON ABEL AS AN EXEMPLUM

Living example or just a predecessor?

Maarten Kater

It is a pressing question how to preach Old Testament characters. This chapter aims to be of service to contemporary preaching on Abel as found in the letter of the Hebrews, but also to preaching from history as related by Genesis 4. This is performed in the manner of the *lectio christiana*, which has a reciprocal direction - 'from old to new and subsequently from new to old' -not as two separate movements but more or less as warp and weft[1]. Surely, a 'one size fits all' approach cannot work. Nonetheless, lessons can be learned from one example towards preaching on other *exempla*.

The Hebrews sermon represents to the congregation present *coram Deo* in terms of a congregation whose people lived *coram Deo by faith* in the past, the so-called *exempla* in the eleventh chapter. Sitting in their pew then and there the Hebrews congregation is to realise herself that she is on route to the city of God, while others have already arrived at the finish line, some of them - these *exempla* - a very long time ago. So, this preacher does not use *direct speech* in Hebrews only (see chapter 1), but he confronts the audience with examples of people from ages and ages past and places them, so to speak, in the same building as they sit there in the first century; and we in our millennium.

The passage that concludes this magnificent list of *exempla* is found in Hebrews 11:39 - **12:2**:

Yet, all these [the 'heralds of faith', the exempla], though they were attested through faith, did not receive the promise, because God had provided something better [the new covenant] so that they would not, apart from us, be made perfect.

---

1 H.G.L. Peels, "'Hoe leest gij?' [How does on read?] Een *lectio christiana* van het Oude Testament," *Theologia Reformata* 52, no. 3 (2009): 236-259.

Therefore, since we are surrounded by so great a cloud of witnesses, let us lay aside every weight and sin which clings so closely, and let us run with endurance the race that is set before us, looking to Jesus, the founder and perfecter of our faith (my emphasis).

Are Abel, Abraham, Isaac and Jacob and all that are enumerated in the eleventh chapter our supporters? Yes, indeed. They sit around us, as the sermon tells us, by means of the metaphor of the stadium. How does this public - these *exempla* - from the eleventh chapter of Hebrews function in our worship services, and what lessons can be gleaned from that chapter for the homiletical field today?

Surely, Abel is not a kind of 'everyman', and this actually is a great privilege to know, because 'everybody' so often disappears in 'anybody', and so 'nobody' at all. Abel is not my neighbour, not in fact even my contemporary as such. He occupies instead a unique place in the history of salvation. It is striking that Jesus summarizes the entire period of the Old Testament in the well-known and stirring words concerning the guilt that people heaped upon themselves because of innumerable killings, 'from the blood of righteous Abel to the blood of Zechariah, son of Berechiah, whom you murdered between the temple and the altar' (Matt. 23:35)[2]. In addition to this, we encounter Abel as the first of the list of *exempla* in the letter to the Hebrews: 'By faith Abel offered to God a more excellent sacrifice than Cain, through which he obtained witness that he was righteous, God testifying of his gifts; and through it he being dead still speaks'[3].

Since I was curious about a number of questions surrounding preaching on such an *exemplum*, particularly questions concerning the position that Abel occupies in the eleventh and twelfth chapter of the Hebrews, I examined sermons from the Dutch sermon series entitled *From the Fountain of Life*[4] around the history of Abel and how it is translated and applied to our time[5].

---

2 So I assume that this commentary points to Zechariah, the son of Jehoiada, who is mentioned as the last prophet who was killed at the end of the Tanach (2 Chron. 24:22), who dying, also speaks about the revenge of God, which links his blood with Abel's blood. There still is much difference in opinion on this detail.

3 Here I ignore the argumentation which could be adduced to prove that this letter has the nature of a sermon. In addition this New Testament writing will conveniently be denoted as *Hebrews*, in which the words 'the letter to' or 'sermon to' are omitted.

4 The Dutch name of this series of sermons from ministers of the CGK: *Uit de Levensbron* [From the Source of Life] (digital versions: www.tua.nl).

5 *Uit de Levensbron*: 9/505 (text Hebr. 11:4), 45/348 (text Gen. 4:3-5a, Hebr. 11:4), 58/125 (Gen. 4:1-16; HC Lord's Day 40), 64/348 (no text, Scripture reading Gen. 4:1-17 and Hebr. 11:4, Thanksgiving Day sermon), 65/359 (no text, Scripture reading Gen. 4:1-16, Hebr. 11:1-4; Advent sermon), 68/330 (Gen. 4:1-5a; Thanksgiving Day sermon) and

7.1 Abel's place in God's speech

He who desires to proclaim the message of a text will of course read it carefully and let the words sink in. Thereupon follows meditation on the words and analysis of the text. The questions that these words evoke, the joy elicited and sometimes also the pain experienced are considered and incorporated in the expression of the message. The preacher will place the text within the context of a pericope, the complete writing and the entire Scripture. Without discussing all the details of a homiletic exegesis, the most important moments are offered to come to sound preaching on what Hebrews says about Abel.

7.1.1 Abel in the letter to the Hebrews

The corresponding introduction to the part in which Abel is mentioned centres on a quote from the prophet Habakkuk: 'the just shall live by faith' (10:38a). These very words are underscored by the continual refrain 'by faith' in the eleventh chapter[6]. The use of this trope (*anaphora*) greatly amplifies the message of this chapter. This becomes apparent especially when we read it out loud. Therefore the moment when Scripture reading occurs in a worship service should not be regarded as a 'build up' to the sermon, but is essentially a proclamation in itself.

The secret of these lives, these righteous, cannot be explained outside the meaning carried in the phrase reading 'by faith.' The direct reason for the quoted words from Habakkuk is given just prior to the phrase: 'For you have need of endurance, so that after you have done the will of God, you may receive (the fulfilment of) the promise' (10:36).

The text that focusses on Abel, as found in the eleventh chapter, belongs in the broader context to be found in the second part of Hebrews, which begins with 10:19: 'Therefore, Brothers, since we have confidence to enter the holy places [...] let us draw near'. The 'by faith'-texts resort

---

85/183 (no text, Scripture reading Gen. 4:1-16). The Scripture reading in 64/348 is a remarkable one: Genesis 4 including verse 17, the first verse of a new pericope. This evokes the question as to whether Scripture reading has been correctly defined and can be accounted for. Eventually, I did not come across a sermon on the meaning of Abel's still speaking as Hebr. 12:24 says.

6 See Mathias Rissi, *Die Theologie des Hebräerbriefs*, Wissenschaftliche Untersuchungen zum Neuen Testament (Tübingen: Mohr, 1987), 104-113 on the characterization of faith in this part, 105: 'The concept of faith takes on a special nuance when the author speaks to the conscience of his readers with regard to one of their particular problems, namely their aversion to suffering. In his introduction to the great faith chapter 11, he contrasts faith with fainthearted retreat (10:39). Here the concept of faith is given a sound that brings it close to the concept of 'endurance' in suffering (10:36). In this way, an element of faith comes into play: faithfulness, reliability (...). It is this component in the concept of faith that is particularly taken up in Faith Chapter 11.'

under this rubric, which Van Bruggen summarizes as perseverance on the way to the heavenly Zion[7]. In this understanding, the section in chapter 10 (19-39) forms a prelude to the theme of faith as perseverance, being convinced by what cannot be seen, but is already reality: life in the city that has foundations. For, considering this, Hebrews is indeed a word of exhortation (13:22)[8].

Furthermore, it is useful to note that, at the end of the text, 11:4, Abel *speaks* in the present tense! This recurs in the text of 12:24. So, one cannot preach from 11:4 without involving 12:24, and vice versa[9]. Additionally, it comes to mind that the verb 'to speak' occupies an extremely important place in the Hebrews. As we have seen, Hebrews (1:1-4) starts with God speaking. God's speaking portrays a highest Word, the last Word, spoken in the Son[10]. And to hear Him speak without listening is fatal, according to the close of the twelfth chapter. Abel is a telling example that points from the old world to the future that has been opened in Jesus[11].

7.2 Abel as *exemplum* and contemporary

It is truly surprising to see Abel's name mentioned first. This first name from the list of the 'heroes of faith' would not have been our choice. When we keep the history from Genesis 4 in the back of our minds, we hear the delight of mother Eve at the birth of her first son, but the naming of Abel does not evoke great expectation. Yet God reverses the order, just as he will do later on around Esau and Jacob. This shows that the way in which God values things is different than our way. We see things superficially, myopically. This quite often makes a heart fail, and is the shortcoming by which the believers addressed in Hebrews were intrinsically broken.

---

7 See Van Bruggen's contribution in: H.R. van de Kamp, *Hebreeën: Geloven is volhouden*, Commentaar Nieuwe Testament (Utrecht: Kok, 2012), 255, for an overview of the structure.

8 It is impossible to do justice to the manifold meaning of the verb παρακαλεω in a translation.

9 It is either recommended to explicitly mention 12:24 with 11:4, or to preach about Abel twice from the *Hebrews*: for instance, during the morning service about 11:4 and separately about 'Abel's speaking' in the second service.

10 In my opinion it does not seem correct to exclusively regard ἐν to be instrumental (with an appeal to the Hebrew prefix b^e). For God's speaking *in* the Son is a much more adequate expression of the exclusive position of the Son - who is a central figure in this overture.

11 See Harold W. Attridge, "God in Hebrews," in *The Epistle to the Hebrews and Christian Theology*, eds. R. Bauckam et al. (Grand Rapids: Eerdmans, 2009), 95-110, 110: 'As its opening line suggests, Hebrew finds particularly fruitful the notion that God has spoken and continues to speak in a vivid and compelling way. Unperturbed by the metaphysical problems about such claims, this homilist understands God to be doing what he himself aims to do: uttering a word that penetrates human hearts and minds.'

7.2.1 'By faith' is to learn to look through the eye of God's love

How does Abel end up as the first righteous person? Placing him at the beginning of the list turns him into a speaking example of God's unconditional love for his chosen people. This ought to be the liberating starting point of everything to be said about Abel in a sermon. For it is exactly this that could be encouraging in all kinds of situations in which we wrestle with what we- being so often short-sighted - do not see. Could you imagine learning to look with different eyes? For that is what faith is about: the evidence of things not seen (11:1)! 'By faith' means learning to look through the eye of God's love.

Abel is definitely not the hero of a success story. It could even be said that God's love for His chosen ultimately costs Abel his life. So, then, he shares in the words of his great Predecessor (12:2) ages before He came down from heaven: 'They have hated me, they will also hate you'. This hero of faith is killed by the knife of his brother. But is such an example encouraging for a congregation fearing persecution, who is moreover socially - and economically boycotted?! Cain's deed, that is, Abel's death, however, does not serve as the last word. But exactly the fact of Abel's death brings high tension into this sermon. Why then is this witness mentioned as a first example to inspire and encourage us? Is anyone inspired to persevere by pointing to someone who died as a martyr?

7.2.2 Not morality

It is striking that hardly any attention has been paid to this essential element. In the sermons analysed, as taken from the Dutch series *From the Fountain of Life,* the choice is often made to depict Abel as an example of how we should make sacrifice to please God. Sometimes this sounds moralistic. Why does this happen? It seems we want to give a rational explication of what this text says to us[12]. We want to offer an explanation for the verse reading: 'And the Lord respected Abel and his offering, but He did not respect Cain and his offering' (Gen. 4:4-5). Why this distinction? It appears from the Dutch sermons that we examined that we are looking for an explanation in Abel himself: why did *he,* according to Hebrews 11:4, receive God's approval on *his gifts?* - and because we don't know how to deal with that line of thought, we quickly move on to the answer: 'by faith'. So was Abel a better person because he gave more or

---

12 R. Walter and L. Moberly, "Exemplars of Faith in Hebrews 11: Abel," in *The Epistle to the Hebrews and Christian Theology*, eds. R. Bauckam et al. (Grand Rapids: Eerdmans, 2009), 353-363, 357 points to the account in the LXX where Cain is reproached because he sacrificed incorrectly: 'when you sacrifice correctly, but do not divide correctly, isn't that sin?' Here the 'morality of the story' is immediately put into words.

gave differently? You will not-usually hear a reformed preacher say this. Usually therefore, a direct reference is made to the refrain, the chorus phrase as found in chapter 11: 'by faith'. It is faith that makes the difference. Then we have the matter neatly constrained again for the sake of our feelings and it does not hang disturbingly in the air.

In any case, this reference to the phrase 'by faith' remains closer to the text than all kinds of fantastic interpretations about how things went when Abel and Cain made their sacrifices to the Lord. As an illustration of what I mean by such fantasies, here is a fragment from one of the sermons *From the Fountain of Life*[13]:

Cain takes just a moment to make his sacrifice. He sets to work almost impulsively: from what is stated it seems like he performs the thought immediately as it arises and takes what is within reach. He performs an official ceremony but does not think long about it [...] almost like: oh yes, that is something which I also have to do [...].

But things are very different with Abel: He takes special care to see that the first thing which he received and also the best part of it, is given back to the Lord. He is totally involved, does it consciously, deliberately and royally [...].In this conscious act, that inner disposition of Abel, God sees, as it were, a portrayal of what He does and bestows: God who so loved us, gives the best He has: His Son as His confession: My eye is on you and I want you to live, to enjoy yourself and to exist, with Me and for Me.

In contrast to such fantastical interpretations, a sermon should always be theologically sound. Therefore, a theological approach to the text on the offerings of Cain and Abel seems to be the most liberating method to preach on Abel. He who takes God's searching love as a starting point, may speak without restraint about the gifts of Abel. Also the expression 'by faith' says that we are encouraged by what God has given and still gives to to testify and witness. After all, it is through faith that the power of God's speaking is manifested. That is what it is all about and that is how people are encouraged to persevere. Just as all things were created by the Word once, so faith is the proof and evidence of the power of God's speech. To be included in the line of those who preceded us at the race course (12:1), to participate in the pilgrimage to the heavenly homeland (11:14-16) is not an achievement, but a matter of grace.

Yet - one could object - it is expressly stated that Abel received God's approval for his gifts and that he brought a πλειονα Θηυσιαν [more (acceptable) or better abundant sacrifice] by faith. Does that word really mean a better, a more abundant sacrifice in the quantitative sense of a

---

13 Cf. note 485 on this series Dutch sermons; here cited sermon 64/348.

'more than'? Yes, it does, but that need not be a problem at all when we start with what God gives, thus avoiding an anthropological commitment as a starting point. When we think in terms of what grace is, we can fullheartedly speak without any concern about the gifts that receive God's approval. Then we really are talking about a more qualitative 'more than'. 'God has appointed them as witnesses (*emarturèthèsan*), they have been acknowledged by God, only *because* they have lived their lives in obedience to His promises'[14]!

7.2.3 The function of the exempla

Before the message of Hebrews reached the church in the second half of the first century, galleries of examples had been created. In the apocryphal books *Wisdom* (10:1-11, 14), *Jesus Sirach* (44-50) and *1 Maccabees* (2:49-70), we encounter lists with names of those who occupied an important place in the history of the people.

The purpose of using such a list in the rhetorical field is to challenge listeners to act as they did[15]. So the message is: be and live like a believing people, in spite of everything that can make you lose heart; therefore, look at these former people of God. Eisenbaum emphasises that these are people who were actually all marginalized in their own lifetime, such as the New Testament believers who are addressed here in their time. It is about more than naming several 'national heroes'[16]. With this in mind, the phrase 'heroes of faith' seems to be a regretful choice. That actually does place these 'heroes' at a great distance from the hearer, who is not such a famous hero of the faith.

It is worth mentioning that, according to the rules of rhetoric, the use of imitation of *exempla* does not so much direct our gaze backwards to the past, but is particularly intended to attract our view to the future[17]. That is exactly what Hebrews aims at! Because of the similarities between the present and the past, the *exemplum* is associated with the future. Sermons on Abel do not transport us to an ancient grey past, but to the bright future. This thought underlines both aspects of faith that receive emphasis in Hebrews: perseverance and seeing what lies ahead of us, what has been promised. By means of the *exempla* as the 'cloud of

---

14 H. van Oyen, *De brief aan de Hebreeën*, Prediking Nieuwe Testament (Nijkerk: Callenbach, 1962).
15 Thus M.R. Cosby, *The Rethorical Composition and Function in the Light of Example Lists in Antiquity* (Macon: Mercer University Press, 1988).
16 P.M. Eisenbaum, "The Jewish Heroes of Christian History: Hebrews 11 in Literary Context," *Journal for the Study of the New Testament* 148 (1997).
17 See summarizing Gudrun Holtz, "Besser und doch gleich: Zur doppelten Hermeneutik des Hebräerbriefes," *Kerygma und Dogma* 58 (2012): 169-170.

witnesses' there is a connection with the 'Author and Finisher of our faith', Jesus (12:2). He endured the cross, that is, demonstrated enormous perseverance, 'for the joy that was set before Him': this is distinctly oriented to the future. He is the *exemplum* par excellence! Abel points to Jesus. In this way Abel points forward, to the future in Christ Jesus, even though he was gagged by Cain.

7.2.4 Contemporary
There are two reasons to characterize Abel as a contemporary when preaching on *exempla*. These are related to the eschatological nature of preaching and the Christian faith itself. In view of this eschatological nature, very often depicted in the tension between 'now already' and 'not yet - 'we do not yet see' and 'we see Jesus [...] crowned with glory and honour', as found in the second chapter. Over the last decades, a broad consensus has emerged on the view that Hebrews does not contain a platonic or dualistic worldview[18]. No contradiction is made between 'here' below and up 'there'; nor between 'here' in the present and 'there' later in eternity. Time and space seem to be stretched to an all-encompassing unity within which the people of God from all ages receive a place[19]. This is one of the most important hermeneutical keys to this sermon. In this way, the parabola of the 'first' and the 'second' tabernacle, the Holy and the Holy of Holies, may be used to indicate the two parts of the history of salvation of the old and the new covenant, namely the period until Christ's finished work and the time after. But these two parts, two periods, are profoundly one.

This is wonderfully illustrated by the border crossing between the end of the chapter of the faith heroes and the twelfth chapter, which brings them all onto the stage at the very beginning. This underlines how the conjunction *kai* forms the transition and thus establishes a close connection between the people on their way in chapter 11 on the one hand, and the ones called 'us' on the other, that is, the congregation in the New Testament. The *expositio* in chapter 11 connects with the *exhortatio* as *applicatio* in chapters 12 and 13, in which regular reference is made to histories from the Old Testament. For that matter, it is typical of Hebrews that, although the first part as a whole strongly bears the character of an *exposition* and the second part that of an *application*, these two are not strictly separated. Also, in the first part, all kinds of 'exhortations' resound,

---

18 Commentaries from the last decades rarely state this anymore, but older commentaries often move along this trail.
19 See Marie E. Isaacs, "Sacred Space: An Approach to the Theology of the Epistle to the Hebrews," *Journal for the Study of the New Testament* 73 (1992).

while there are also moments in the second part that explain what happened then and there (see the introduction of Esau and the Sinai in chapter 12).

The second reason may be found in the significance of bringing the *exempla* up to date. Around this actualizing process, consider the relevance of the verb 'remember'. It does not appear out of the blue, because in the final chapter the exhortation to remember the predecessors is heard (13:7). The verb remember implies that something of the past becomes present, with the intention that we may discern the 'present of the future'. In this way we may become a 'contemporary' of Abel; he is our predecessor. The crux of this is that Abel occupies his place at the beginning of the history that God unfolds in this world. In that movement of God the congregation of 'today' is included. This could also be expressed as follows: the letter to the Hebrews regards the text - for example the text about Abel - as a window on history, a history in which the listener partakes[20]. This is therefore not about the story in the text, but about the text as a window through which we look at the speaking past.

7.3 Abel as predecessor and passer-by

'Abel still speaks' (Hebr. 11:4). What does this speaking of Abel refer to according to this text? Several possibilities have been mentioned, such as for instance, his faith, his faith as it is expressed in his sacrifice or his blood. We will see how each reference does justice to the text and the context.

If we now want to know what this speech of Abel relates to, it seems correct to examine an important *inclusio* in the pastoral address. After all, there appears to be a well-considered composition here, which is another reason to assume that this is a sermon. Which *inclusion* sheds light on the phrase 'still speaks'?

11:4   ... he being dead still speaks.
12:24 ... that speaks better things than that of Abel.

It is striking that the voice of Abel right at the beginning of the list of *exempla* is connected to his speaking at the end of the sermon (12:24). But Abel's speaking serves the speaking of God. After mentioning Abel's speaking in chapter 12, the sermon arrives at a climax in the line commencing with the message of the speaking of God in and through the Son (1:1-4). A similar effect occurs in the line that runs from the climax, namely that this speaking is from him who now as the King-Priest sits at

---

20 See Ken Schenck, "God Has Spoken: Hebrews' Theology of the Scriptures," in *The Epistle to the Hebrews and Christian Theology*, eds. Richard J. Bauckham et al. (Grand Rapids: Wm. B. Eerdmans, 2009), 321-336, 323.

the right hand of the Father (8:1-2). After all, that confession is the heart of what Hebrews focusses on. Thus Hebrews comes to the conclusion, in the light of the fact that 'Abel still speaks', that you should see that 'you do not reject Him who speaks' (12:25). The motivation or even reason for this? Jesus speaks!

Let us first ascertain that it is Abel himself who speaks and not Abel's *blood*, as has been incorrectly adduced to 12:24 in a number of translations[21]. Then the comparison made becomes this, that 'the blood of sprinkling' surpasses the speaking of (the blood) of Abel. To substantiate that it cannot be the blood, sometimes reference is made to the LXX. In that translation of the Hebrew Bible the verb βοαω [to crie] is used in Genesis 4 or, according to Genesis 4, this blood cries out to God from the ground. However, this skews the equation: the blood of Jesus speaks to us, the blood of Abel cries to God.

It seems to be a fundamental fact that the comparison is read in the light of the word κρεῖττον [superior, excellent]. For when this comparison is made in Hebrews, it appears that there cannot be a discrepancy between the two objects contained in the comparison. So, there is no discrepancy between the blood that proclaims forgiveness and the blood that calls for revenge[22]. An example can clarify this, because this κρεῖττον appears earlier in the sermon. 'Of a so much κρεῖττον covenant Jesus has become a surety'(7:22; see 8:6) or 'Therefore it was necessary that the copies of the things in the heavens should be purified with these, but the heavenly things themselves with *better* sacrifices than these' (9:23; my emphasis in italics). When the comparison is made with regard to the covenant, then there is absolutely no discrepancy, but a *besser und doch gleich* [German for: a better and yet equal][23]. The *new* covenant is not very different from the *old* covenant. It is κρεῖττον when compared with the old: more powerful, richer, better or whatever other synonym we could use to make clear that the new surpasses the old. Similarly in the case of the sacrifices: the first were 'necessary', indicating accord, but the necessity of a 'better'

---

21 Apart from that, this does not mean that what Genesis 4 states about the *blood* of Abel would no longer apply, only that it does not apply in preaching on *Hebrews*. Surely, it is true that according to the testimony of the Scriptures that the shed blood in the earth calls for the revelation of God's righteousness (Rev. 6:9-10)!

22 Compare various commentaries, but also more recently: Tim Keller, *Preken: Geloof overbrengen in een sceptische tijd* [Preaching. Bring about faith at a time of skepticism] (Franeker: Van Wijnen, 2015), 76. He discusses the rule 'Preach Christ in every important person from the Bible' and then gives the following reflection: 'Jesus is the true and better Abel, who, although he was innocent when he was killed [...], blood that calls for our absolution, not for our condemnation' (Hebr. 12:24).

23 Holtz, "Besser und doch gleich."

sacrifice remained, that is, it is superlative. The expression 'how much more' echoes as a *cantus firmus* about the excellence and the superiority of Jesus Christ and the new covenant founded in his blood, as found throughout the entire letter. That is the one hand. But on the other, κρείττον also presupposes an agreement, an analogy. For otherwise there is nothing to compare. This prevents a separation between the two testaments as if the old would have been replaced by the new. The superlative of the second emphasises the good of that which is mentioned first. It is not as if the first was 'bad' and was not 'good' until now, but it was 'good' and now it is 'better'. In this way, we may speak of an *unfolding* of what has been handed down to us in the Old Testament, so that the purport of 'how much more' becomes apparent.

Abel speaks through the faith with which and through which he brought his sacrifice. How does he speak, what makes him speak? He speaks, because this voice apparently still sounds today - again the remarkable use of the present tense! - from the history of Genesis 4. We can state that the Scripture presents the speaking of God through Abel. And in this way Abel, as a witness of faith, speaks to us from the Scriptures and the testimony that God gave about his gifts. A second line may be mentioned in the words that state that he still speaks, even after his death. In the opening paragraphs above I briefly mentioned the question as to whether this really does amount to such an encouraging example for the believers, who should be inspired. They all knew that Abel entrusted himself to God, which signified his death. And then the stunning phrase: 'he being dead *still speaks*' 1? (my emphasis). Is it therefore indeed true that the righteous shall live by faith!? The words of Habakkuk apparently apply to this witness as a living witness[24].

Abel still speaks. But he is a passer-by. By saying this, I allude to the fact that the true Predecessor is superior to him. For Jesus (and his sacrifice) speaks more powerfully than Abel (and his sacrifice). Preaching about Abel in a Christ-centred way does not mean following the method of bringing out the contrast, but that of the *Steigerung* [increase]. Jesus' life, which he sacrifices, is infinitely more glorious, that is, '*perfect*', than Abel's. His complete submission to the Father, His *active obedience* is the way of obeying in perfect trust of faith (5:8-9).That is the first line of Abel's speaking to Jesus' speaking. Abel was drawn into this Jesus'trail (12:2). That trail and the parts in that path receive practical specification

---

24 The 'cloud of witnesses' (12:1) to which Abel belongs, may also be indicated here. It is characterized as 'the general assembly and church of the firstborn' and 'the spirits of just men made perfect'. We draw near to them when we come to the congregation of God, when we gather together in the name of the Lord.

in chapter 12, but it does not occur before the 'runners' have first been encouraged and roused by their predecessors and especially by the Predecessor. In this way Abel, as a predecessor, is a passer-by. We in the in our twenty first century do not look to Abel, but are urged to look to Jesus. The second connection between Abel and Jesus is that of Jesus' sacrifice, which cleanses completely. With His *passive* obedience He has forever sanctified all those who come to God through Him. His perfect sacrifice speaks of a perfect atonement (9:14; 10:22). In this way Jesus speaks more powerfully to us than Abel could ever speak. As mentioned, 'how much more' intends to illuminate the beauty and the glory of the Son. Jesus' speaking is more powerful, because it points to his glory. This gives the *paranesis* in this letter an even more powerful impetus.

The actual *Predecessor* who, historically speaking, fulfils the race - to which Hebrews urges us- later than Abel, essentially precedes all when viewed from the perspective of the movement that God initiates, which shall lead to the finish.

7.4 Some homiletic notes on preaching exempla

- *Theological preaching*. Beginning with the inquiry after the theological meaning of the text, that is to say the inquiry after the revelation of and the knowledge of God, should guard against exemplary preaching that has only a moralizing character: 'I wish to be like Abel'.
- *Do not preach from the Old Testament and New Testament references simultaneously*. It is striking that, on a number of occasions, no text had been chosen for the sermon, but rather a more thematic approach was taken on Abel, which title could read as follows: 'Lessons to be learned from the life of Abel'.
- This does not deserve any recommendation: the message of Hebrews 11:4 does not come into its own right when Genesis 4 is commented upon in great detail, nor do unique personal accents from the history achieve this, In this way, sermons about this *exemplum* take a general character, with very little surprises in store.
- Preaching about Abel from Hebrews should proceed from the *inclusio* of 11:4 and 12:24.
- *Show* the wonderful *connection* between the *exempla* and the *Predecessor*:
- If there is one writing in the New Testament that shows Christ as an example (*exemplum*) and as a sacrament (*sacramentum*), it is this sermon to the Hebrews. Jesus' *active* obedience, that is, his role as *exemplum* and his *passive* obedience, his *sacramentum*, belong together.

- Preaching is about how God speaks in the present tense:
    o Service of atonement:
    o Abel's speaking is surpassed by Jesus' speaking; Jesus' speaking is accompanied by the 'blood of sprinkling' and as such the ministering of the Word is the ministering of atonement;
    o Who calls Abel to remembrance and listens to his speaking, should be called to remember the 'how much more' of listening to the voice of Jesus in the ministry of atonement.
    o The κρείττον and consequences:
        • No discrepancy between the Old Testament and New Testament; neither is the Old Testament replaced by the New Testament; it 'merely' surpasses the Old Testament;
        • the aim of continually applying 'better' is to put Jesus in the first and highest place.
- *Argue* from the *'inferior'* to the *'superior'*. This is a good means to convince listeners of the richness and fullness of the 'how much more' in the present, and show the beauty and the greatness of salvation which has been revealed in Christ, the sublime excellence of who he is and what he did and does. This Christ-centred manner of speaking excludes a so-called Christomonism, because of the analogy that precedes the naming of the 'how much more'.

REFERENCES
(N.B. Commentaries are not mentioned).
Attridge, H.W. "God in Hebrews."
In *The Epistle to the Hebrews and Christian Theology*, edited by R. Bauckham, D. Driver, T. Hart, and N. MacDonald, 95-110. Grand Rapids: Wm. B. Eerdmans, 2009.
Cosby, M.R. *The Rethorical Composition and Function in the Light of Example Lists in Antiquity*. Macon: Mercer University Press, 1988.
Eisenbaum, P.M. "The Jewish Heroes of Christian History: Hebrews 11 in Literary Context." *Journal for the Study of the New Testament* 148 (1997).
Holtz, Gudrun. "Besser und doch gleich: Zur doppelten Hermeneutik des Hebräerbriefes." *Kerygma und Dogma* 58 (2012): 159-177.
Isaacs, M.E. "Sacred Space: An Approach to the Theology of the Epistle to the Hebrews." *Journal for the Study of the New Testament* 73 (1992).
Keller, T. *Preken: Geloof overbrengen in een sceptische tijd*. Franeker: Van Wijnen, 2015.
Moberly, R. and L. Walter. "Exemplars of Faith in Hebrews 11: Abel."

In *Hebrews and Christian Theology*, edited by R. Bauckham, D. Driver, T. Hart, and N. MacDonald, 353-363. Grand Rapids: Wm. B. Eerdmans, 2009.

Peels, H.G.L. "'Hoe leest gij?' Een lectio christiana van het Oude Testament." *Theologia Reformata* 52, no. 3 (2009): 236-259.

Rissi, M. *Die Theologie des Hebräerbriefs*. Wissenschaftliche Untersuchungen zum Neuen Testament. Tübingen: Mohr Siebeck, 1987.

Schenck, K. "God Has Spoken."
In *Hebrews and Christian Theology*, edited by R. Bauckham, D. Driver, T. Hart, and N. MacDonald, 321-336. Grand Rapids: Wm. B. Eerdmans, 2009.

Van Oyen, H. *De brief aan de Hebreeën*. Prediking Nieuwe Testament. Nijkerk: Callenbach, 1962.

CHAPTER 8

REMEMBRANCE AS PROPELLANT FOR THE ACT OF SEEING IN PERSUASIVE PREACHING THAT EVOKES A CHANGE IN ATTITUDE

Ferdi Kruger

The Hebrews message that God has spoken in Christ in the last days is not primarily aimed at understanding, but rather on creating new meaning under circumstances where listeners experienced doubt. The preacher enables listeners to engage in a dialogue between their own life-stories and the words of this sermon. Therefore, a reminder of all past promises is evident. Papkpahan[1] stresses that remembrance is powerful in the sense that it enables people to live their lives and enjoy a sense of the self through vivid memories. Remembrance actually prevents the past from fading and is linked to the future to illuminate memories. One could also say that a merging process between listeners' concrete circumstances and the sermon is evident. The sermon allows one to think about a seasoned teacher approaching students with the following comment: *I am going to tell you what I am going to tell you. Afterwards I will tell you about this exact issue and then I'll tell you what I have told you. Eventually I will review this very matter.* The teacher knows that repetition of content is a major key in teaching. Therefore, the educational principle of starting with familiar things to proceed to unfamiliar territory is adhered to. In Hebrews, the preacher utilises the opposite of a progressive form or a syllogistic form of argumentation, namely the so-called repetitive form of argumentation. In other words, there is indeed a logic behind the argumentation. A sameness of thoughts is evident rather than a mere linear progression. One could also say that a restatement of an important matter occurs and it is done in more than one way. Some

---

[1] B.J. Pakpahan, *God Remembers: Towards a Theology of Remembrance as a Basis of Reconciliation in Communal Conflict* (Amsterdam: VU University Press, 2013), 33.

thoughts are repeated, but each time with greater and closer force. This a typical figure that is sometimes also used in the musical environment to evoke a response or emotion from listeners.

Listeners of the Hebrews sermon were inclined to romanticize the past. The idea of remembrance is central to Christian faith, mainly because believers are called to remember the saving acts of God in Christ[2]. Volf [3] helps us to see that it is important to invoke matters that tend to transpire and memories that slip away. Memories of the past are important, because part of the identity of people is integrated in what they remember. Therefore, the sermon is purposefully constructed to indicate that Christ alone fulfilled everything that the Old Testament pointed to. The priesthood, the sacrifices, the familiar aspects described and all of the religious rituals found their fulfilment in him. This idea is constructed along the careful trajectory of an arrow. The preacher wants listeners to remember something poignant about the influence of their past memories in daily life. They have to remember the past experiences, even the rituals of the past, rather than forgetting these. One should immediately add that it is the aim of the sermon to help listeners to edit memories in the light of God's communication in Christ. The preacher therefore piles up a number of synonymous phrases that show either what the law with its sacrifices could not achieve on a negative plain or, positively, what Christ's sacrifice did indeed accomplish:

10:1   The sacrifices of the Law could never make perfect those who draw near.

10:2   Those sacrifices could not completely cleanse the worshippers and take away their consciousness of sins.

10:3   Those sacrifices provided a yearly **reminder** of sins.

10:4   Those sacrifices could not take away sins.

10:10   By God's will through the cross, we have been sanctified once for all.

10:12   Christ offered one sacrifice for sins for all time.

---

2 Pakpahan, *God Remembers*, 21.
3 M. Volf, *God's Forgiveness and Ours: Memory of Interrogations, Interrogations of Memory* (Garden City: Doublebay, 2007), 188.

10:14 By one offering He has perfected for all time those who are being sanctified.
10:17 God promises **to remember** their sins and lawless deeds no more.
10:18 Where there is forgiveness, there is no longer any offering for sin.

These items show the close interweaving of remembrance and understanding of the meaningfulness of God's communication in Christ. It is also evident that the three aspects have to do with God's promises that have been fulfilled already. From the perspective of the New Testament, remembrance (anamnesis) is closely related to significance or the meaningfulness of events and words[4]. Through the act of remembrance, the person or deeds that are remembered are brought into the realm of the here and now[5]. One could also say that remembering the present, past and future is what Christians ritually practice every week in their participation in liturgy, and especially during the celebration of the eucharist. It is simultaneously a ritual to remind us to remember every day the future, that is, the last days of Hebrews 1:1. The action of *anamnesis* entails to re-member or to put the pieces of memory constructively back together, because no one can claim that a particular memory is necessarily the correct or all-encompassing version of facts. Bruce[6] therefore rightly highlights that to cultivate remembrance, a distinct line of argumentation is adhered to in the Hebrews sermon, namely considering the value of the message of Jesus Christ in their lives (see Hebrews 3:1 and also 12:2-3). This could in fact be regarded as a central line within the sermon.

The mediation of meaning through remembrance is created in this process and listeners should understand the meaningfulness of remembrances. Through remembrance, the meaningfulness of the active God of the past is remembered as active in the present. This very idea provides a dynamic hope for the future. It moves like a wheel that can move backwards but also forwards. A striking challenge in the Hebrews sermon is to persuade believers who have lost the energy and the sense of the meaningfulness of typical actions aspects such as encouraging each other, communion with each other and meeting each other. The listeners have, after all, longed for the memories of the good old days (*in memoriam*).

---

4 Pakpahan, *God Remembers*, 139.
5 R. Brouwer, "Preken in context over de homiletische situatie," in *Als een leerling leren preken*, eds. M. Barnard et al. (Zoetermeer: Uitgeverij Boekencentrum, 2009), 25.
6 F.F. Bruce, *The Epistle to the Hebrews*, New International Commentary of the New Testament (Grand Rapids: Eerdmans, 1990), 5.

The writer of the Hebrews sermon does not adhere to the contours of communicating via the lines of *in memoriam*. Contrary to the *in memoriam* idea, the Hebrews sermon underlines the aspect of what it entails to live in the last days or to remember the future[7]. The sermon now motivates a deeper-lying change in attitude based on the idea that the present circumstances of the listeners' lives are anchored within the past of God's promises as fulfilled in Christ. This very fact provides a life-line for intrinsic hope in the future[8].

The present chapter will try to elucidate that the main aim of listening to sermons is not a mere mental understanding of words, but rather a new understanding, that is, meaning-identification by participants who act as meaning-seekers where, for example, listeners' own stories enter into dialogue with the words uttered. The words utilised unveil and activate remembrance of experiences. One word, even one concept, could unveil many things. The listeners to the Hebrews sermon were longing for the good old days and their nostalgic memories in a one-sided manner. The preacher of this sermon does not, however, communicate with the emphasis on the good old days, as mentioned, because God can simply not be kept captivated in a memory of a temple in Jerusalem[9]. The memory of God is not a memory of a static God but rather of a dynamic God who is present in the listeners' contemporary circumstances. The emphasis of the preacher is to underline what it takes to live in the last days and the importance of the here and now[10]. The emphasis on the here and now, or what Cilliers[11] describes as the synchronisation of times, is evident in this sermon. Cilliers proceeds by saying that God is not a monument, but rather a God on the move, so that preaching from a particular passage delineates a certain movement in terms of God's movement. God, who speaks through the ages and in the last days in Christ, is actually offering sermons to listeners for them to acknowledge *eureka*; because of what has been communicated in the sermon, listeners

---

7   F.P. Kruger and C.J.H. Venter, "Die prediking van geloofsverantwoordelikheid: homiletiese perspektiewe vanuit Hebreërs [Preaching responsibility in faith: homiletical perspectives from Hebrews]," *Praktiese Teologie in Suid-Afrika* 21, no. 1 (2006): 65.

8   Ferdi P. Kruger, "Prediking en gesindheidsverandering: 'n Prakties-teologiese studie in die lig van Hebreërs," ThD thesis (Potchefstroom: North-West University, Dept. Practical Theology, 2002), 65.

9   Ferdi P. Kruger, "Rekognisie as meganisme vir die identifisering van die betekenis van liturgiese elemente in die erediens," *Verbum et Ecclesia* 38 (2018): 4, a1694, from https://doi.org/ 10.4102/ve.V38i1.1694.

10 Kruger and Venter, "Prediking van geloofsverantwoordelikheid," 65.

11 Johan H. Cilliers, *Timing Grace: Reflections on the Temporality of Preaching* (Stellenbosch: Sun Media, 2019), 23.

could say that it is their sermon from now on.

8.1 The influence of memories on listeners' difficulty in understanding a problematic praxis of temporality

The contours of the problematic praxis that the historical listeners of the Hebrews sermon faced were influenced by the following aspects:

- The listeners initially lived according to their religion and their faith. They had proved their willingness to care for the community of believers (Hebrews 6:10-11). They stood firm when their properties were confiscated. They even accepted this severe disappointment with gratitude (Hebrews 13:32-34).
- When this sermon was addressed to the listeners, the situation had changed drastically[12]. Limp hands and lame knees (Hebrews 12:12-13) were the result of their understanding and response to the difficulties they were facing. A decline in spiritual growth posed a profound threat to the listeners (Hebrews 12:3). Their former vitality and enthusiasm were lost.
- The problematic praxis of the listeners began to take its toll. On the one hand, they had become disheartened due to the severe challenges they experienced on a daily basis, while profound hope for the future unfortunately functioned like a pie in the sky. It was truly an existential crisis, or crisis of faith, that they were facing.

One can also say that the problematic praxis centred on the meaning of life and the meaning of believing. It also influenced the listeners' willingness to listen and to participate in liturgical activities. The deeper-lying question whether it really still was worth believing as Christians. The shine of being a Christian had been lost and the listeners were faced by the issue of what they should do with their faith in life's reality. The listeners had a vivid memory of the past. One could also say that their memories were holding fast on to the good old days of Jewish liturgical practices. An intriguing question to raise would therefore be whether the visibility of the liturgical elements with its sacrificial system in Jerusalem and the memory of these matters could have influenced the listeners around the dilemma they faced. One of the core problematic aspects in their attempt to understand arose from the functioning of their percepions. It was their perception, for instance, that in the old dispensation, God's presence was visibly part of formation activities and sacrifices

---

12 Anrie du Toit, *Hebreërs vir vandag [Hebrews for today]* (Vereeniging: CUM boeke, 2004), 18.

performed in the temple. Rituals and symbols in the good old days offered a reassuring framework for their understanding of life.

In short, the listeners of the Hebrews sermon faced a problematic praxis of doubting the meaning of being a Christian here and now, but they also longed for the memories of the good old days. Now, one can also understand why the preacher of the Hebrews sermon makes it clear that this sermon is all about encouragement of exhortation (Hebrews 13:22) rather than a brutal nit-picking process. This sermon does not want to provide comments from a distance, but rather offers a purposeful effort to, proverbially speaking, put the arms on the shoulders of listeners and encourage them to find meaningfulness in remembering what God has done exactly over the years. We could also formulate this slightly differently by saying that tension between cognition and recognition, understanding and memory, was evident. Concepts such as memory, remembrance and the difference between remembrance (anamnesis) and nostalgia were emergent. The punch-line of this sermon has to deal with the idea that, in Christ, we receive a complete, final and once-and-for-all pardon for all of our sins, while this influences the past, present and future.

Vosloo[13] emphasises that the past does not simply mean the past tense, but rather the past is actively present in our memories and in our imagination; it lives positively and negatively in our bodies, in our thoughts and in our dreams. The past is indeed present in a powerful and a complex way so that one should admit the past is not dead and that it is not even sleeping. This very idea is a challenging reality that preachers face daily. The question regarding what and how Christians should remember and what and how they should forget is a difficult matter to reflect on.

In the Hebrews sermon, the preacher discusses this and makes it clear that listeners should not forget their past, but should instead integrate their understanding of the past and the meaningful framework of the present and the future. Vosloo[14] helps us to contextualise this theoretical idea of a shift in western temporality that is still unfolding. Assmann[15] also underlines a shift in temporality, saying that the future has lost its shine for many Christians and has indeed become a source of concern. He continues in this vein and offers an answer to this matter by saying

---

13 R. Vosloo, "Commemoration, Rememoration and Reformation: Some Historical-Hermeneutical Celebrations of the Dutch Reformed Church," *Studia Historiae Ecclesiasticae* 41, no. 3 (2015): 3, https://.doi.org/10.17159/2412-4265/2015/764.

14 Vosloo, "Commemoration," 4-8.

15 A. Assmann, *Der lange Schatten der Vergangenheit: Erinnerungskultur und Geschichtspolitik* (München: C.H. Beck, 2006), 7.

that the reason for renewed focus on the past coincides with the violence and horror characteristic of the twentieth century. The growing moral appeal not to forget the past that was characterised by inhumanity and injustice is furthermore audible.

Listeners normally remember pieces of an event (liturgy and preaching) but tend to forget others, and the event-details recalled are shaped by their current mindset and moulded by thoughts and experiences that occurred between the original event and the moment of remembering[16]. Most people would not be surprised to realise that memory is not perfect. Experiences that elicit arousal are more likely to be remembered than experiences that do not evoke an emotional response. Negative information is remembered with a greater sense of vividness than positive information[17]. People often claim that they remember the details of negative events whereas they are more likely to only know that a positive event occurred without remembering the details[18]. Memories are in need of editing and this is exactly why the research field of remembrance is influential here. The act of listening in liturgy that takes place regularly offers glimpses of the potential to stir someone's memory[19]. When it comes to the formation of a community of faith through a sermon, the remembrance of Christ's functioning as Priest or Liturgist (Hebrews 8) stands central. The choice of the sermon utilised in Hebrews has to do with persuasion for people to gain an understanding of their own and unique situation.

8.2 Remembrance as a set of perspectives for encouragement as found in the Hebrews sermon

In this section it is important to take note of the fact that the memories are not neglected by the preacher of the Hebrews sermon. In fact, memories are closely interwoven with cultic or (one can say) liturgical aspects[20]. Remembrance enjoys a constructive functioning within the Hebrews sermon. The argument in the Hebrews sermon has been, in exposition and application, that the sacrifice of Christ was superior to Old Testament sacrifices. By his blood Christ renewed and completed the

---

16 E.A. Kensinger, "Remembering the Details: Effects of Emotion," *Emotion Review* 1, no. 2 (2009): 8, https://doi.org/10.1177/1754073908100432.
17 S.A. Dewhurst and L.A. Perry, "Emotionality, Distinctiveness and Recollective Experience," *European Journal of Cognitive Psychology* 12, no. 1 (2000): 545, https://doi.org/10.1080/ 09541440075005022.
18 K.N. Ochsner, "Are Affective Events Richly 'Remembered' or Simply Familiar? The Experience and Process of Recognizing Feelings Past," *Journal of Experimental Psychology* 29, no. 1 (2000): 244.
19 J.D. Arthurs, *Preaching as Remembering* (Illinois: InterVarsity Press, 2018), 5-6.
20 Du Toit, *Hebreërs*, 104.

promised reconciliation of God's covenant that had been ministered formerly by the Levite priests in the blood of the Old Testament sacrifices. When Jesus came, he did not abolish the old covenant, but gave new meaning to it, and thus became the minister of a renewed (καινή) covenant[21]. Notably, the old and new are not arranged in a contradictory framework, but are intimately linked in the careful exposition and application of the work of the High Priest, Jesus Christ. The tenses of past, present and future are therefore merged into a meaningful arrowhead where the memory of the past and the expectation of the future that has already started are functional and vivid in the experiences of the here and the now. It is a kind of re-membering or essential connection of things related to the past, present and future.

In previous chapters, it has been indicated that the preacher of this sermon is committed to persuade the listeners to have earnestness in their lives of faith. Hence, active listening provides the opportunity for the disheartened listeners to become silent for the memory of the Saviour, Jesus Christ, to flourish[22][23]. The preacher of the Hebrews sermon is skilful in his deliberate attempt to enable the listeners to edit their memories. The problematic praxis of the listeners was that the message about Christ had become audible, but was not visible in their minds, because they struggled to see the concreteness of the message about Christ. The preached message of Christ was in danger of becoming the proverbial pie in the sky, without penetrating their lives. Preaching of the living Christ lies at the centre of Christian belief and, underlying this idea, the Bible is clear that if Christ is not raised, faith is indeed in vain. The Hebrews sermon underlines this and therefore aims at persuading the listeners to really see the relevance of God that has spoken in and through his Son within the last days.

The Hebrews sermon is constructed in such a manner that powerful memories and the vivid remembrance of Christ can emerge. A good example of picturing vivid remembrances is found in Hebrews 5:11-6:20. The utilisation of an intermezzo in Hebrews 5:11-6:20 to connect Hebrews 5:1-10 and Hebrews 7:1 is a good example of this purposeful approach towards editing the memories of the listeners. The hook-on technique is a reminder of the fact that the preacher has not lost focus of something that was announced in Hebrews 5:10[24]. Scholars describe the utilisation

---

21 G.J.C. Jordaan, "Some Reflections on the 'New Covenant' in Hebrews 12:24," *In die Skriflig* 50, no. 4 (2016): 3, a2140, http://dx.doi.org/10.4102/ids.v50i4.2140.
22 Stanley Hauerwas, *The Hauerwas Reader* (London: Duke University Press, 2002), 149.
23 J.K.A. Smith, *Liturgy as a Way of Life: Embodying the Arts in Christian Worship* (Grand Rapids: Baker Academic, 2013), 19.
24 Du Toit, *Hebreërs*, 104.

of the intermezzo as the preacher's attempt to enable the listeners to understand the difficult matters that were described in Hebrews 5:11, therefore the preacher reminds listeners to understand the meaningfulness of memories of the old days in the light of what God has done in the last days.

8.2.1 Anamnesis (remembrance) of familiar things - Hebrews 10:3 and Hebrews 10:32

In the sermon, remembrance centres on the recognition of things that people are familiar with[25] [26]. In the context of anamnesis, memory and to be familiar with something should be highlighted as two focal points, and in the context of preaching the two focal points can never be overestimated. The first reference to the concept of anamnesis is made in Hebrews 10:3 where the concept is utilised in the context of the mentioning of the recurring ritual of the Day of Atonement, which involves a reminder of sins year by year[27]. It is important to say that this reminder involves far more than merely calling something to mind. Instead, a particular kind of activity is at stake. In preaching to disheartened listeners, the preacher includes the remembrance of sin within the message of exhortation. The conjunction of αλλα [but] denotes a contrast between an unreal situation and reality[28]. The recurring sacrifices of the old dispensation have not complied fully with the removal of sins[29]. In the old dispensation, sacrifices could not remove the sins of people. The reminder of the *'yom kippur'* [Day of Atonement], maintained once every year, denotes that a connection has to be made in the minds and hearts of the participants between what is currently happening and what has happened in the past[30]. This connectivity does not materialise in an empty space, but points to something that is going to materialise in the next year[31]. The participants were reminded to recall their sins, and in this sense, considering also anamnesis, it is implied that something significant should be re-connected or re-membered. Above all, remembrance of sins

---

25 Kruger, "Rekognisie," 3.
26 S.E. Wood and E.G. Wood, *The World of Psychology* (Boston: Allyn and Bacon, 1999), 199.
27 Bruce, *Epistle*, 237.
28 P. Ellingworth, *Commentary on Hebrews*, New International Greek Testament Commentary (Grand Rapids: Eerdmans, 1993), 273.
29 Simon J. Kistemaker, *Hebrews*, New Testament Commentary (Grand Rapids: Baker Book House, 1996), 273.
30 J.M. Flanigan, *Hebrews: What the Bible Teaches*, Ritchie New Testament Commentaries (Kilmarnock: John Ritchie, 1997), 197.
31 Kruger, "Rekognisie," 4.

has to do with believers' memory of God as the God who wants to remember his children. In this process, powerful memories of the past that includes God's effort with his children and believers' own shortcomings, should be evident. Therefore, the act of remembrance unlocks and brings certain important memories about God to the fore[32].

The contrast between the remembrances of the sacrifice for sins, year after year, the perfect offer of Christ, once and for all, stands central here[33]. Remembrance of sin has to do, after all, with remembering God's appropriate action, which he bestowed on his children[34]. In Hebrews 8:12 where God says that He will not remember their sins anymore, one is struck by the contrast between the old order of the annual reminder of sins and the new covenant. In the old order, the annual recapitulation of sins had to remind participants of the annual removal of sins[35]. Hebrews 8 indicates that the priests in the old dispensation served as a *copy and a shadow* of heavenly things. The tabernacle and temple were a shadow; the official priesthood of the Old Testament was a shadow; the animal sacrifices were a shadow and the feasts and dietary laws were a shadow. When Jesus Christ came, because God remembered about his promises and about the right time to send his beloved Son, the shadows began to fall away, because Christ himself was the Reality. The listeners of the Hebrews sermon are urged to remember that the earthly sanctuary was designed from the outset to be a copy and a shadow of heavenly reality[36].

It is important to realise that the priests' work was never finished in the Old Testament, therefore they went in and out of the sanctuary[37]. The High Priest of the new covenant and of the heavenly sanctuary is entitled to sit at the right hand of the Father. He is described by the Hebrews preacher as the *leitourgos* [liturgist] of the heavenly sanctuary[38]. The listeners should remember that Jesus brought his offering once and for all, entered the heavenly sanctuary and began his priestly ministry (liturgy) in the presence of God[39]. The reference to the memory of the tabernacle is striking. It is made clear however that it was literally pitched (set-up) by man. This word for pitched is used only once in the New

---

32 L.H. Evans, *Hebrews*, Communicator's Commentary (Washington: Macmillan, 1984), 173.
33 Thomas G. Long, *Hebrews*, Interpretation: A Bible Commentary for Teaching and Preaching (Louisville: John Knox Press, 1997), 102.
34 Bruce, *Epistle*, 237.
35 Bruce, *Epistle*, 237.
36 Bruce, *Epistle*, 82.
37 J. Vines, *The Believers Guide to Hebrews* (New Jersey: Loizeaux, 1993), 1145.
38 Flanigan, *Hebrews*, 147.
39 Kistemaker, *Hebrews*, 216.

Testament and it occurs in Hebrews 8:2. It means to fix or to make fast, typically when pitching a tent[40].

Hebrews 8:10-12 debates this very idea of God's better promises (Hebrews 8:6) by providing seven-fold promises. The use of the concept 'covenant' is again notable. It is again striking that the preacher of the Hebrews sermon refers to the listeners' memory of Jeremiah 30:7. It is done to indicate that the new covenant indeed reveals better promises. Why is this so? Hebrews 8:12 states that God will forgive the people's wickedness and he will no more remember their sins[41]. Three concepts are utilised to describe the wrong-doing of people, and they are offered in the plural form, namely *adikiais* [injustice], *hamartion* [missing the mark] and *anomion* [iniquities]. The memory of sin is typical of the old covenant. From the perspective of the new covenant, it is striking that the old covenantal sacrifices could not remove sin. Sin has been dealt with in the once-and-for-all offering of Christ, therefore those sins are no longer remembered[42]. It is a divine prerogative of His people not to remember the sins, ever[43]. The listeners' remembrance (anamnesis) cannot be separated from a distinct memory of the sacrifice and atonement of Christ[44]. Their remembrance of their sin should bring them to the remembrance of the once-and-for-all offer of Christ and the memory of him who is the *leitourgos* in the new covenant. The attitude of boldness to enter into God's presence is based on the remembrance of the improved promises of the new covenant[45]. This kind of remembrance is like a coin with two sides. Remembrance of sin enables listeners to remember what Christ did, and the remembrance enables listeners to acknowledge and confess their daily sin.

The Hebrews sermon calls on listeners to remember those earlier days. The exhortation to remember is the opposite of dwelling in the past only[46]. The preacher is trying to ignite the memories of the listeners to ask whether they still do remember. The preacher's purpose is to help them remember the early days and the good beginning in their lives of faith[47]. Hebrews 10:26-31 is clearly not utilised to manipulate the listeners, but rather to encourage them, as seen in the word of exhortation in Hebrews

---

40 Flanigan, *Hebrews*, 147.
41 Flanigan, *Hebrews*, 160.
42 Vines, *Believers Guide*, 161.
43 Flanigan, *Hebrews*, 161.
44 Du Toit, *Hebreërs*, 161.
45 W.B. Johnston, *The Epistle to the Hebrews,* Calvin's Commentaries (Grand Rapids: Eerdmans, 1994), 133.
46 Flanigan, *Hebrews*, 220.
47 Du Toit, *Hebreërs*, 181.

10:32-34[48]. Listeners' perseverance during the severe circumstances of earlier days that were dis-amputated is a reminder that something could still be done about poignant memories. Three important aspects of listeners' memories are highlighted, namely that they stood their ground in the face of suffering, were publicly exposed and were persecuted (insulted). The positive memory amid these calamities was that they were able to stand by the side of other believers and that they joyfully accepted the confiscation of their property, mainly because of the hope of something better in Christ[49]. Remembrance of these fond memories should enable listeners to persevere in what they were experiencing.

8.2.2 Remembrance of Christ as Mediator of the new covenant (memoria Christi) - Hebrews 12:24

8.2.2.1 Preaching as the revisiting of the storehouse of memories

Augustine once elaborated on a particular aspect of the interpersonal participation of listeners by saying '*I came into the fields and spacious palaces of my memory, where are treasures of countless images of things of every manner*'[50] (my emphasis). Augustine describes human memory as a stomach that holds both pleasant and less pleasant memories[51]. The senses of human beings have conveyed memorable things to the storehouse of memory[52]. Augustine also compares memory to a storehouse and a field. His most striking metaphor for memory may be the 'stomach of the mind' (*venter animi*), where food is stored without tasting, but later brought forth for rumination. This metaphor strikes the ear as odd and even repulsive, but the image is brilliant. It implies that memories are held and digested, eventually nourishing the whole body.

The act of preaching points to and reminds listeners of the astonishing fact that God is remembering them, therefore he has spoken in the last days[53]. The Hebrews sermon revisits the storehouse of memories, but now within a framework of the dynamic of God's communication in the last days. Smit[54] therefore rightly indicates that preaching (also liturgy) should help listeners to see things differently for them to start doing things

---

48 Bruce, *Epistle*, 267.
49 Du Toit, *Hebreërs*, 182.
50 E.S. Casey, *Remembering: a Phenomenological Study* (Bloomington: Indiana University Press, 1987), 2.
51 P. Venter, J. Symington, and A. van Wyk, *Augustinus se belydenisse* (Wellington: Lux Verbi, 2007), 45.
52 Casey, *Remembering*, 11.
53 D.E. Saliers, *Worship as Theology: Foretaste of Glory divine* (Nashville: Abingdon Press, 2010), 11.
54 D.J. Smit, *Geloof en openbare lewe* (Stellenbosch: Sun Press, 1997), 257.

differently. It correlates with Calvin's underlining of the idea that, in listening, listeners are learning to really see[55]. Preaching of God's Word acts like the lenses of glasses for listeners to see clearly. In listening to sermons, remembrance of God's Work in and through Christ is so important as to carry a profound hope, therefore they are really becoming transformed[56].

In rehearsing the memory of the past, preaching assists listeners of the Hebrews sermon in truly understanding the creative tension between past, present and future. The memory of Christ dominates the argumentation. Piper[57] underlines that God's glory in Christ is, after all, the Gospel. Greidanus[58] also elaborates on the idea that a sermon without Christ-preaching cannot be regarded as preaching, but he is afraid of the confusion in preachers' minds about what this entails. To preach Christ as in the Hebrews sermon is much more than mentioning his name in the sermon. Preaching the good news, according to the meaning of the text, entails keeping in mind that God's Kingdom is indeed always related to the King, Jesus Christ[59]. This idea reckons with the recognition that the new day (last days) is ours in Jesus Christ our Lord. The vividness of our memory of Christ will therefore influence present experiences and our expectation of the future. The importance of remembrance of the remembered, Christ, should stand central in preaching for listeners to hear the living voice of God. Remembrance of our experiences of what God has done in Christ is the most considerable need the world probably has[60].

8.2.2.2 Remembrance of the Mediator of the new covenant-memory of the old and cognizance of the new

In the Hebrews sermon, references to the new covenant appear quite frequently, in particular from chapter 7 onwards (see Hebrews 8:8, 13; 9:15; 12:24). In all of these instances, the new covenant is referred to as a διαθήκη καινή, the only exception being Hebrews 12:24, where it is called a διαθήκη νέα. Hebrews 12:24 calls Jesus the mediator of a διαθήκη νέα (new covenant), instead of a διαθήκη καινή, as elsewhere in the New

---

55 Smit, *Geloof*, 259.
56 Smit, *Geloof*, 260.
57 J. Piper, "Inspirational Preaching," in *The Supremacy of God in Preaching*, eds. J. Piper et al. (Massachusetts: Hendrickson, 2005), 13.
58 S. Greidanus, *Preaching Christ from the Old Testament* (Grand Rapids: Eerdmans, 1999), 2-4.
59 Greidanus, *Preaching Christ*, 8.
60 Piper, "Inspirational Preaching," 17.

Testament[61]. Hebrews 12:24 uses the phrase διαθήκη νέα since, in contrast to the rest of Hebrews, it does not compare the new covenant to the old covenant with Israel but to the situation of humankind in their depravity after the fall into sin. Although God's promise of a seed (Christ) in Genesis 3:15 already brought a shimmering of hope for salvation to fallen humankind, the blood of the murdered Abel witnessed to the fact that, in itself, humankind was destined for God's judgement without a possibility of reconciliation with him[62].

Hebrews 12:24 describes the unique nature of the new covenant. It speaks of Jesus 'as mediator of a new covenant' (διαθήκης νέας μεσίτῃ Ἰησοῦ) and makes a direct connection between this and the 'sprinkled blood' (αἵματι ῥαντισμοῦ). This description is in agreement with the rest of Hebrews (see Hebrews 9:18-28), since it compares Jesus' blood to the blood of the sacrifices in accordance with the Mosaic laws. However, Hebrews 12:24 introduces a new comparison, namely to the blood of Abel: '*We have now come to Jesus, the mediator of a new covenant, and to the sprinkled blood that speaks a better word than the blood of Abel*' (my emphasis). It seems feasible that Hebrews 12:24 should be taken as a subsection of the part of the sermon that focusses on applying the message[63]. Hence also the comparison between the blood of Abel and the sprinkled blood of Christ, which can then be taken as part of the purpose of the sermon. Pertinently, the comparison seems to contribute to the *since*-part of its usage. It explains either how, being in Christ, we approach God in a way superior to the Old Testament believers, or how, being in Christ, we are in a position before God that is superior to the Old Testament believers' position[64].

Why the concern around this covenant in the sermon (see Hebrews 9)? The reason is that it is mind-boggling in what it offers, namely a deeper-lying answer to the listeners' experiences of difficult circumstances[65]. The listeners should remember that this covenant is indeed new and not merely a renewed version of the old one. The Christological emphasis of this sermon cannot be ignored. Therefore, remembrance of Christ does not occur *in memoriam*, but is vivid and is the remembrance of a living Christ. Ellingworth[66] underlines that Hebrews 12:24 takes the argumentation of Hebrews 12:18-24 to a climax. The memory of Moses, also described as mediator of the old covenant, emerges. In contrast with

---

61 Jordaan, "Reflections," 1.
62 Jordaan, "Reflections," 1.
63 L.D. Pettegrew, *The New Covenant* (Grand Rapids: Zondervan, 1999), 252.
64 Jordaan, "Reflections," 6.
65 Pettegrew, *New Covenant*, 256.
66 Ellingworth, *Commentary on Hebrews*, 681.

a mere human being, the work of Christ in mediating the new covenant at God's right hand encourages the listeners to persevere[67]. In this sense, they should remember that they are now brought into the presence of God because of Christ's offering, once and for all, and that he is now the *leitourgos* in the heavenly sanctuary.

The title *mediator* (μεσίτης) that is given to Christ in Hebrews 12:24 equally takes the listeners back to chapters 8-10. Hebrews 8:6 calls Him 'mediator of a better covenant' and 9:15 'mediator of a new covenant' (διαθήκης καινῆς). The new covenant is referred to as a διαθήκη νέα, and the comparison to the blood of Abel is related to the topic of reconciliation[68]. This message, says Hebrews 12:24, is better than the message spoken by the blood of Abel. The blood of Abel speaks a message of vengeance without any reconciliation. Thus these two messages are opposed in Hebrews 12:24. On the one hand, the message of Abel's blood is a message of no reconciliation and, on the other, the message of Christ's blood is a message of graceful reconciliation. Thus it seems that Hebrews 12:24 indeed adds something new to the argument of Hebrews 8-12. It adds an aspect that up to that stage has not been elucidated, that is, the reality of no reconciliation without Christ. Up to this point of the book, the argument has been (in exposition as much as in application) that the sacrifice of Christ was superior to the Old Testament sacrifices. By his blood Christ renewed and completed the promised reconciliation of God's covenant that had formerly been ministered by the Levite priests in the blood of the Old Testament sacrifices. When Jesus came, he did not abolish the old covenant, but gave new meaning to it, thus becoming the minister of a renewed (καινή) covenant[69]. In this renewed covenant, the grace of God, who brought Christ as our reconciliation into the world, is emphasised: otherwise, there is no possibility of being reconciled with God[70].

Gaarden[71] indicates that the aim with preaching is not merely a mental understanding of words, but a new understanding (meaning-identification) where listeners' own stories should enjoy a dialogue with the words of the sermon. The preacher acts as listener amongst listeners, so

---

67 J. Phillips, *Exploring Hebrews* (New Jersey: Loiszeaux Brothers, 1992), 186.
68 Jordaan, "Reflections," 8.
69 Jordaan, "Reflections," 8.
70 B. Witherington, "The Conquest of Faith and the Climax of History (Hebrews 12:1-4, 18-29)," in *The Epistle to the Hebrews and Christian Theology*, ed. R. Bauckham (Grand Rapids: Eerdmans, 2009), 435.
71 M.L. Gaarden, "The Emerging Sermon. The Encounter between the Words of the Preacher and the Listeners' Experience," (paper presented at Aarhus University, Denmark, 2014), 28.

that ownership of sermons can be exchanged, and he or she should first of all wade into the waters of remembering[72]. Based on the preacher's own remembrance and experience of the text, something Spurgeon has called earnestness, preaching as reminding could spur a new kind of dynamic. Each word and section of the formulation will be carefully scrutinised to enrich people's memories. Like ancient Israel that has erected monuments and shrines, believers are also assembled within worship services to participate in liturgy with one purpose and that is to remember God's presence[73]. The words and also the style used in a sermon unveil and activate the remembrance of experiences.

Remembrance should create opportunities to experience anew the reality of Christ. The power of remembrance (anamnesis) lies in reliving the saving acts of God in such a powerful manner that it enables us to appropriate all God's promises. Remembrance, as viewed from a liturgical angle, has to do with the memory of familiar aspects or persons that are established for living memories and vivid experiences to take place[74]. Remembrance therefore amounts to drawing people into the reality of the fullness of the life in Christ. Moltmann[75] indicates the importance of this kind of remembrance when he says that *'without the memory of Christ's passion there is no Christian meditation on the future life and conversely, without hope for the coming of Christ and therefore the remembrance of Christ loses its power'* (my emphasis). Remembrance is a prominent building block in people's expectation of here and now and the future. Remembrance stimulates hope against hope.

Vorster[76] furthermore highlights the importance of knowing that remembrance is not a passive activity of bringing something into memory, but rather a confrontation with the living and present, mediating Christ. Welker[77] defines remembrance as an act or even a re-enactment of Christ's triumphant sacrifice and the grace to make its benefits available to believers in the present. Remembrance functions like a photograph. On seeing the photograph, it is not only the person itself, but also what the person did, that surfaces.

---

72 Arthurs, *Preaching*, 116.
73 Arthurs, *Preaching*, 126.
74 M. Welker, *What Happens in Communion?* (Grand Rapids: Baker Academic, 2000), 126.
75 J. Moltmann, *A Broad Place: An Autobiography* (Minneapolis: Fortress, 2008), 103.
76 Koos M. Vorster, *Menswaardigheid, versoening en vergiffenis* (Potchefstroom: Teologiese Publikasies, 2011), 64.
77 Welker, *What Happens?*, 126.

8.3 Homiletical perspectives on the importance of remembrance
8.3.1 The preacher should share remembrances with listeners
Augustine uses Cicero's famous dictum to point out that there are different ways of communicating truth: an eloquent man has to speak to teach, delight and persuade[78]. His ability to use words in provocative and evocative ways was carried over into his preaching ministry. He employed a variety of rhetorical devices in his preaching, using analogies, word-pictures, similes and metaphors in his explaining and application of the Scriptures[79]. In the fourth book of *De Doctrina Christiana*, which Augustine wrote towards the end of his life, he elaborates on how one should preach. He emphasises that the content of the sermon should be thoroughly biblical, because God is speaking through it to us. It is necessary to have a detailed knowledge of the Bible before setting out to present one's findings[80]. Furthermore, a good general understanding is required of mathematics, music, history, geography, botany, geology, astronomy and, among other areas, dialectics and rhetoric (*eloquentia*). Augustine further emphasises that eventually, the fire blazing in the Word of God is the glow of the Holy Spirit. If the preacher does not glow as he preaches, he cannot fire up the one to whom he is preaching[81].

For Augustine, as spiritual food, God's Word was humanity's daily bread. In sermons on the Lord's Prayer, he tells us that the words '*Give us this day our daily bread*' refer to natural bread, the bread of the Eucharist *and* the Word. 'What I explain (*tracto*) to you is also daily bread, just as the Scriptural readings you hear daily are daily bread. And the hymns you hear and sing are also daily bread'[82]. 'The Word of God that is preached daily is also bread'[83]. For Augustine, preaching is the breaking of bread:

> *When we explain the Scriptures to you we are, as it were, breaking the loaves. What I hand out is not mine. What you eat, I eat. What you live on, I live on. We have together our storeroom in heaven. For that is where the Word (verbum) of God comes from*[84] *(my emphasis).*

---

78 J.A. Sypert, "Redeeming Rhetoric: Augustine's Use of Rhetoric in His Preaching Ministry," *Eleutheria* 4, no. 1 (2015): 26.
79 Sypert, "Redeeming Rhetoric," 31.
80 J. van Oort, "Augustine, His Sermons, and Their Significance," *HTS Teologiese Studies/ Theological Studies* 65, no. 1 (2009): 4, Art. #300, DOI: 10.4102/ htsv65i1.300.
81 Van Oort, "Augustine," 5.
82 E. Rebillard, "Sermones," in *Augustine through the Ages: An Encyclopedia*, eds. Allan D. Fitzgerald et al. (Grand Rapids: Cambridge, 1999), 33.
83 C. Mohrmann, *Augustinus: Preken voor het volk* (Utrecht en Brussel: Het Spectrum, 1974), 21.
84 Mohrmann, *Augustinus*, 22.

It is striking that he uses the same terminology for the preaching of the Word as for the celebration of Holy Communion. He speaks of a 'banquet of the Scriptures' that is prepared at 'the table of the Lord'[85] and of 'food' as well as spiritual 'bread'[86]. Augustine thus elaborates on a particular aspect of the interpersonal participation of listeners when he says: '*I came into the fields and spacious palaces of my memory, where are treasures of countless images of things of every manner*'[87] (my emphasis). It is against this background that he describes human memory as a stomach that holds both pleasant and less pleasant memories[88]. He suggests that human senses convey memorable things to the storehouse of memory[89] As mentioned, his most striking metaphor for memory may be the 'stomach of the mind' (*venter animi*), where food is stored without tasting but later brought forth for rumination. Again, this metaphor may strike the ear as odd and even repulsive, but the brilliance of the image resides in the notion that memories are held and digested, eventually to nourish the whole body.

Food is deeply intertwined with the core tenets of Christian identity in numerous ways[90]. Biblical themes such as the fruit in the Garden of Eden, the Passover meal, the provision of manna in the desert, the food regulations in the Torah, the notorious meals that Jesus enjoyed with outcasts, the declaration of Jesus that he is the Bread of Life, the celebration of the Holy Communion and the coming wedding feast of the 'Lamb that was slain', are examples of how central the image and the idea of food is. Conradie[91] convincingly elaborates on the idea of *kenosis* and of eating for enjoyment and connects this idea with glorifying God himself. It is therefore striking that, so long ago in history already, Augustine connected preaching with such a central theme in the Bible. The elements of joy and celebration that are important within a liturgical context are therefore highlighted. Applied to preaching and the metaphor of eating, it seems that the attitude of celebration should be evident, mainly because the joy in a present God that is no monument but a living God, should be celebrated.

Augustine is adamant about the fact that the preached Word generated its eloquence, an eloquence parallel with Scripture itself. Preaching is

---

85 Rebillard, "Sermones," 34.
86 Van Oort, "Augustine," 7.
87 Casey, *Remembering*, 2.
88 Venter, Symington, and Van Wyk, *Augustinus*, 45.
89 Casey, *Remembering*, 11.
90 E.M. Conradie, "What We Do When We Eat," *Scriptura* 115, no. 1 (2016): 1.
91 Conradie, "What We Do," 5-7.

wisdom proceeding out of her own home[92]. What does the role of the preacher entail in this respect? In conjunction with Augustine's view, the phrase *'The Lord's Remembrancers'* was coined by Lancelot Andrewes, chaplain to Queen Elizabeth and King James I[93] [94] (my emphasis). Andrewes drew his metaphor from the royal court. The king's (or queen's) Remembrancer is the oldest judicial position in continual existence in Great Britain, having been created in 1154 by Henry II. Today it amounts to a ceremonial position, but for centuries the Remembrancer's job was to put the lord's treasurer and barons of court in remembrance of pending business, taxes paid and unpaid and other matters pertaining to the benefit of the crown. This historical situation reminds liturgists (preachers) of their responsibility to enable participants to see the old and the new of remembrances to enjoy new perspectives for the future. The storehouse of listeners' memories is invaluable. By enabling listeners to remember, valuable aspects of God's treasury are offered and editing or engramming of memories eventually takes place.

8.3.2 Remembrance as propellant to stir memories in preaching
Preachers are therefore Remembrancers. They stir memories of listeners by utilising words. Style is important, because careful utilisation of style enables listeners to see. A theory by Perelman and Olbrechts-Tyteca focusses on the minds and feelings of listeners as well as on what the preacher, the persuader, expects from them[95]. This theory elaborates on more compelling and less compelling argumentation. The building blocks in this process are direct sensory experience, memories and imagination[96]. Words and the style of sermons should evoke attention and concrete events for memories to be evoked. In this way, the preacher enables listeners to remember things that they have forgotten or enables them to taste memories anew. The vivid use of language, that is, one important aspect of sermon style, cannot be over-emphasised, since memory enjoys a passive and active aspect. When we are confronted in the present time with an emotion, or persons, places and times from the past, the passive kind of memory becomes an active kind of memory[97]. We recall those experiences of the past, and they come to the fore, especially through

---

92 Thomas G. Long, *Preaching from Memory to Hope* (Louisville: John Knox Press, 2009), 40.
93 Arthurs, *Preaching*, 2.
94 Casey, *Remembering*, 12.
95 Arthurs, *Preaching*, 67.
96 Arthurs, *Preaching*, 67.
97 Paul Ricoeur, *La Mémoire, L'Histoire, L'Oubli* (Paris: Seuil, 2000), 183-186.

images[98]. Religious language, when it reflects the biblical message, opens up a new horizon for people to see a problem in a new light. It can turn things upside down in an unexpected, surprising way, as in the parables of Jesus, for instance. It disorients the listener, because it confronts the listener with something paradoxical, something not to be expected, that functions as a breaking point to orient him or her in new way[99] [100].

After all, stirring of memories is one of the primary responsibilities of preachers[101]. In proclaiming well-known facts from the Bible, preachers have to realise that the Word enjoys performative power. The Remembrancer stirs the memories of listeners by bringing the past into the realm of the present. The power of remembrance is in that telling or stirring of familiar things[102]. The aim of stirring memories through remembrance is targeted at one's heart, leading to a context where the dichotomy between mind and emotion can no longer be upheld. Arthurs[103] even describes one's heart as a motivational structure of which thinking, feeling and doing are integral parts. Preaching to listeners in the manner of preachers acting as Remembrancers has to do with cutting one's heart, where 'heart' enjoys the meaning of 'the whole person'. This exposition shows that preaching according to Augustine is indeed a purposeful act of persuasion. In the listening process, listeners are therefore connected to the heavenly storeroom. It is the preacher's responsibility to help listeners see old and new things, to re-chew, in Augustinian imagery, and celebrate the new perspectives that are created.

8.3.3 The power of remembrance in preaching

From the perspective of the New Testament, remembrance is closely related to the idea of God in the sense that it is he who remembers and is taken to fulfilment in and through Jesus Christ's suffering and victorious resurrection[104]. Through the act of remembrance, the person or the deeds remembered are brought into the realm of the here and now with a close connection to celebration[105]. The relevance of the message proclaimed is that it is good and joyful to know what it entails to be one in Christ's suffering and His victory. The power of anamnesis therefore lies in

---

98 Ricoeur, *La Mémoire*, 63.
99 Paul Ricoeur, *Exegetical and Hermeneutical Studies* (Chicago: University Press, 1998), 3.
100 Paul Ricoeur, *The Conflict of Interpretations* (Evanston: Northwestern University Press, 1974), 381-467.
101 Arthurs, *Preaching*, 48.
102 Arthurs, *Preaching*, 55.
103 Arthurs, *Preaching*, 57.
104 Pakpahan, *God Remembers*, 139.
105 R. Brouwer, "Preken in context," 25.

reliving the saving acts of God in such a powerful manner that it enables us to appropriate all God's promises. Remembrance as a means of acknowledging the past in a way that is inspirational for the present and life-giving for the future is pivotal in the New Testament.

Through remembrance, the active God of the past is remembered as active in the present. This very idea provides dynamic hope for the future. It is like a wheel that can move backwards and also forwards. A much-cited Dutch scholar, Gerrit Immink[106], hits the nail on the head when he avers that Christ is expected in the worship service, while he is not simply there at people's command. Preachers are servants and not mere magicians. Therefore, the idea of epiclesis, the invocation of the Holy Spirit, is important. It is the Holy Spirit who opens people's minds and provides receptivity in people's hearts.

As part of this process, words or language are functional and aimed at linking people's memories with remembrance. This is what Wiersbe[107] describes as the purposeful process of turning listeners' ears into eyes to realise what is expected from them. Careful planning of words and of the sermon should re-connect dis-amputated things in listeners' lives. As part of the preacher's approach to introducing an important focal point gradually and in a structured way, in the Hebrews sermon he or she utilises Old Testament quotations on at least 35 occasions, as has been indicated[108]. The emphasis on Christ that is greater than prominent leaders from the old dispensation is striking. Vivid memories of the past provide dynamic perspectives for the present. For instance, this author enumerates various figures from the Israelite tradition to encourage first listeners or readers to remain loyal to themselves[109]. Hebrews 2:1 emphasises that listeners should take heed to things that they have heard, since it is linked to salvation in Christ.

These notions make it clear that the delivering of sermons as well as listening to sermons are matters that move through one's intestines, bearing witness to spiritual digestion. They indicate that the homiletical challenge indubitably involves an exchange of ownership in a sermon. When listening to preaching, the listener should be able to admit that this sermon is now exchanged, an exchange of *aha!* - It is my sermon that has

---

106 Gerrit Immink, *The Touch of the Sacred: The Practice, Theology, and Tradition of Christian Worship* (Grand Rapids: Wm. B. Eerdmans, 2014), 53-55.
107 W.W. Wiersbe, *Preaching and Teaching with Imagination* (Grand Rapids: Baker Books, 2006), 42.
108 Ellingworth, *Commentary on Hebrews*, 37.
109 M. Cromhout, "The 'Cloud of Witnesses' as Part of the Public Court of Reputation in Hebrews," *HTS Teologiese Studies/Theological Studies* 68, no. 1 (2012): 1, Art. #1151, 6 pages. http://dx.doi.org/10.4102/hts.v68i1.1151.

occurred. Listening and re-chewing what is heard should be cultivated for vivid remembrances to connect listeners' memories with new perspectives provided. However, homiletical instruction has traditionally centred on sermon-building that entails restriction to a merely cognitive approach. The preacher has been trained to construct logical outlines and to write a logical sermon before constructively delivering the sermon according to sound communicative principles. Such training has commonly produced sermonisers rather than preachers. Preachers are normally instructed to prepare sermons that are logical in structure and polished in the execution, but utterly harmless when it comes to touching people's lives.

However, to preach, as demonstrated here, has to do with a particular kind of communication that is aimed at the participation of the listener by means of effective listening that also includes an organic process of memories that will be edited according to the functioning of remembrance. This is exactly where the optical lens of remembrance offers a helpful mechanism for participatory involvement in the act of preaching. Participants are indeed then taking part in the act of listening and remembering memories about Christ[110]. Memories are part of stories that people tell themselves and each other about the past. People are constantly in the process of writing and rewriting the stories of their lives to make sense of the world around them. Listeners' memories become part of their sense-making efforts[111]. Re-chewing during the listening process, and during the week after, of what has been communicated could further enhance a participatory experience around vivid remembrances that should enable listeners to see new perspectives on daily life.

Gaarden[112] is convinced that remembrance is not merely about a mental understanding of words, but rather about a new understanding and of meaning-identification where listeners' own stories could enter into dialogue with what is being communicated in the sermon. The preacher, who must uphold an attitude of being a listener among listeners, should first of all wade into the waters of remembering[113]. Each word and section of his or her formulation of the message has to be carefully scrutinised and formulated to enrich people's memories[114].

---

110 Rudolf Bohren, *Predigtlehre* (Gütersloh: Gütersloher Verlagshaus, 1974), 159. Refers to this idea as *'Die Geistesgegenwart umfast die Zeiten [presence of mind includes the times]'*.
111 G. Rosenwalt and L. Rochberg, *Storied Lives* (New Haven, CT: Yale University Press, 1992), 22.
112 Gaarden, "Emerging Sermon," 28.
113 Arthurs, *Preaching*, 116.
114 Arthurs, *Preaching*, 126.

A memorable participation or listening to sermons as such invites people to look and see that new perspectives on daily life are indeed necessary. The beauty of this resides in offering new perspectives on reality as well as stirring memory, and not simply repeating threadbare platitudes[115]. Preachers are aware of the fact that the words utilised will connect with previous experiences (often referred to as schemata) in listeners' lives. Listeners frequently refer to this connection when they talk about sermons afterwards. Moreover, they are not always able to remember the exact formulation or the words the preacher used in the sermon, but they can link the sermon with a concrete situation in their lives[116]. An associative interaction takes place when listening results in remembrance of a new set of questions and challenges in listeners' minds. This new understanding does not necessarily always stem from the exact intent of the preacher, which is why what is remembered could differ from what has been communicated.

An additional aspect of the kind of involvement that remembrance offers to listeners could further be called critical interaction with the content. This critical interaction would occur, for instance, when a preacher's understanding and exposition of a text are not consistent with listener's interpretation[117]. This clash between what is preached and what is true according to people's inner speech could nonetheless pave the way for a new kind of understanding to arise. Gaarden[118] proceeds to indicate that there is a further kind of participation in the listening process, namely a kind that is beyond human words. This could be called contemplative participation, where listeners know they have listened, but afterwards cannot recall the relevant information. Listeners are convinced of the fact that the liturgy enjoys considerable meaning, but they cannot retrieve that information. They are nonetheless adamant about what the worship service has meant. They feel relaxed and silenced in their state of being. It is clear that participation is more mysterious than what the naked eye believes.

8.4 Conclusion

This chapter has discussed the concept of αναμνησις was discussed and it became clear that remembrance is more than a mere remembrance of the cross of long, long ago. The memory of the message about Christ should

---

115 Arthurs, *Preaching*, 7.
116 Bert de Leede and Ciska Stark, *Ontvouwen: Protestantse prediking in de praktijk* (Zoetermeer: Boekencentrum, 2016), 141.
117 Gaarden, "Emerging Sermon," 22.
118 Gaarden, "Emerging Sermon," 25.

become a remembrance of its essential meaning. Although listeners hear words, vivid images come to the fore. Listeners also have memories of Christ. In the act of preaching and especially within the Hebrews sermon, this idea is emphasised. The emphasis is not primarily on the crucified Christ, but on the cognizance that he is the risen Lord who allows us to experience his redemptive presence while listening to sermons. While listening to a sermon, the listener is not remembering alone, but engages in close interaction with other listeners. In realising that remembrance is influential in persuading listeners to change their attitudes, preaching offers the unique opportunity for listeners to edit their memories of the past within the present. Remembrance of Christ and past memories are functional towards providing hope for the future amid present experiences.

Applied to what people experience in the challenging circumstances of the Covid-19 pandemic, one should realise that preaching has to cultivate remembrances. Arduous circumstances evoke memories. Emotions such as desire, hope, anger, fear and disgust reflect appraisals that goal attainment or failure is either anticipated or threatened[119]. These emotions, irrespective of their positive or negative valence, are characterized by high motivational intensity and an impetus to act. When they experience these kinds of emotion, people's attention narrows to information that is central to their goals[120]. For example, anger prepares people to remove obstacles to their goals and fear prepares them to avoid or escape threats to their goals. Because the angry individual focuses on the agent obstructing a goal, and the fearful individual on the source of threat, the range of information attended to, encoded in or retrieved from memory is narrow. This narrow focus leads to poorer memory for details that are not relevant to the individual's current goal, resulting in greater vulnerability to misinformation concerning those details. In contrast, emotions such as happiness and sadness are lower in motivational intensity, because they reflect appraisals that goal attainment or failure has already occurred. When they experience these emotions people's attention broadens as they consider the consequences of goal attainment or failure, change their beliefs and expectations and orient themselves towards new goals.

People's memories are shaped, after all, by knowledge, attitudes and beliefs, all processes that are influenced by their emotion--memories can

---

[119] R.L. Kaplan, I. van Damme, and L.J. Levine, "Motivation Matters: Differing Effects of Pre-Goal and Post-Goal Emotions on Attention and Memory," *Frontiers in Psychology* 3, no. 404 (2012): 11-13, DOI: 10.3389/ fpsyg.2012.00404.

[120] Kaplan, Van Damme, and Levine, "Motivation Matters," 27.

therefore also be mis-shaped, warped or thwarted. People's most vivid and lasting memories are typically emotional ones. These memories are selective, however. This is exactly why remembrance as an editing process of memories could be regarded as influential. The Hebrews sermon provides a framework for listeners to become involved in remembrances that are influential with a view to their experiences of meaningfulness.

REFERENCES
Arthurs, J.D. *Preaching as Remembering*. Illinois: InterVarsity Press, 2018.
Assmann, A. *Der lange Schatten der Vergangenheit: Erinnerungskultur und Geschichtspolitik*. München: C.H. Beck, 2006.
Bohren, Rudolf. *Predigtlehre*. Gütersloh: Gütersloher Verlagshaus, 1974.
Brouwer, R. "Preken in context over de homiletische situatie."
In *Als een leerling leren preken*, edited by M. Barnard, F. Borger, K. Bregman, R. Brouwer, G. van Ek, and G. Immink. Zoetermeer: Boekencentrum, 2009.
Bruce, F.F. *The Epistle to the Hebrews*. The New International Commentary of the New Testament. Grand Rapids: Eerdmans, 1990.
Casey, E.S. *Remembering: A Phenomenological Study*. Bloomington: Indiana University Press, 1987.
Cilliers, Johan H. *Timing Grace: Reflections on the Temporality of Preaching*. Stellenbosch: Sun Media, 2019.
Conradie, E.M. "What We Do When We Eat." *Scriptura* 115, no. 1 (2016).
Cromhout, M. "The 'Cloud of Witnesses' as Part of the Public Court of Reputation in Hebrews." *HTS Teologiese Studies/Theological Studies* 68, no. 1 (2012): Art. #1151, 6 pages. http://dx.doi.org/10.4102/hts.v68i1.1151.
De Leede, Bert and Ciska Stark. *Ontvouwen: Protestantse prediking in de praktijk*. Zoetermeer: Boekencentrum, 2016.
Dewhurst, S.A. and L.A. Perry. "Emotionality, Distinctiveness and Recollective Experience." *European Journal of Cognitive Psychology* 12, no. 1 (2000). https://doi.org/10.1080/09541440075005022.
Du Toit, Anrie. *Hebreërs vir vandag [Hebrews for today]*. Vereeniging: CUM boeke, 2004.
Ellingworth, P. *Commentary on Hebrews*. New International Greek Testament Commentary. Grand Rapids: Eerdmans, 1993.
Evans, L.H. *Hebrews*. The Communicator's Commentary. Washington: Macmillan, 1984.
Flanigan, J.M. *Hebrews: What the Bible Teaches*. Ritchie New Testament Commentaries. Kilmarnock: John Ritchie, 1997.

Gaarden, M.L. "The Emerging Sermon: The Encounter between the Words of the Preacher and the Listeners' Experience." Paper presented at Aarhus University, Denmark, 2014.

Greidanus, S. *Preaching Christ from the Old Testament*. Grand Rapids: Eerdmans, 1999.

Hauerwas, Stanley. *The Hauerwas Reader*. London: Duke University Press, 2002.

Immink, Gerrit. *The Touch of the Sacred: The Practice, Theology, and Tradition of Christian Worship*. Grand Rapids: Wm. B. Eerdmans, 2014.

Johnston, W.B. *The Epistle to the Hebrews*. Calvin's Commentaries. Grand Rapids: Eerdmans, 1994.

Jordaan, G.J.C. "Some Reflections on the 'New Covenant' in Hebrews 12:24." *In die Skriflig* 50, no. 4 (2016): a2140. http://dx.doi.org/10.4102/ids.v50i4.2140.

Kaplan, R.L., I. van Damme, and L.J. Levine. "Motivation Matters: Differing Effects of Pre-Goal and Post-Goal Emotions on Attention and Memory." *Frontiers in Psychology* 3, no. 404 (2012). DOI: 10.3389/fpsyg.2012.00404.

Kensinger, E.A. "Remembering the Details: Effects of Emotion." *Emotion Review* 1, no. 2 (2009). https://doi.org/10.1177/1754073908100432.

Kistemaker, Simon J. *Hebrews*. New Testament Commentary. Grand Rapids: Baker Book House, 1994.

Kruger, F.P. and Venter, C.J.H. "Die prediking van geloofsverantwoordelikheid: homiletiese perspektiewe vanuit Hebreërs [Preaching responsibility in faith: homiletical perspectives from Hebrews]." *Praktiese Teologie in Suid-Afrika* 21, no. 1 (2006).

Kruger, Ferdi P. "Prediking en gesindheidsverandering: 'n Prakties-teologiese studie in die lig van Hebreërs." ThD thesis. Potchefstroom: North-West University, Dept. Practical Theology, 2002.

Kruger, Ferdi P. "Rekognisie as meganisme vir die identifisering van die betekenis van liturgiese elemente in die erediens." *Verbum et Ecclesia* 38 (2018): a1694. https://doi.org/ 10.4102/ve.V38i1.1694.

Long, Thomas G. *Hebrews*. Interpretation: A Bible Commentary for Teaching and Preaching. Louisville: John Knox Press, 1997.

Long, Thomas G. *Preaching from Memory to Hope*. Louisville: John Knox Press, 2009.

Mohrmann, C. *Augustinus: Preken voor het volk*. Utrecht en Brussel: Het Spectrum, 1974.

Moltmann, J. *A Broad Place: An Autobiography*. Minneapolis: Fortress, 2008.

Ochsner, K.N. "Are Affective Events Richly 'Remembered' or Simply Familiar? The Experience and Process of Recognizing Feelings Past." *Journal of Experimental Psychology* 29, no. 1 (2000).

Pakpahan, B.J. *God Remembers: Towards a Theology of Remembrance as a Basis of Reconciliation in Communal Conflict.* Amsterdam: VU University Press, 2013.

Pettegrew, L.D. *The New Covenant.* Grand Rapids: Zondervan, 1999.

Phillips, J. *Exploring Hebrews.* New Jersey: Loiszeaux Brothers, 1992.

Piper, J. "Inspirational Preaching."

In *The Supremacy of God in Preaching*, edited by J. Piper, G. Macdonald, S. Chapman, B. Wilkerson, H. Robinson, J. Arthurs, J. Ortberg, and C.B. Larson. Massachusetts: Hendrickson, 2005.

Rebillard, E. "Sermones."

In *Augustine through the Ages: An Encyclopedia*, edited by Allan D. Fitzgerald, John C. Cavadini, and Marianne Djuth. Grand Rapids: Cambridge, 1999.

Ricoeur, Paul. *The Conflict of Interpretations.* Evanston: Northwestern University Press, 1974.

Ricoeur, Paul. *Exegetical and Hermeneutical Studies.* Chicago: University Press, 1998.

Ricoeur, Paul. *La Mémoire, L'Histoire, L'Oubli.* Paris: Seuil, 2000.

Rosenwalt, G. and L. Rochberg. *Storied Lives.* New Haven, CT: Yale University Press, 1992.

Saliers, D.E. *Worship as Theology: Foretaste of Glory Divine.* Nashville: Abingdon Press, 2010.

Smit, D.J. *Geloof en openbare lewe.* Stellenbosch: Sun Press, 2008.

Smith, J.K.A. *Liturgy as a Way of Life: Embodying the Arts in Christian Worship.* Grand Rapids: Baker Academic, 2013.

Sypert, J.A. "Redeeming Rhetoric: Augustine's Use of Retoric in His Preaching Ministry." *Eleutheria* 4, no. 1 (2015).

Van Oort, J. "Augustine, His Sermons, and Their Significance." *HTS Teologiese Studies/Theological Studies* 65, no. 1 (2009): Art. #300. DOI: 10.4102/ htsv65i1.300.

Venter, P., J. Symington, and A. Van Wyk. *Augustinus se belydenisse.* Wellington: Lux Verbi, 2007.

Vines, J. *The Believers Guide to Hebrews.* New Jersey: Loizeaux, 1993.

Volf, M. *God's Forgiveness and Ours: Memory of Interrogations, Interrogations of Memory.* Garden City: Doublebay, 2007.

Vorster, Koos M. *Menswaardigheid, versoening en vergiffenis.* Potchefstroom: Potchefstroomse Teologiese Publikasies, 2011.

Vosloo, R. "Commemoration, Rememoration and Reformation: Some Historical- Hermeneutical Celebrations of the Dutch Reformed Church." *Studia Historiae Ecclesiasticae* 41, no. 3 (2015). https://.doi.org/10.17159/2412-4265/2015/764.

Welker, M. *What Happens in Communion?* Grand Rapids: Baker Academic, 2000.

Wiersbe, W.W. *Preaching and Teaching with Imagination*. Grand Rapids: Baker Books, 2006.

Witherington, B. "The Conquest of Faith and the Climax of History (Hebrews 12:1-4, 18-29)."

In *The Epistle to the Hebrews and Christian Theology*, edited by R. Bauckham, D. Driver, T. Hart, and N. MacDonald. Grand Rapids: Wm. B. Eerdmans, 2009.

Wood, S.E. and E.G. Wood. *The World of Psychology*. Boston: Allyn and Bacon, 1999.

CHAPTER 9

HEARING AND BEING IN CHURCH

Preaching in worship services

Maarten Kater

Up to the Spring of 2020 we took for granted the close connection between preaching and being in a church building. We listened, among other things, within the community of the congregation. Surely, we realise anew now that, in the past, there were no-go areas in this world for Christians, where they could not meet each other as a congregation, mainly because of ideologies translated into laws; and this situation has gone one into the present, of course. So many Christians were persecuted, even in the 21st century, when large parts of our world could only imagine a so-called 'just' world.

But during the Spring of 2020, most church services were banned more or less for months. We had not thought this possible in our part of the world. The restrictions happened because of the by now much-discussed Covid-19 pandemic. What was left was just a broadcast in front of a camera from a church building, mostly in the presence of very few people. This new phenomenon brings an important question to our attention: do we lack something essential without a congregation assembled? Surely, one could argue that the congregation actually did come together, although scattered through a great area, listening in their homes, especially as viewed from a theological and ecclesiological perspective. Nevertheless, the sermon has always been seen as part of the liturgy as a whole, and in a profound sense:

'The sermon is part of the liturgy [...]. Sermon and the whole liturgy, service of Word and Sacrament, service of the W/word and answer in the prayers, songs and gifts are together a whole. Together they form a directed sacred play. The pastor in worship is the orchestrator of the sacred. Preachers work on the unachievable'[1].

---

1 Bert de Leede and Ciska Stark, *Ontvouwen: Protestantse prediking in de praktijk* (Zoetermeer: Boekencentrum, 2018), 133. See F. Gerrit Immink, *The Touch of the Sacred: The Practice, Theology, and Tradition of Christian Worship* (Grand Rapids: Wm.

In this chapter, therefore, some elements of our worship services in connection to preaching are discussed. What does the relation between preaching and being in church mean? How do they connect?

In response to these vital questions, the chapter will first examine, on the basis of a minor phenomenological exploration, some characteristics of a gathered congregation to make clear why our liturgy and ecclesiology should be connected to body and soul, because preaching cannot be reduced to a one-sided phenomenon propelled from a pulpit to a 'public': instead, it has the character of a dialogue (9.1).

Second, I take a wider biblical perspective to make one or two critical comments that are substantial, in biblical-theological terms, to what our worship services are about (9.2). In the final part of the chapter, some special characteristics from Hebrews are taken into consideration that aim at what reality ultimately is. To be sure, the open doors of a church building and an open heavenly gathering belong together (9.3).

9.1 A phenomenological exploration

As mentioned, we briefly sojourn here along an insightful phenomenological study of the differences and similarities between in-church and televised worship, as conducted at the end of the 20th century[2]. The study offers a useful base for further research around the possibilities and shortcomings of digital worship and digital preaching within the decade to come, although much has changed in the last two decades in our world-wide-web world. Recent investigations in connection with the consequences of the digitalization of worship in a lock-down period are however still superficial due to a lack of distance from current events, and often these rush to conclusions[3]; these will therefore not be used in the present scientific context. Furthermore, I consult one or two extant illustrations from literature on being present bodily in worship and the meaning of corporeal worship experiences in which we approach God with body and soul.

9.1.1 Capturing the complexity of the in-church worship experience
In his research, Wolff (1999) used a methodological schema spread across

---

B. Eerdmans, 2014).

2 Richard F. Wolff, "A Phenomenological Study of In-Church and Televised Worship," *Journal for the Scientific Study of Religion* 38, no. 2 (1999): 219-235.

3 During the spring of 2020, almost all newspapers around the world carried surveys on social distancing and the connected digitalizing of life (work and worship, dealing with isolation and lack of being touched and so forth) were published from different points of view (such as from the perspective of psychological, philosophical, social and religious sciences). In a few years to come, surely more grounded new insights could be published.

three legs: description based on transcribed interviews, reduction based on thematizations and interpretation based on hermeneutic reflection[4]. In this way he found three thematic categories to be emergent from the process of reduction, embodying three essential constituent elements of ecclesiastical experience: hierarchy, immersion and freedom.

In the lived complexity of ecclesiastic experience, that is, in-church experience, there appear to be important characteristics found in at least three areas[5]:

- Ecclesiastical experience in contrast with 'everyday' experience:
- Church as different from work, everyday conflicts and ordinary experiences of time. In contrast with the everyday chaos and everyday jostling, humdrum and 'hubbub', church provides a well-structured and peaceful environment. One of the interviewees remarked: 'At church I am not expected to be a wonderful person, I'm expected to be a sinner to be forgiven and somebody who's going to go out and try to be a better Christian and live out their faith in a better life, where at your work you don't have that ability to necessarily fail and be readily forgiven, you're expected to do the best and not fail, and people don't necessarily forgive you if you do fail'. One of the interviewees said about the experience of time: 'it's a sort of suspension of time'.
- Ecclesiastical modes of corporeal experience:
- Defocussing on the passage of time goes along with heightened focus on sense. 'Senses are foregrounded in relation to what is experienced as a neutral horizon forming the background. Thus. Silence is the background against which speech is foregrounded; seatedness is the visual background against which a person standing commands attention; nearness is the tangible background against which touching is foregrounded'.
- Although it is not possible to give a complete survey of all the findings, some of them are quite instructive, for instance that the intertwining of quietness and self-focus of the church is dependable as is the auditory element: 'It's very comforting to hear the same words'. Respondents say that their concentration comes about by a conscious effort to be intentionally directed towards sound, the voice of one reading the prayers, and in terms of bracketing the visual by not looking at the printed word, the reader or the

---

4 See R.L. Lanigan, *Phenomenology of Communication: Merleau-Ponty's Thematics in Communicology and Semiology* (Pittsburg: Duqueen Unversity Press, 1988).
5 Wolff, "In-Church," 222-225.

congregants. As far as the matter of tactility and bodily presence are concerned, a sense arises in which worshippers experience the God whom no-one has seen as concretely present and touchable. After the sermon someone feels better 'that I'm in touch with God'. One further important aspect for the in-church experience: the presence of others directing the awareness to what connects them all serves metonymically to connect all things and all people, because of physical proximity and tangibility: 'I think you can probably feel the mood of people'.
- Ecclesiastical modalities of intersubjective awareness:
- Interviewees mentioned, among others, the experience of the preacher as 'a spokesman for God' in contrast with that preacher when visiting their home and the self as willingly separated from itself: 'with a church service I hope that I'm a different person when I come out'. The self is renewed as a different form from the one who entered the service, the influence of others and especially the 'Great Other', God himself. The God 'out there' comes in 'in here'.

Consider here again that Wolff's research shows, as mentioned, that the three essential constituent elements of ecclesiastical experience are hierarchy, immersion and freedom. Hierarchical relationships present themselves in a number of ways, for instance between God and men, pastor and congregation, old self and new self, church time and everyday time. 'It puts things in a better perspective', one of the interviewees said. Ecclesiastical time is experienced as a temporal point of demarcation, a time that sets apart that which came before from that which comes after. God is experienced as separate from and connected to congregants. God's high status is protected through his invisibility. We are unable to see God, but are seen by God perpetually.

This hierarchy and awareness of separation forms the background against which immersion comes into focus. In the perception of the interviewees, an item was brought up which is quite striking, centring on the difference between the visual and the auditory. The visual emphasises separation, difference and hierarchy. On the other hand, the auditory emphasises a bringing together, a filling of gaps, a homogenization. Sound surrounds and is present to all persons in a way that makes each of them its centre. Sound binds and unifies within its invisible presence[6].

---

6 See Stephen H. Webb, *The Divine Voice: Christian Proclamation and the Theology of Sound* (Grand Rapids: Brazos Press, 2004) based, among others, on Walter J. Ong, *The Presence of the Word: Some Prolegomena for Cultural and Religious History* (Minneapolis: University of Minnesota Press, 1967).

In the framework of immersion - where the 'I' is incorporated in the 'we' and 'us' - several distractions are to be considered, however, especially when the visual may overpower the auditory and suddenly re-establish, as an example, awareness of the isolation of the 'I' among the 'we'. Community identity is experienced as easily broken by apparently simple matters such as the gaze of another. Nevertheless, the sense of community is maintained and congregants gain an identity beyond that of an isolated self. A communal self is established during the worship service particularly in relation to hearing words spoken or sung[7]. Therefore, a practical theological consideration of what 'interest' really and literally means *inter esse* will be helpful in research on in-church and digitalized worship; namely, being among others, being *inter alia*.

Respondents experience immersion as freedom from their ordinary experience, of self, time, world. They are freed from that which is limiting and are able to experience what is encompassing. Coming into the service, the self is experienced as limited and this sets the background for freedom. There is a movement from anxiety to hope. That shift separates and gives value to a new week. There are in the lived experience different planes within which one may find oneself, that is, 'in' which one is such as the church and the everyday. Although the churchly plane is apart from the everyday, it affects life 'in' the everyday.

Careful hermeneutical reflection on the three themes shows that they can be reduced to a phenomenological definition of in-church worship as related to the participants' phrases. In sum, ecclesiastical experience involves a *conformation (making one form, complying with a group expression) and concentration (making one centre, making stronger) involved in an act of transformation (of self, time, world)*. Church service brings about a transformation of self and time by means of conformity and concentration.

9.1.2 Some descriptions of in-church worship and corporality
Phenomenological explorations do have a real treasure trove in literature of all kinds, in stories and histories, in essays and sermons, in prose and poetry. Some examples, some treasures, will therefore be taken on board here as a reminder of practical theological lessons from Hebrews.

---

7 For the meaning of singing and music, see R. Voladesau, *Theology and Arts: Encountering God through Music, Art and Rhetoric* (New York: Paulist Press, 2000); D. Ihde, *Listening and Voice: A Phenomenology of Sound* (Athens: Ohio University Press, 1976); Viktor Zuckerkandl, *Man the Musician*, trans. N. Guterman (Princeton: University Press, 1976).

The passionate American writer, preacher and theologian Frederick Buechner published more than thirty books, among which *Secrets in the Dark. A Life in Sermons* (2006). In a sermon on Exodus 3:1-6 and Luke 19: 37-40, he gives some descriptions of going to and being in church that are fruitful for further theological considerations around our presence in church in relation to a concern informed by the burning bush:

For those of us who are in the habit of putting on our best clothes and going to church from time to time, maybe it is a good idea to consider what a church is, of all things. What are all these churches we keep coming to, year in and year out? A church in the sense of a building is walls and a roof erected on the proposition that this ancient story of Moses and his burning bush is somehow true - that however you choose to explain that story, you cannot all that easily explain away. Something extraordinary took place a long time ago on the eastern Gulf of Aqaba, and our presence in churches, and the presence of millions like us, is evidence that the reverberations of that event are felt this day. It is the reason why churches exist. It is the reason why we go to them[8].

Buechner then goes on to say that God is everywhere, and in this respect the whole earth is holy. He goes as far as to proclaim that

'God is not more in a church than he is anywhere else. But what makes a church holy in a special way is that we ourselves are more present in it'[9].

The first sentence of this passage should be discussed in light of Matthew 18:20. All places are holy - that I fully agree with - but some places are holier than others. The second sentence of the passage is moving. Buechner describes this 'more present' with words and phrases such as 'more fully and nakedly ourselves', 'with muck on our shoes', 'the dust of life upon us', 'our failures, deceits, hypocrisies' and 'strangers and exiles':

Whatever it is that is truly home for us, we know in our hearts that we have somehow lost it and gotten lost [...]. We come here to acknowledge that in terms of the best we could be we are lost and that we are helpless to save ourselves. We come here to confess our sins'[10].

Buechner comes, subsequently, to a wonderful description of a Pascal-like - and as will be shown, even a Hebrews-like - experience of what happens during a worship service in the lives of the participants:

That is the sadness and searching of what church is, of what we are in a church - and then suddenly FIRE! The bush bursts into flame, and the voice speaks our names, whatever they are - Peter, John, Ann, Mary. The

---

8 F. Buechner, *Secrets in the Dark: A life in Sermons* (New York: Harper Collins Publishers, 2006), 75.
9 Buechner, *Secrets*, 75.
10 Buechner, *Secrets*, 76.

heart skips a beat. 'YOU! YOU!', the voice says. Does it? I think so. I think if you have your ears open, if you have your eyes open, every once in a while some word in even the most compromising sermon will flame out, some scrap of prayer or anthem, some moment of silence even, the sudden glimpse of somebody you love sitting there near you, or of some stranger whose face without warning touches your heart, will flame out - and these are the moments that speak our names in a way we cannot help hearing[11].

All this, and more, makes the ground on which we stand holy, because we heard that voice here which called us by name. Buechner is convinced of the reality that happens even through the boredom arising when we come to church just because of habit, and indeed even through our thoughtlessness while being in church. From a preacher's perspective in the building he describes this as follow:

'...[N]ot wanting, most of them, to be there at all, and showing it. But as I looked out at their faces the way I look out now at yours, I had again and again the uncanny sense that from time to time, in spite of themselves, they were truly listening....'[12].

How important it is to bring our bodies to the church, as demonstrated by Tish Harrison Warren's book on *The Liturgy of the Ordinary*. If worship services are not about any more than listening to the sermon and just belonging to a passive audience we reject the idea that Christianity is a thoroughly embodied faith and not just a bit of brainy subculture.

Scripture values and honours the body, which is integral to our worship. Christians are often accused of two wrong-headed views of the body. One is that we ignore the body in favour of a disembodied, spirits-floating-on-clouds spirituality. The other is that we are obsessed with bodies, focusing all our attention on policing sexual conduct and denigrating the body as a dirty source of evil.

Jesus redeems us, and that redemption occurs in our bodies. The biblical call to an embodied morality - sexual purity, moderation in food and drink, comes not out of a disdain for the body, but out of the understanding that our bodies are central to our life in Christ, as temples of the Holy Spirit.

Referring to Romans 12:1, Warren writes:

We learn how our bodies are sites of worship, not as an abstract idea, but through the practice of worshiping with our bodies. During seminary, I occasionally visited a little Anglican church that some of my friends attended about forty minutes north of my house. There was a lot of movement in the service - processing, sitting, walking, standing, kneeling,

---

11 Buechner, *Secrets*, 76.
12 Buechner, *Secrets*, 80.

eating, making signs of the cross, reading aloud, bowing. I had been longing for an embodied faith and this church felt like some kind of spiritual Pilates class[13].

Although the comparison with a Pilates class is not the most attractive one, this vivid anecdote nonetheless urges practical theology to think through the bodily aspects of our worship services, because 'if the church does not teach us what our bodies are for, our culture certainly will'[14].

This short twofold phenomenological exposé brings to the surface one or two aspects of the vital connection between hearing the Word of God and being in his presence:

a) **Ecclesiastical experience:**
Contrasts with everyday experience (time and performance);
Is connected with modes of corporeal experience (senses, silence, proximity);
Leads to modalities of intersubjective awareness (God and others 'out there' who come 'in here');
Has three constituent elements: hierarchy, immersion and freedom.

b) **Bodily attendance:**
influences our response to God's presence as shown in the burning bush;
underscores the holiness of the in-church service;
underpins the fact that Christianity is an embodied faith and not just a bit of brainy subculture: Jesus Christ delivers body and soul.

9.2 Some key elements characteristic of being in church

It is striking that the Bible does not literally use the term 'church service' anywhere. Our 'worship services' - another term the Bible does not use - are best typified by the word *congregation* (Lat. *congregare*: bring together, unite) or *synagogue* and derivatives, as used in the famous exhortation reading 'not neglecting to meet together' (Hebr. 10:25)[15]. But then the simple and intriguing question is, who comes together, with whom, and why[16]?

---

13 Tish Harrison Warren, *The Liturgy of the Ordinary* (Illinois: InterVarsity Press, 2019), 43.
14 Warren, *Liturgy*, 44.
15 John Paul Heil, *Worship in the Letter to the Hebrews* (Eugene: Wipf and Stock, 2011).
16 See on 'worship': Leland Ryken, James C. Wilhoit, and Tremper Longman, eds., "Worship," in *Dictionary of Biblical Imagery: An Encyclopedic Exploration of the Images, Symbols, Motifs, Metaphors, Figures of Speech and Literary Patterns of the Bible* (Downers Grove: InterVarsity Press, 1998), 969-973 for a concise summary; Nicholas Wolterstorff, *The God We Worship: An Exploration of Liturgical Theology* (Grand Rapids: Wm. B. Eerdmans, 2015); Hetty Zock, ed., *At the Crossroads of Art and Religion: Imagination, Commitment, Transcendence* (Leuven: Peeters, 2008).

Around any planned meeting we can abstract some characteristics. Perhaps the most important aspect to start with is the convener who initiates the gathering. Only as a result of convening people can such meetings be planned for a fixed time and even at a fixed place, should you actually want to meet each other bodily. Of course, this sounds all too logically systematic and obvious. You are called somewhere and when others are called there as well, you come together. But from a theological point of view, as we think about worship services this are not self-evident, the question arises as to who orders people to come together.

In the Old Testament, meetings of the people of Israel are held on the initiative of the God of Israel, as the Pentateuch frequently shows. A gathering between the LORD and the people who belong to him, the people of his covenant, is unthinkable without the *convocation* of the LORD. Apparently this official gathering has not been of interest to some, who decided to organize their own religious gatherings with the intention of sacrificing, singing, listening to a 'story' and such. But, where men have taken the initiative in history, often service to idols makes its appearance. Such a meeting would be no more than a mere product of our own thinking and religious feelings, preferably aimed at making us comfortable.

The LORD calls all kinds of people by means of his convocations, whereby he himself always is the First as the convener. In this way, He seeks Adam and Eve, calling them out of their hiding place to meet Him (Gen. 3). He engages Moses at Mount Sinai, to whom He gives the prescriptions of the service of the meetings (Ex. 19-24). God has chosen places where he calls people together, especially at the tabernacle and the temple (Deut. 12). He also engages priests and Levites in the sanctuaries and, closer to home, calls on parents to fulfil His invitation to come to the congregation.

So, the conviction that God calls together his people even throughout the whole world (Isa. 45:22) is essential for dealing with our church services. The meetings of the congregation in our time are held because God still wants people to come together to meet with them. A church council is just a facilitation to make sure that, practically speaking, that calling can be fulfilled by means of arranging a time and place for the meeting.

9.2.1 The congregation of the LORD
The designation for the assembled covenant people in the Old Testament is the *qahal YHWH* [17]. This is the community formed at the invitation of the LORD. They are called together. A similar verb is used in the New

---

17 Cf. '*qhl*' in: William A. van Gemeren, ed., *New International Dictionary of Old Testament Theology and Exegesis*, vol. 3 (Carlisle: Paternoster Press, 1996), 888-891.

Testament. There we speak of the ecclesia of Jesus Christ. The word *ecclesia* (which we usually translate with the word 'church') stems from a verb with the meaning 'to be called out'. So again we see the thought of being 'called' (from darkness to light) and 'holy' (set apart with a special purpose: to proclaim the virtues of God). In this context it is important to bear in mind that the word *synagogue* has the same meaning: you go on the same path together and thus come together, forming a meeting. What does one do when going to the meeting of the congregation? To express it first from the perspective of an Israelite in the Old Testament: one does not actually go to a tent or a temple, not to the priests or Levites, not to an altar, shining gold or fragrant wood, but the worshipper comes to God and so into his presence. That is, we come to His presence, we come into His ears, we hear words from His mouth, and there we see His lips moving, as it were. Hearing Him while in his presence, while being before his face.

9.2.2 The presence of God

The biblical expression the 'face of God' acts as an indication of the personal presence of God. When we turn to Mount Sinai, the first thing we realise is the command that reads: do not approach Me! I am present on this mountain, so do not touch, do not come near. Nobody could meet the living God on the mountain. The lively description given in Hebrews speaks volumes (Hebr. 12: 18-21) in this respect. Even Moses trembles with fear. From that mountain sounds the voice of the living God. Being together as a congregation while listening to the Lord is a tremendous event at the foot of Sinai, a moving worship service.

The LORD wants to meet people not just in private and in a personal manner, but also as a congregation. The word 'congregation' already indicates that there is a meeting that has a *personal* character. Perhaps the most beautiful expression for meeting is the phrase 'approaching *before My face*'. By means of this expression the LORD makes it clear that when people come to him, they may think of him as a real person. God adapts, that is, accommodates his way of speaking to us[18]. The LORD knows well that we cannot understand that he always sees us when there was never any mention made of the 'eyes of the LORD'. In the same way, we can think of the 'ears of God'. Through this expression we understand that God hears us. Gathering in the worship service has its kernel in 'approaching before the face of God'.

---

18 Arnold Huijgen, *Divine Accommodation in John Calvin's Theology: Analysis and Assessment* (Göttingen: Vandenhoeck & Ruprecht, 2011).

But how can there be any meeting and so *communion* between God and his people? Old Testament bestows a great gift to that exact end: the 'tent of encounter' outside the camp. Above it, the column of cloud stands as a sign of God's presence as soon as Moses enters the tent. 'The LORD spoke to Moses face to face, as a man speaks to his friend' (Ex. 33:11). If Moses does not want to go on without God's presence, the LORD asks him, 'Must My face go with him to reassure you?' Moses replies, 'If your face does not go, let us not go up from here' (Ex. 33:14-15). The Hebrew word *panim* means first of all face, but it also indicates the personal 'presence' of someone. In the language of the New Testament we encounter this expression more often. Someone's 'face' is someone 'in person'[19]. In the situation described at Mount Sinai, the question is whether God will indeed be the 'God with us' - our Immanuel. The people give Him reason enough not to be in their midst any longer. Communion with God is only possible as gracious communion, a communion in grace.

A fine New Testament example of the meaning of gathering 'before God' can be found in the history of the Roman centurion Cornelius (Acts 10). What does this important man say when he has called all his household together and Peter is standing before him? (Acts 10:33) 'We are all here before God now, to hear all that has been commanded of you by God'. The expression 'in the presence of God' literally reads 'before (the face of) God'. The phrase saying that we are 'in the presence of God' is more than a general indication of place. On the contrary, it indicates the reality of God's presence. Thus, those present can hear the words of Peter as the words of God while sitting in God's presence in Christ by his Spirit.

9.2.3 On earth as it is in heaven

Old Testament liturgy is bound to very detailed prescriptions. Literally everything about the tabernacle and what is to be placed in it is described: altars, crockery and tools. The numbers and dimensions, use of materials, and so on - these are fixed. It is also striking that everything had to be richly decorated with symbols: think for instance of the many palm trees in the carvings. Artisans listened closely; work came down to a millimetre and an ounce. God says it himself: 'And see that you make it after the example shown to you on the mountain' (Ex. 25:40). This is reminiscent of the saying 'as in heaven, so it is on earth'. God determines to perfection how he wants to be served.

---

19 See '*panim*' in: William A. van Gemeren, ed., *New International Dictionary of Old Testament Theology and Exegesis*, vol. 3 (Carlisle: Paternoster Press, 1996), 637-639.

According to His precept, the place where He wants to live among the people and gather with them is divided into three parts. The court, accessible to the congregation, the holy place, accessible only to the priests and the holy of holies (most holy of all), only accessible to the High Priest, once a year. It is important to understand that the worship in the tabernacle was first and foremost a service of the priests. They functioned as mediators between God, who lived in the sanctuary, and the people, who stood in the court. God was approached in terms of the separate spiritual status of priests and Levites. The 'common people' stood at a distance and remained passive.

What does the New Testament say about this Old Testament liturgy? We are probably inclined to think that the sacrifice of Jesus on the cross brought this earthly worship to an end. After all, the torn veil shows that access is now completely open. Though this is this is true, there is more to this matter. Hebrews gives considerable attention to Old Testament worship. There we find the answer to the question: What is the meaning of the service in the tabernacle or temple in light of the history of salvation?

Hebrews sings the highest song about Jesus Christ as the High Priest in heaven. There He has entered and there He is 'the minister of the sanctuary, of the true tabernacle, which the Lord established, and no man' (Hebrews 8:2). Before the title 'minister' literally stands 'Liturgist'! The Liturgist is in heaven. There the actual service is performed.

In this context, however, the sermon returns to the earthly sanctuary. Hebrews 8: quotes the words of Exodus 25: 'See that you make it according to the image (example) shown to you on the mountain'. However, it emphasises that the priests in this earthly sanctuary have only done their work as a reflection and shadow of the heavenly sanctuary. The whole ceremonial service of the Old Testament is a shadow, a premonition, pointing to the actual worship that takes place in heaven.

A core passage in this sermon, which also points to the great significance of the service of the heavenly High Priest in the actual heavenly sanctuary, states it this way: 'For Christ did not enter into the sanctuary made with hands, which is an antithesis of the true, but into heaven itself, to appear before God before us now' (Hebrews 9:24). To be perfectly clear, a 'mirror image' is not an 'opposite', but a characterization[20]. Joseph, for example, can be seen as a type, a portrayal of the Lord Jesus. When you read back from the New to the Old Testament, you recognize in him

---

20 Otfried Hofius, *Der Vorhang vor dem Thorn Gottes*, Wissenschaftliche Untersuchungen zum Neuen Testament (Tübingen: Mohr Siebeck, 1972). *Wissenschaftliche Untersuchungen zum Neuen Testament*

a number of patterns from Joseph's life, special moments that are typical for who Jesus is. Joseph, then, is a counter-image of Jesus.

In sum, we can see that ceremonial worship is a shadow or pattern of the work of Jesus Christ, especially of his work in heaven. An important conclusion is therefore that Old Testament worship is an example for worship in heaven rather than only for the New Testament church on earth. This worship on earth is no longer determined by the example shown to Moses on the mountain. That liturgy is fulfilled. So we cannot simply call upon the Old Testament worship services to be reintroduced into the New Testament congregation today. This is evident from the fact that you will not find the instructions and designations given in Exodus anywhere in the New Testament.

Key elements in our vision on what being in church means therefore may be said to centre on three c-words: congregation, convocation and communion. The presence of God is the face of God.

9.3 Preach while they have come

There is much more happening on earth, as we can see. What happens in church services during the sermons preached and before and after these services could not be presented just by (social) psychology, sociological methods or even statistical methods. Surely, the use of qualitative research has its merits. Nevertheless, what is noticeable is more than what is measurable or what could be expressed in simple words[21].

Hebrews says much about heaven, but shows that it is definitely connected to earth perpetually. One of the most valuable insights here is that a sermon has to sound as a song, a song for our heavenly High Priest Christ Jesus. But one of the most surprising things is that Hebrews upgrades a worship service to a heavenly level. Homiletics is embedded within ecclesiology at a very high level.

'See that you do not refuse him who is speaking', states Hebrews 12:25. This is what homiletics is about: Him who is speaking, continually and in real time. When does this admonition, 'See', reach the ears and hearts of the listeners? When the congregation is gathered in their building, their sanctuary, as the room is sometimes called within the church building where the congregation sits in their pews. Yes, but this is not looking along the wonderful lines which Hebrews 12 offers us in relation to our church meetings. Where have their partakers of their services come to according to this Hebrews preacher? It sounds unbelievable and like

---

21 See John Swinton and Harriet Mowat, *Practical Theology and Qualitative Research* (London: SCM Press, 2006), 38-46, on the important features of *ideographic knowledge* (as opposed to *nomothetic knowledge*) for the practice of practical theology.

language from another planet indeed. They have come or approached (*perfectum*!) heaven, the heavenly congregation, and ultimately to Jesus as the climax of it all:

You have come to:

- Mount Zion;
- The city of the living God, the heavenly Jerusalem;
- Innumerable angels in festal gathering;
- The assembly of the firstborn enrolled in heaven;
- God, the judge of all;
- The spirits of the righteous made perfect;
- Jesus, the mediator of a new covenant and his sprinkled blood.

With this list the stage is set for 'him who is speaking' (12:25). The New Testament congregation has come to 'Mount Zion'. This of course is not literally true, but meant as a metaphor: the mountain of the theophany, the dwelling place of God. They actually did come to a building where they were congregating in the name of Jesus[22]. But being in church actually means being in the 'city of the living God', being amongst 'innumerable angels' and 'the assembly of the firstborn' or 'spirits of the righteous made perfect' , that is, all people mentioned before in the eleventh chapter! - and, ultimately, to 'Jesus, the mediator'. Being in church on earth is being connected with God and all heavenly spirits, and with all believers who have reached the finishing line already and are at rest (Hebr. 4). What a great benefit we should understand ourselves to enjoy when we realise that hearing the Word of God while being in church includes this heavenly reality[23]. In this way homiletical insights - besides all other aspects of our worship services ad liturgy - are helpful towards (re)gaining this awareness in our services.

Liturgy, however, also has a formative value, as we saw earlier in this volume. Liturgy forms a certain image of God. How we pray and sing expresses what we believe. That is true, but what about the reciprocal movement? What we pray and sing is what we believe. This is how the creeds came to be. The first Christians were convinced by the Spirit that Jesus is the Son of God. This is how they started praying to Him and

---

22 On the meaning of special places: Christian Grethlein, *An Introduction to Practical Theology: History, Theory, and the Communication of the Gospel in the Present*, trans. U. Rasch (Waco: Baylor University Press, 2016), 197-206.

23 Marie E. Isaacs, "Sacred Space: An Approach to the Theology of the Epistle to the Hebrews," *Journal for the Study of the New Testament* 73 (1992).

worshipping Him. Thus came a confession in which the Godhead of Jesus was emphatically confessed. The liturgy communicates directly, by means of a so-called 'first order theology'. The reflection on this within theological science (a 'second-order theology') only takes place afterwards.

If we look at being in church in this way, we see that a certain liturgy can lead to a certain image of God. At a low threshold, to enter our services appears to mean that it all has to be a bit loosely, our language must be popular, not 'stiff', but nonchalant; but what does that say about our image of God? What image of God do we sing? Does someone who comes from outside get a biblical image of God through the way we sit in church, sing, listen, pray, stand up? Before the service, during the service and after the service? Do we experience a deep sorrow and an unspeakable and delightful joy in our divine services? Consider that there is therefore a downside to the plea for approachability. If the accessible God 'lowers', the worship service loses its appeal. No-one is waiting for a God on a human scale. A 'God-who-fits-me' is merely one among many gods.

Liturgy forms, but can also deform. This applies to services in which the low threshold has lowered God to a 'God-who-fits me', but also to services in which stiffness is confused with reverence, in which hardly any emotions are expressed and in which language use ensures that the God of the Bible becomes (re)known. In short, the attractiveness of worship services is a theme that arouses longing for the presence of Christ himself, of his Spirit. Only in this way will God's paternal face shine upon us (Num. 6).

Our services are exercises in awe and reverence precisely because of the connection between the earthly and heavenly services and especially the nearness of God and Christ or, perhaps better, God in Christ. Admittedly, on first sight the author appears to contrast the fright of the Israelites at Mount Sinai at the sight and voice of God (vv. 18-21; see Ex. 20:18-19) with the assurance that the new-covenant people have approached Mount Zion. However, the concluding appeal for reverence and awe as the reminder that 'God is a consuming fire' forces us to reconsider this interpretation. Employing the well-known rabbinic method of arguing from the lesser to the greater, the preacher suggests that if the encounter with God at Sinai evoked such great awe, how our entrance into the heavenly Jerusalem at 'Mount Zion' should do so all the more[24].

---

24 Therefore it is wrong to say with George H. Guthrie, "Hebrews," in *Commentary on the New Testament Use of the Old Testament*, eds. G.K. Beale and D.A. Carson (Grand Rapids: Baker Academics, 2007), 919-994, 988 that the 'striking picture of the old covenant sets up a beautiful contrast seen in description of the new-covenant mountain, Zion, in 12:22-24t, a mountain of joyful celebration, community, and relational closeness to God himself.' Surely it is, but God remains a consuming fire.

9.4 Homiletical lessons to be learned again and again

What do we learn from these aspects of Hebrews for preaching? In the first place, that our homiletics have do justice to this aspect of God's revelation, namely as 'fire', in all our worship, including preaching. This metaphor conveys a reality that has been revealed in the burning bush in which God was present for the redemption of his people from the bondage of Egypt (Ex.3: 2-3).

Thus the LORD descends upon Sinai in fire (Ex 19:28). This fire has actually continued to burn throughout the centuries within Israel on the altar in the tabernacle and in the temple. JHWH himself lights the first sacrifice on the altar (Lev.10:1) on which he himself substitutes life for atonement (Lev.17:11).

What Hebrews makes clear is that after the perfect sacrifice of Christ we should not think that we can play with fire in the church. Not to Sinai, but to Zion means 'much more'. In that respect, it calls for sermons that are on fire, for fiery sermons. Hebrews itself is a wonderful example of such a sermon. Sermons are not religious essays performed in well written prose or recited in a well-voiced manner. Long puts it sharply:

Almost every Christian preacher desires to speak the gospel, to bear witness to God's presence and action in the world. What has happened to the pulpit is more like a habit of speech, being accommodated to the way our culture uses religious language, namely, as holy sounding talk with all the edges filed away, so that *it refers not to the wild, undomesticated presence of the living God*, but only to us, to our sincere hearts, spiritual intentions, and our desire to do good things in life. In other words, there is a plenty of morality and good counsel, *but no desert bush bursting into flame*[25].

In the second place, the sermon is an 'appearance space' for the Holy One. The presence of God is not a commonplace, not self-evident nor suppositional. God cannot be packaged in a sermon. The presence of God, however, is a reality as an event to which we give testimony. 'Either God is present and active in our preaching, or we are poseurs and pathetic fools [...]. If we do not seriously raise the possibility and run the risk of being a damn fool, then we will never get near the possibility of being a fool for Christ'[26].

---

25 Thomas G. Long, *Preaching from Memory to Hope* (Louisville: Westminster John Knox Press, 2009), 34.

26 Long, *Preaching*, 37-38. See Miskotte: 'The moment the change takes place (in the Eucharist), there is a clear, mighty shriek through the Church and all fall to their knees: they experience the real, tangible Representation. In the ministry of the Word, through the human words, there can also be a clear shriek in the hearts: 'God is present, God is in our midst, let us worship deep in the dust.' (K.H. Miskotte, *To the Living Word*).

Third, the sermon should have room for the fear of the Lord as well. God's people do not serve any domesticated God[27]! Once again, preaching without shoes in the presence of God as once happened at a burning bush is of the essence, offering space for fear-filled people. The preaching of (this part of) the Gospel can be an opening up of a 'homiletical space' in which someone is allowed to scream his or her fear and, while screaming, may hear the 'I am He'[28]. Or, to use another metaphor, this is preaching as 'being drawn into the cloakroom' where a person's fear would be changed in its very character. The same fear can be experienced in another way by different feelings, because of having been in the room of the fear of the Lord[29].

Fourth, the considerations given in this chapter will remind us that theological reflection as a deliberate process aims to enable us to discern the wisdom of God in the scriptures for faithful living, both in hearing and preaching in church, as well as outside the worship services as well. To do this properly requires critical understanding, spiritual depth, patient listening and reflection to catch the vision anew and afresh.

The temptation, however, is to try avoid the blood, sweat, and tears, to see the method as the substance, and to accept the short cut and easy response. The Bible, in all its diversity and even perversity, is not an easy companion, even if it also invites us to enter in the joy of the Lord[30].

---

27 David H. Kelsey, "Picturing God Theologically," in *Preaching as Picturing God in a Fragmented World*, Lucy Hogan and Theo Pleizier (Delft: Eburon, 2012), 21-34.

28 See Leif Andersen, "The Language of Hopelessness in Preaching: Pastoral Care in the Preaching of Hope," in *Preaching as a Language of Hope*, Studia Homiletica 6, eds. C. Vos, L.L. Hogan, and J.H. Cilliers (Pretoria, 2007), 203-213; Alexander Deeg, "Preaching God's Wisdom: Response to Marilynne Robinson," in *Viva Vox Evangelii: Reforming Preaching*, Studia Homiletica 9, eds. J. Hermelink and A. Deeg (Leipzig, 2013), 43-53, 52; 'Christian preaching needs a new language again and again - a language that interrupts and disturbs. That breaks open the boundaries of this world and opens up a new perspective. Martin Luther once called it the 'nova sprach de resurrection mortuorum', the 'new language of the raising of the dead.'

29 M.J. Kater, "*Mark 6:45–52, As a Fear-Increasing and Fear-Decreasing Passage*. A Homiletical Analysis From a Biblical-Theological Perspective," *International Journal of Homiletics* 4 (2019): 91-100.

30 Paul Ballard, "The Use of Scripture," in *The Wiley Blackwell Companion to Practical Theology*, ed. Bonnie J. Miller-McLemore (Malden/Oxford: Wiley Blackwell, 2014), 163-172, 169.

REFERENCES

Andersen, L. "The Language of Hopelessness in Preaching: Pastoral Care in the Preaching of Hope."
In *Preaching as a Language of Hope*. Studia Homiletica 6, edited by C.J.A. Vos, L.L. Hogan, and J.H. Cilliers, 203-213. Pretoria: Protea Books, 2007.
Ballard, P. "The Use of Scripture."
In *The Wiley Blackwell Companion to Practical Theology*, edited by B.J. Miller-McLemore, 163-172. Malden/Oxford: Wiley Blackwell, 2014.
Buechner, F. *Secrets in the Dark: A life in Sermons*. New York: Harper Collins Publishers, 2006.
Deeg, A. "Preaching God's Wisdom: Response to Marilynne Robinson."
In *Viva Vox Evangelii: Reforming Preaching*. Studia Homiletica 9, edited by J. Hermelink and A. Deeg, 43-53. Leipzig: Evangelische Verlaganstalt, 2013.
De Leede, B. and C. Stark. *Ontvouwen: Protestantse prediking in de praktijk*. Zoetermeer: Boekencentrum, 2018.
Grethlein, Christian. *An Introduction to Practical Theology: History, Theory, and the Communication of the Gospel in the Present*. Translated by U. Rasch. Waco: Baylor University Press, 2016.
Guthrie, G.H. "Hebrews."
In *Commentary on the New Testament Use of the Old Testament*, edited by G.K. Beale and D.A. Carson. Grand Rapids: Baker Academics, 2007.
Heil, J.P. *Worship in the Letter to the Hebrews*. Eugene: Wipf and Stock, 2011.
Hofius, O. *Der Vorhang vor dem Thorn Gottes*. Wissenschaftliche Untersuchungen zum Neuen Testament. Tübingen: Mohr Siebeck, 1972.
Huijgen, A. *Divine Accommodation in John Calvin's Theology: Analysis and Assessment*. Göttingen: Vandenhoeck & Ruprecht, 2011.
Ihde, D. *Listening and Voice: A Phenomenology of Sound*. Athens: Ohio University Press, 1976.
Immink, F.G. *The Touch of the Sacred: The Practice, Theology, and Tradition of Christian Worship*. Grand Rapids: Wm. B. Eerdmans, 2014.
Isaacs, M.E. "Sacred Space: An Approach to the Theology of the Epistle to the Hebrews." *Journal for the Study of the New Testament* 73 (1992).
Kater, M.J. "Mark 6:45-52 as a Fear-Increasing and Fear-Decreasing Passage: A Homiletical Analysis from a Biblical-Theological Perspective." *International Journal of Homiletics* 4 (2019): 91-100.
Kelsey, D.H. "Picturing God Theologically."
In *Preaching as Picturing God in a Fragmented World*, L. Hogan and T. Pleizier, 21-34. Delft: Eburon, 2012.

Lanigan, R.L. *Phenomenology of Communication: Merleau-Ponty's Thematics in Communicology and Semiology*. Pittsburg: Duqueen Unversity Press, 1988.

Long, T.G. *Preaching from Memory to Hope*. Louisville: Westminster John Knox Press, 2009.

Ong, W.J. *The Presence of the Word: Some Prolegomena for Cultural and Religious History*. Minneapolis: University of Minnesota Press, 1967.

Ryken, Leland, James C. Wilhoit, and Tremper Longman, eds. *Dictionary of Biblical Imagery: An Encyclopedic Exploration of the Images, Symbols, Motifs, Metaphors, Figures of Speech and Literary Patterns of the Bible*. Downers Grove: InterVarsity Press, 1988.

Swinton, J. and Harriet M. Mowat. *Practical Theology and Qualitative Research*. London: SCM Press, 2006.

Van Gemeren, William A., ed. *New International Dictionary of Old Testament Theology and Exegesis*. Vol. 3. Carlisle: Paternoster Press, 1996.

Voladesau, R. *Theology and Arts: Encountering God through Music, Art and Rhetoric*. New York: Paulist Press, 2000.

Warren, Tish Harrison. *The Liturgy of the Ordinary*. Illinois: InterVarsity Press, 2019.

Webb, S.H. *The Divine Voice: Christian Proclamation and the Theology of Sound*. Grand Rapids: Brazos Press, 2004.

Wolff, R.F. "A Phenomenological Study of In-Church and Televised Worship." *Journal for the Scientific Study of Religion* 38, no. 2 (1999): 219-235.

Wolterstorff, N. *The God We Worship: An Exploration of Liturgical Theology*. Grand Rapids: Wm. B. Eerdmans, 2015.

Zock, H., ed. *At the Crossroads of Art and Religion: Imagination, Commitment, Transcendence*. Leuven: Peeters, 2008.

Zuckerkandl, V. *Man the Musician*. Translated by N. Guterman. Princeton: University Press, 1976.

CHAPTER 10

THE DETERMINING DIMENSION OF ENCOURAGEMENT AS PART OF THE ESCHATOLOGICAL DIMENSIONS IN THE HEBREWS SERMON

Ferdi Kruger

Up to this stage, the present book has emphasised the importance of developing and strengthening of listeners through preaching in arduous times. The church has to be thankful for the continuous functioning of preaching, since the origin of the church is integrally connected to preaching. Furthermore, one should acknowledge that the continued existence of the church is dependent on listening to God's speaking within the last days[1]. The listeners to the Hebrews sermon were encouraged to grow spiritually and not neglect God's voice. The problem was however that they found the afflictions in their lives overwhelming. The sermon utilises the explication-application approach but adopts an astonishingly colourful sketch comprised of eschatological strokes. In fact, the eschatological references are arranged in strategically important places for listeners to understand that the coming of the Lord and the final day of salvation are the origins of comfort under arduous circumstances. The Christological dimension of this sermon offers profound motivation for the exhortation to persevere in faith[2]. The message about Christ is excellent, and when the relaxation in listeners' faith-lives is scrutinized, the preacher tries to motivate them with firmness in the sense that the realisation of what God has done in Christ, is real[3]. The firm conviction about what Christ has done is a prominent milestone in this sermon.

---

1 H. Ridderbos, *Paul: An Outline of His Theology* (Grand Rapids: Eerdmans, 1985), 482.
2 B.A. Russell, "Fixing Your Eyes on Jesus," *South African Baptist Journal of Theology* 5, no. 1 (1996): 140-148.
3 Ferdi P. Kruger, "Prediking en gesindheidsverandering: 'n Prakties-teologiese studie in die lig van Hebreërs," ThD thesis (Potchefstroom: North-West University, Dept. Practical Theology, 2002), 102.

Christ is described as one who enters before us into the heavenly sanctuary as a *prodromos*. This concept denotes the idea that Christ is the Precursor to the heavenly sanctuary. He entered this sanctuary and His children have the assurance that they will follow Him. The certainty about His promises is not a mere pie in the sky, but rather a reminder that God does not forget about what he is doing in the last days in which he is speaking. The message about Christ and God's profound speaking in him offer the solid foundation for the listeners to the Hebrews sermon to persevere in arduous times.

The eschatological dimension of God's speaking in Christ is utilised in a purposeful manner. The preacher utilises positive expectations about the future (Hebrews 4:1-11, 9:28, 10:37), but also mentions the importance of realistic expectations about consequences if listeners continue to be disobedient[4]. Barton et al.[5] underline that the eschatological characteristics of this sermon emphasise the importance of keeping in mind the rich heritage they already have in God. Thomas[6] explains that the word 'eschatology' indicates ultimate things and not just last things. Therefore, ultimate reality is not just what will transpire at the end of time, but what God apparently has always sought to make a present reality. The expectation of the future stimulates and empowers human life in the present dispensation[7] [8] [9]. The hastening the day of the Lord entails that effort is made to establish peace and righteousness in anticipation of the *parousia*[10]. Long[11] argues that vibrant Christian preaching depends on the recovery of its eschatological voice. Preaching has the task to share and spread hope in Christ to the world. In the resurrection of Christ, God has already opened the future for his church. Believers share this hope in

---

4   Russell, "Fixing Your Eyes," 143.
5   B.B. Barton, D. Veerman, and L.K. Taylor, *Hebrews*, Life Application Bible Commentary (Wheaton: Tyndale House, 1997), 3.
6   G.J. Thomas, "A Holy God Among a Holy People in a Holy Place: The Enduring Eschatological Hope," in *Eschatology in Bible and Theology: Evangelical Essays at the Dawn of a New Millennium*, eds. K.E. Brower and M.W. Elliot (Downers Grove: InterVarsity Press, 1997), 53-60.
7   J.H. van Wyk, "Die nuwe hemel en die nuwe aarde: dogmatiese en etiese oorwegings oor 'n aspek van die eskatologie," *In die Skriflig* 32, no. 3 (1998): 324.
8   H.W. Robinson, *Expository Preaching: Principles and Practice* (Grand Rapids: Baker, 2001), 93.
9   F. Janse van Rensburg, "Die eskatologie van 1 Petrus: hoop en vindikasie vir tydelike en permanente uitlanders," *In die Skriflig* 44, no. 1 (2010): 226.
10 T.C. Rabali, *The Motif of Hastening the Lord's Coming: II Peter 3:11-13 and Its Alleged Parallels and Background* (Pretoria: Unisa, 1992), 324.
11 Thomas G. Long, *Preaching from Memory to Hope* (Louisville: John Knox Press, 2009), 123.

Christ, therefore they embody a new reality and new community in this world. The eschatological dimension in preaching unites the facts of the advent, that is, the coming of Christ in us, with us and through us right to the end of all things. This view of a new future in Christ inevitably shapes a new look on the present[12][13].

In this chapter, I will pay attention to some of the important eschatological markers in the Hebrews sermon as well as perspectives on rest as found in Hebrews 4. If a biblical view of eschatology falls away in preaching, sermons easily become legalistic[14]. That means that human potential replaces God's promises. In legalistic preaching, a distorted apocalyptic is used to coerce people in a certain direction by using several concealed threats about the future. Changes in people's lives and in society that originated from fear, do not last. Threats around the future cause tension but do not console[15]. Long[16] distinguishes between two kinds of eschatology, namely the first of which depends on a literalistic grip on biblical images and results in a gospel that is intellectually implausible, stuck in the clouds of a pious and irrelevant heaven that never touches earth. If that is our only option, the retreat into a self-contained present tense is our only ethical choice. The second, however, allows eschatological affirmations that 'Christ is risen!' and 'Jesus is Lord!' to exercise their influence on the present tense, generating judgement and promise at once, creating the possibility of ethical action in a world sustained by hope.

10.1 Colourful eschatological dimensions of the rainbow of the Hebrews sermon

The frequency of the author's utilisation of exhortations helps us sense the sermon's urgency. These exhortations are implicit at times, but appear explicitly at least 30 times. On many occasions, the Hebrews preacher utilises the hortatory subjunctive. These verbal forms implore and are often translated with the phrase '*let us*' (do this or that). The preacher is clear about that this sermon did not only inform the audience of theological doctrines in general. Instead, by using important doctrines he persuades them to adopt changed attitudes regarding the meaningfulness

---

12 Bert de Leede and Ciska Stark, *Ontvouwen: Protestantse prediking in de praktijk* (Zoetermeer: Boekencentrum, 2016), 10.
13 B.A. Müller, "Eskatologiese prediking," in *Riglyne vir eskatologiese prediking*, eds. C.W. Burger, D.J. Smit, and B.J. Müller (Pretoria: N.G. Kerk-Uitgewers, 1995), 11.
14 Johan H. Cilliers, *The Living Voice of the Gospel: Revisiting the Basic Principles of Preaching* (Stellenbosch: Sun Press, 2004), 82.
15 Cilliers, *Living Voice*, 83.
16 Long, *Preaching*, 123.

of the essence of being a follower of Christ. The church as a dynamic process of remembering the fact that they are a wandering people[17] is striking. This idea leads to further reflection. Orepeza[18] underlines a common denominator with many other New Testament writings that present or presuppose the emergent Christian life as a journey or a new exodus-wilderness pilgrimage in which eschatological salvation overlaps the two ages of present and future. Based on this insight, Christ-followers may be viewed as those who have a liminal existence between intersecting macro-eras in which faithfulness and perseverance are necessary if their salvation is to be fully realised at the culmination of time when Christ returns.

The eschatological directedness of the Hebrews sermon offers a meaningful space where listeners can understand the field of tension surfacing from their being underway as pilgrims. Powerful building blocks starting with vivid memories about God's speaking to their fathers (Hebrews 1) and liturgical memories about the tabernacle and the reality of the heavenly sanctuary (Hebrews 9) offer insight into the arrow-movement of God's involvement in time. The meaningfulness of fulfilment in Christ that depicted as *better* (see the concept of *kreitton*) is striking. This idea is also illustrated in the contrast between Sinai and Mount Zion (Hebrews 12) and becomes even more evident in the comparison between the pilgrims in the desert and the pilgrims of today who are on their way to the heavenly homeland[19]. Living between the borderlines of time entails becoming aware that all believers participate in the faith-marathon. The anchor of living between the borderlines of time has the firm foundation of Christ who is always the same, even around dynamics between the past, the present and future (Hebrews 13:8). Between prominent transitions in time the idea of God's speaking in Christ should be the focal point. Preaching in the eschatological sense of the word, that is, speaking as communication or voicing of what is and what will come serves as indicator of God's meaningful direction about what listeners should do in the last days (Hebrews 1).

---

17 E. Käsemann, *Das wandernde Gottesvolk* (Gottingen: Vandenhoeck & Ruprecht, 1984), 30-31.
18 B.J. Orepeza, *The Warning Passages in Hebrews* (Tübingen: Mohr Siebeck, 2011), 31.
19 M.J. Kater, "Mark 6:45-52 as a Fear-Increasing and Fear-Decreasing Passage: A Homiletical Analysis from a Biblical-Theological Perspective," *International Journal of Homiletics* 4 (2019): 30.

*10.1.1 Active listening to the message of Christ in these last days
(Hebrews 1:1-3)*

Hebrews should be seen as a good example of a typical first century sermon. In saying this, it is important to realise that the introduction or first words of this sermon announces the sermon's essence (see Hebrews1:1-3). It purposefully starts with emphasis on what it is about, namely God who has spoken in Christ in the last days. It is not a sermon holding up a once-upon-a-time God. On the contrary, as du Toit[20] indicates, mentioning the last days denotes the urgency of responding to God's voice in the framework of Messianic time. This time is related to His coming to earth and His return. God has spoken in the old dispensation through his Son and has sent prophets and apostles to make his voice audible. He has spoken in an unsurpassed manner in the last days through his Son. The *Aoristus* tense indicates that He has spoken once and for all. It is of further significance that the relationship between the past (old) and the present (last days) is not one of a tension between good and bad, but should rather be seen as a relationship between good and that which is much better[21]. If you have received the best, namely God's voice in and through his Son, why would you choose the good of the old dispensation? In fact, the coherence between the old dispensation (past) and the last days signifies an intimate link between God's presence and his influential voice. This contrast highlights God's eschatological speaking that is *complete* and *perfect*, as indicated by ἐν υἱῷ, which is a major theme throughout Hebrews. In other words, that which God has spoken to us (ἐν υἱῷ) is his complete communication over against prior partial disclosures. The implication is that when God spoke ἐν υἱῷ, it was no longer in many parts and many ways, but was instead a *perfect* revelation and one the author expected the audience to willingly receive[22].

The importance of God's voice in the past as well as in the present is accentuated in a meaningful stylistic approach. In Hebrews 1:1-2 the mentioning of *polumeros kai polutropos* is notable. The repetitive pattern is evident. It is notable that the pattern of alliteration of the letter 'p' underscores the contrast between the past and present. Bruce[23] brings clarity around this by underlining that God has spoken his revealing and redeeming Word for people to see life differently. The eschatological view

---

20 Anrie du Toit, *Hebreërs vir vandag [Hebrews for today]* (Vereeniging: CUM boeke, 2004), 35.
21 Du Toit, *Hebreërs*, 35.
22 R. Boyd, *The Role of Hebrews 1:1-4 in the Book of Hebrews* (Cambridge: Asberry Technological College, 2017), 153.
23 F.F. Bruce, *The Epistle to the Hebrews*, New International Commentary of the New Testament (Grand Rapids: Eerdmans, 1990), 45.

of the Hebrews sermon is after all not restricted by viewing the communication as centring on a mere pie in the sky, nor does it adhere to an escapist approach. It is around God's decisive speaking in Christ that the preaching of the Gospel should be understood by the listeners. God chose spokesmen in the old dispensation, but in the last days he has chosen to proclaim the fulfilment of his last word to people through Christ. The fact that God has not spoken once but numerous times denotes a progression towards a destination. God has revealed himself in numerous ways by means of, for instance, dreams and visions, but has also utilised various manners to express himself. He utilised various modes such as encouragement, instruction and exhortation. Circumstances and people's unique challenges were incorporated in the manner in which He spoke. The directedness of preaching on people's unique circumstances within the framework of the last days is something to reflect on. It is clear that God's eschatological speaking in Christ takes people's actual experiences into consideration. Therefore, His speaking to listeners is purposeful and directed.

Bruce[24] emphasises that Christ is viewed as God's final revelation of salvation (Heb. 1.1-4), superior to what was revealed before, whether through angels (1.5-14), Moses (3.1-6), the Levitical and Melchizedek priesthoods (4.14-16; 7.15-28) or the old covenant (8.8-13; 10.1-10). Guthrie[25] refers to this idea from the viewpoint of a hermeneutics of the living voice and therefore indicates that the preacher is speaking 'old' words from the Old Testament to denote a dynamic meaning that encompasses all dispensations. Hebrews 2:1-4 underlines this idea by pointing out that listeners should pay careful attention to what they have heard for them not to drift away. Toussaint[26] expresses the notion of salvation that functions as an important theme in Hebrews 2:1-4. The expression of paying careful attention could also be translated with the formulation of a dedicated or focussed kind of attention[27]. The focussed way of listening and of reacting to what is heard will ensure that listeners will not drift away. The metaphor of a ship that drifts away from the harbour is notable. It could also be connected to a ring that could easily slip from a finger. The urgency and seriousness of reacting to what is heard is tangible in this exhortation.

---

24 Bruce, *Epistle*, 47.
25 Donald Guthrie, *Hebrews Use of Old Testament* (Washington: Union University, 2003), 188.
26 S.D. Toussaint, *The Eschatology of the Warning Passages in the Book of Hebrews* (New York: Grace Theological Seminary, 2011), 68 (was 1982).
27 Du Toit, *Hebreërs*, 47.

Bruce[28] emphasises the importance of acting responsibly to what is heard, because it is after all a matter of life and death. The preacher connects to the listeners' framework by referring to the law at Sinai. If the sanctions given at Sinai were inescapable, neglecting the words of salvation should be seen in a serious light (Hebrews 2:2). After all, the message of salvation was not communicated in a distinct manner by angels but by Christ Himself[29]. We could also say that it was proclaimed by humans and by angels but Christ announced the good news. The preacher utilises the technique *a minore ad majus*, that is, moving from a smaller thought to a bigger idea, to indicate the eschatological tension that arises when listening to sermons[30]. The two verbal ideas that link up with an eschatological dimension, namely of drifting away in the present tense and of escaping in future as found in Hebrews 2:3 are therefore closely connected. The danger of drifting away in the present could lead to the inevitable reality of not escaping in future. The urgency of listening to preaching to make it your own is debated in the sermon within this unique eschatological field of tension. The sermon emphasises that our response to sermons indeed enjoys determining consequences for the future. Preaching of the message of salvation in sermon has the meaning of certainty about salvation from sin and struggles, but it simultaneously refers to the eternal rest[31]. This kind of salvation is also called the future world (Hebrews 2:5 and 6:5) as well as the heritage we will inherit (Hebrews 4:1, 9:15, 10:36 and 11:39). Preaching about God's promises that includes the past, the present and the future is something that should ignite listeners to become involved in what is proclaimed for them.

The eschatological vision on what has realised in Christ as well as the heritage that should come plays an important role in the sermon[32]. Hebrews 2:5 explicitly mentions the world to come. The consummation of salvation will occur when Christ appears to bring believers into its final blessings. This new world was inaugurated by Christ's enthronement, although it is not yet present in its fullness[33]. God's Word and the preaching of the Gospel could therefore not be ignored. It is also striking that the preacher not only mentions the eschatological Word or voice in terms of negative warnings, but also makes an effort to indicate the positive side of what listeners should practically do with what is heard. The profound functioning of present, past and future could not be ignored

---

28 Bruce, *Epistle*, 66.
29 Bruce, *Epistle*, 68.
30 Du Toit, *Hebreërs*, 48.
31 Du Toit, *Hebreërs*, 49.
32 Du Toit, *Hebreërs*, 49.
33 Bruce, *Epistle*, 71.

in the act of preaching. In the last days, God's voice encompasses the foundation of what he did in his Son, what the listeners should do today with what is heard, all of which points to the wonderful heritage still to come.

10.1.2 The eyes focussed on the reality of the sabbath-rest - Hebrews 4
The sermon further announces the preaching-text or the topic in relation to the Old Testament, as found in Hebrews 3:7-11, then to elaborate on this topic at the hand of two sub-headings, as found in Hebrews 3:12-19 as well as Hebrews 4:1-11. The first of these pericopes contains a typical serious warning, also called a negative warning, while the latter distinctly offers a positive outlook on what listeners could expect[34]. The notion of the church as a wandering people is connected to the passage from Psalm 95:7-11. Preaching about listeners' expectation around the future is therefore connected with what one could call a *total'* understanding about what God already indicated in the Old Testament. The listeners understood the language and the message of Psalm 95, therefore the preacher links up with their memories. The preacher utilises this point of departure to explain the similarities between Israel in the dessert and the people living in the last days. These striking similarities are described by du Toit[35]:

- The listeners are similar to Israel underway to the promised land;
- The vision of what should still come is something to look forward to in anticipation;
- Participation in being the wandering people of God includes calamity and challenging circumstances;
- Disobedience will always be a challenging factor;
- Focussed attention regarding listening to God's Word in today's life should be regarded as pivotal.

Mentioning *today* should be seen in the light of an eschatological framework[36]. Today could be described as a decisive moment regarding what is heard. Bruce[37] stresses that, because Christ is bigger than Moses, one should acknowledge that rejection of the message of salvation should simultaneously be seen in a serious light. The preacher has repeated *today* three times in a very short period of time (Hebrews 3:7, 3:15 and also in

---

34 Bruce, *Epistle*, 77.
35 Du Toit, *Hebreërs*, 75.
36 Du Toit, *Hebreërs*, 77.
37 Bruce, *Epistle*, 99.

4:7). This is done to indicate the eschatological importance of this concept. The point is that God's promise of entering rest remains open for his children[38]. The listeners are urged to obtain this Sabbath rest of Canaan while there is still the possibility of a today. The people in the desert have heard the good news of rest and even expected it to realise. The mere hearing of the good news was not lasting, because the listeners of Psalm 95 did not appropriate the good news by faith when they heard it[39]. Listeners who appropriate the good news by faith could however be assured that rest is intended for them[40]. The preacher addresses the matter of coming or falling short of this promised rest, which could be described as the *crux interpretum* of this section in the sermon. Experiencing the promised rest, the sabbath, is however not only a matter for the future but part and parcel of the present reality when listeners approach the good news in faith[41]. The words for *appropriation or combining* in Hebrews 4:2 enjoy the literary meaning of *mixing* something[42]. It denotes the process when different colours of paint are mixed to provide a vivid picture.

An eschatological dilemma is evident in Hebrews 4[43] [44]. Because of the lack in a mixing between hearing and faith, the promise of the Sabbath-rest as relief from the bondage of sin had been due for ages to come. Within the last days and within today God has changed this dilemma[45]. Preaching of the Gospel has the purpose to proclaim this good news and that is why active and responsive listening today is so pivotal. Obtaining this Sabbath-rest is a matter of making every effort to do achieve it (Hebrews 4:11). It is a matter of earnest endeavour and should result in obedience to God's Word[46]. Long[47] raises the valid argument that the preacher is in fact addressing a disheartened congregation, tired of struggle. The grit of reality has worn down their faith. In Hebrews 3:7 - 4:11 a sermon within a sermon is utilised that in fact discusses the theme of rest[48]. The deeper background could metaphorically be described as a struggle between the listeners' ears and their eyes that has created

---

38 Bruce, *Epistle*, 106.
39 Bruce, *Epistle*, 109.
40 Toussaint, *Warning Passages*, 70.
41 Toussaint, *Warning Passages*, 71.
42 Du Toit, *Hebreërs*, 83.
43 M.O. Oyetade, "Eschatological Salvation in Hebrews 1:5-2:5," *Ilorin Journal for Religious Studies* 3, no. 1 (2013): 77.
44 Du Toit, *Hebreërs*, 84.
45 Du Toit, *Hebreërs*, 85.
46 Bruce, *Epistle*, 111.
47 Thomas G. Long, *Hebrews*, Interpretation: A Bible Commentary for Teaching and Preaching (Louisville: John Knox Press, 1997), 54-55.
48 Long, *Hebrews*, 54.

immense challenges. The listeners have seen turmoil and arduous circumstances and consequently struggled to listen[49]. The sermon enables them to understand that today does not merely refer to the current date on the calendar but rather to the present tense in human experience. Therefore, every day is today. This is critical or a determining moment when looked at from the perspective of the listeners' faith-lives. They have to make their decision within the *kairos*, the eternal now[50]. Although the concept of rest is multi-dimensional in its essence, it denotes that God's will is brought to completion. It refers to God's Sabbath-rest on the seventh day, but also points to the completed work of redemption. It should be clear that rest is not only something that has to be applied to the beginning and end-times, but rather as related to the middle of time, too[51]. To rest in the middle of time, that is, today, has to do do with the intrinsic joy of assurance that by the grace of God all our labour and all our effort fall under the fulfilment of God's promises.

By referring to the situation of Psalm 95 and the scenario of Israel in the wilderness, the preacher evokes listeners' memories[52]. He assists them to re-member things that have been amputated in their cognizance. By reminding them that Israel did enter Canaan but did not really enter rest because of what they have done in the Promised Land, a reframing of their understanding is facilitated. They are reminded of the importance of being decisive today. It is further important for listeners to realise their responsibility regarding what they have heard within the decisive moment of today. The vivid image of what happened to Israel in the wilderness should be a warning to them not to repeat similar events[53]. In reminding them of their wandering lifestyle in the world, the importance of remembering the danger of faithless wandering should simultaneously be acknowledged. To edit their memories, they have to listen anew to this message in Christ within the last days. They should have the assurance that those who persevere will experience something of a foretaste of eschatological rest[54]. The message is clear that they have to make every effort to enter into that rest today.

With a view to their appropriation of the warning, the preacher ends the sermon with a typical poem, as found in Hebrews 4:12-13[55]. God's Word is after all sharper than a two-edged sword. It is so sharp that it can

---

49 Long, *Hebrews*, 54.
50 Long, *Hebrews*, 55.
51 Long, *Hebrews*, 59.
52 Bruce, *Epistle*, 186.
53 Long, *Hebrews*, 60.
54 Long, *Hebrews*, 61.
55 Long, *Hebrews*, 61.

expose the secrets of the heart and even separate soul from spirit. The living voice of God's Word lays bare all of people's intentions right here, now and today.

10.1.3 Fixed eyes on God's promises needs perseverance - Hebrews 10:19-39
Once he has expounded the Christological foundation of the sermon over the span of three chapters, the Hebrews preacher arrives at preaching the so-called *'so what'* of the sermon[56]. Now the main issue of what listeners have to do with this particular sermon is addressed. He starts by providing a summary of the previous lengthy explanation around Christology in Hebrews 10:19-20[57]. It could be summarized as having confidence to enter now in the most Holy Place by the grace of Jesus Christ. The first section of the sermon (Hebrews 1-9) explains that God has come to us in the last days through his Son. The second section from Hebrews 10 until the end, discusses how listeners could come to God through Jesus Christ[58]. It is Christ who opened a living way into the true sanctuary. The concept of boldness to enter functions in the present tense to denote that we enjoy the necessary boldness here and now[59]. In fact, it is a boldness that should realise in a continuous manner[60]. Long[61] depicts this idea according to what he calls the parabola of salvation. Hence, the idea that listeners are pilgrims towards the true sanctuary where Christ is the Liturgist, and that they have to prepare themselves accordingly.

One of the core aspects of their preparation is holding on to God's promises (Hebrews 10:23). Hebrews 10:19-25 mentions cohoratives three times, namely *let us*. Hebrews 10:23 mentions the second of these, namely 'let us unswervingly hold to the hope we confess'. In a pilgrim-lifestyle the church is indeed of a confessing nature, professing the wonderful message of what God has done in and through his Son in the last days. The confession should realise today, but there is also the future dimension that no one can ignore[62]. The Greek word for *hold on in a firm* (unswervingly) *manner* features here in Hebrews 10:23 only. It has the literal meaning of *not deviating an inch*. It is after all the firm confession of

---

56 Long, *Hebrews*, 103.
57 Du Toit, *Hebreërs*, 168.
58 J.M. Flanigan, *Hebrews: What the Bible Teaches*, Ritchie New Testament Commentaries (Kilmarnock: John Ritchie, 1997), 210.
59 J. Vines, *The Believers Guide to Hebrews* (New Jersey: Loizeaux, 1993), 138.
60 Du Toit, *Hebreërs*, 169.
61 Long, *Hebrews*, 104-105.
62 Du Toit, *Hebreërs*, 170.

profound hope in Christ that defines listeners' lives[63]. Long[64] underlines that they have to live their lives in the reality of daily life. The challenge for them is to determine how to live their lives when they are not really able to visibly see the realisation of God's promises[65]. The answer offered to this challenge is that they are living by hope and eagerly awaits God's future that has become reality in listening to his voice in Christ within the last days (Hebrews 1:1). Hope is after all the strong cord that connects their lives with God's firm promises in the midst of their struggle[66]. Holding on to this confession of hope is much more than a mere holding on to an abstract idea. In fact, it is a holding on to the living Jesus Christ who provides every reason to hope[67]. God's promises express more than empty words. It is after all an assurance that God is committed in every way to his children[68].

Hebrews 10:26-39 continues to utilise warnings as well as words of encouragement. Here one comes across one of the most difficult passages in the Bible, although the preacher's stern attitude is present nonetheless. The proclamation about Christ has realised, and now a grim warning is announced, which has to do with those who have heard and received the living voice of God but wilfully persist in sin[69]. This centres on people who are aware that God has spoken in the last days through his Son but knowingly continue to resist the message. The concept of 'persistence' has the meaning of trampling the message under your feet[70]. Hebrews 10:29 further describes it as an act of contempt for Christ's blood[71]. This kind of resistance eventually means that the listeners insult the Spirit's message of salvation (Hebrews 10:29), involving a terrifying kind of *hubris*, mainly because of the fact that all listeners are aware of their own imperfection. It is important to realise that the sin described here denotes a functional pervasive context of apostacy: it involves a deliberate attempt to reject the Gospel[72].

The preacher in the Hebrews sermon tries to pinpoint the consequences if they continue along their set ways, involving ignorance of the importance of today. This warning enables listeners to refrain from this kind of

---

63 Flanigan, *Hebrews*, 214.
64 Long, *Hebrews*, 106.
65 Flanigan, *Hebrews*, 215.
66 Long, *Hebrews*, 106.
67 Flanigan, *Hebrews*, 215.
68 Du Toit, *Hebreërs*, 170.
69 Long, *Hebrews*, 108.
70 Du Toit, *Hebreërs*, 174.
71 Du Toit, *Hebreërs*, 174.
72 Long, *Hebrews*, 109.

danger. No sacrifice is applicable to those who persist in rejecting the living voice, because Christ's sacrifice was not enough for them[73]. Hebrews 10:32 actually calls a spade a spade by mentioning that it is dreadful to fall in the hands of the living God. This is not a sermon that wants to convey unilateral threats and it does not want to say 'turn around otherwise you will be severely punished'. Rather, it acts as a timely warning not to neglect God's grace and his living voice in the last days. Therefore, listeners are in fact confronted by the living God Himself to take responsibility for what they have heard[74].

Hebrews 10:32-39 utilises the technique of approaching listeners according to an important kind of reflection, namely: do you still remember? It is important for the listeners to remember what they did earlier in their lives[75]. The preacher is introducing a constructive process of asking what went wrong in their lives over a period of time. They are in fact encouraged to persevere in performing God's will until they have finally received what God has promised (Hebrews 10:35-36). The preacher is concerned that they could throw away their confidence and neglect the wonderful assurance of God's promises[76]. The eschatological tension evident in mentioning perseverance is highlighted by referring to two passages, namely Isaiah 26:20 and Habakuk 2:3-4. The idea behind the quotations is to indicate that listeners are living by faith and have the assurance that He who is coming will come and will not delay[77]. In the time between times, namely today or living in the last days, perseverance and patience are needed, because God is not wasting time. This time is filled with action regarding God's living voice. The purposefulness of God's utilisation of time in listeners' lives should not be doubted nor the specific reasons why they are experiencing what they are experiencing[78]. Why should they persevere? Because he who is coming will surely come. The promise of God's blessing is as sure as the promise of Christ's coming and therefore, in eternity, this waiting is a little while[79]. God is after all never late in the fulfilment of his promises. In Hebrews 10:39, the preacher finds a thoughtful way to combine the intense warning with encouragement. The purpose is to indicate that a living expectancy of God's promises brings wheels into action. The emphatic use of 'we' is notable around encouraging listeners to have a commitment towards God's eschatological

---

73 Du Toit, *Hebreërs*, 175.
74 Du Toit, *Hebreërs*, 175.
75 Long, *Hebrews*, 111.
76 Vines, *Believers Guide*, 154.
77 Du Toit, *Hebreërs*, 182.
78 Flanigan, *Hebrews*, 223.
79 Flanigan, *Hebrews*, 223.

voice In Christ. The preacher identifies with them and is saying that we are after all not part of those who shrink back. He continues to encourage them by highlighting their true identity, namely that we are of those who believe and are saved[80]. This is the exact reason why the listeners should persevere in the pilgrim-lifestyle, because they do this with the assurance of a people who have direction and are not astray in this world.

10.1.4 Warning against refusing of the living God who speaks
    - Hebrews 12:14-29
Right at the beginning of Hebrews 12, the preacher introduces the metaphor of an athlete participating in a foot race. Hebrews 12:12 encourages the listeners to lift their drooping hands and to strengthen their weak knees. The notion of seeing the Lord is then announced in Hebrews 12:14. Listening and seeing are now intimately linked to each other. It is clear that it does not denote separate acts, but rather underlines moments of recognition. Bruce[81] indicates that seeing the Lord is the highest blessing any human could possibly enjoy and this privilege is reserved for those who are holy in their hearts and in their lives. After mentioning the reward of seeing the Lord, the preacher mentions the concept of 'seeing' two times, as found in Hebrews 12:15-16. Listeners are encouraged to take care not to apostate from God's grace and not to be guilty of the example of apostasy in the life of Esau. The attention of the Hebrews sermon is focussed on the contrast between Israel's experience of Sinai and the listeners' expectation of Mount Zion[82]. Listening without seeing the living God who is speaking, is therefore dangerous and irresponsible.

    They are reminded of how awesome it was to receive the law at Sinai, but that it has been more awesome to receive the promises of the Gospel[83]. Those listeners who fall back are now reminded of the consequences of despising the Gospel[84]. Hebrews 12:22 states that '*you have come to Mount Zion*' (my emphasis). The fact is that after hearing this message listeners continued to experience the same arduous circumstances and nothing really changed. They were still participating in their pilgrimage. According to du Toit[85], the latter expression offers a good example of how promises of the future become reality in the present through faith. Through faith listeners' eyes in fact see much further than anyone could guess. They can

---

80 Flanigan, *Hebrews*, 225.
81 Bruce, *Epistle*, 349.
82 Du Toit, *Hebreërs*, 220.
83 Flanigan, *Hebrews*, 354.
84 Bruce, *Epistle*, 355.
85 Du Toit, *Hebreërs*, 221.

experience the joy of the heavenly city. The preacher emphasises the importance of not refusing God who speaks (Hebrews 12:25). The way in which this cohortative is stated indicates that they should refrain from something that is probably in progress[86].

It could be concluded that the manner in which the Hebrews preacher utilises eschatological elements is focussed on helping listeners to realise that God's voice in the last days requires an appropriate response from them. The balanced way in which both sides of the coin of God's grace and the idea that he is a consuming fire is preached, provides us with the perspective that the element of promise in a sermon has to contain both these aspects. The eschatological tension of hope that is assured of more things to come should then be reflected on further.

10.2 Homiletical perspectives on the eschatological dimension in preaching

10.2.1 Interest in the concept of prophetic preaching with an eschatological outlook

Lately, preaching that should penetrate current circumstances to indicate God's promises to listeners who struggle around how to engage with societal issues has received reflective attention. The idea of prophetic preaching has been focussed on considerably. Prophetic preaching amounts to aligning the living message of the biblical text with the world in its current state and destiny. Prophetic preaching therefore involves hermeneutical activity with the text in a critical-creative manner[87]. Pieterse[88] formulates the following guidelines for prophetic preaching:

- The preacher becomes a mouthpiece of the dynamic and acting God;
- The preacher interprets the crisis in society with a critical but creative touch in terms of the promises in God's Word to open new and creative options to the hearers;
- Prophetic preaching demands a prophetic style with a close relation between courage and compassion.

---

86 Simon J. Kistemaker, *Hebrews*, New Testament Commentary (Grand Rapids: Baker Book House, 1996), 399.
87 Müller, "Eskatologiese prediking," 65.
88 Hennie J.C. Pieterse, *Preaching in the Context of Poverty* (Pretoria: UNISA Press, 2001), 95.

The purpose of prophetic ministry is to nurture, nourish and evoke consciousness and perceptions that are alternative from the consciousness and perception of the dominant culture around us[89]. McMickle[90] resonates with Brueggemann` of thinking, making the following remark:

In the Old Testament the 'royal consciousness' represents the deeply entrenched forces- political, economic, social or religious- of Israel. These are the status quo, and they only offer to people a vision of the future that allows them to remain in power and requires that the masses of people remain marginalized in society. The work of the prophet is to combat that single vision and to show that God can and will bring about a future different form that envisioned by the ruling elite (my emphasis).

In a context of the apparent incapacity to engage with the challenges of prophetic preaching, Tubbs Tisdale[91] pose searching questions: Why is it that we are sometimes tempted to substitute another god for the God of justice of the Scriptures? Why do we avoid speaking truth in love regarding some of the burning issues of our day? And why are we often fearful of what becoming a prophetic witnesses will mean for our lives? In attempting to get to grips with the problem field opened up by these questions, she indicates seven hallmarks of prophetic preaching:

- It is rooted in biblical witness: both in the testimony of the Hebrew prophets of old and in the words and deeds of the prophet Jesus of Nazareth;
- It is counter-cultural and challenges the *status quo*;
- It is concerned with the evils and shortcomings of the present social order and is often focussed on corporate and public issues rather than individual and personal concerns;
- It requires the preacher to name what is *not* of the God in this world (criticizing) and the new reality God will bring to pass in the future (energizing);
- It offers hope of a new day to come and the promise of liberation to God`s oppressed people;
- It incites courage in its hearers and empowers them to work to change the social order;
- Prophetic proclamation requires of the preacher a heart that breaks with the things that breaks God`s heart; a passion for justice in the

---

89 W. Brueggemann, *The Prophetic Imagination* (Philadelphia: Fortress, 1978), 13.
90 M.A. McMickle, *Where Have All the Prophets Gone? Reclaiming Prophetic Preaching in America* (Cleveland: Pilgrim, 2006), 11.
91 Leonora Tubbs Tisdale, *Prophetic Preaching: A Pastoral Approach* (Westminster, Louisville: John Knox, 2010), 3.

world; the imagination, conviction, and courage to speak words from God; humility and honesty in the preaching moment; and strong reliance on the presence and power of the Holy Spirit[92].

Defining the essence of prophetic preaching amounts, in our view, to the following: it proclaims the biblical message critically in a society that is in the process of deviating from its God-given form and destiny - in the process equipping Christians to radiate the light of the kingdom of heaven and its righteousness revealingly and energizingly with the eye on refocusing the world on its destiny in restored relationship with God.

10.2.2 The eschatological dimension of preaching
Long[93] identifies an important difference between *progress-preaching* and *eschatological preaching*. The former tells people to gird up their lions and use the resources at hand to make the world a better place, and such preaching necessarily condemns people to failure and despair. The later, in contrast brings the finished work of God to bear on an unfinished world, summoning it to completion. Eschatological preaching promises a 'new heaven and a new earth' and invites people to participate in a coming future that, while it is not dependent upon their success, is open to the labours of their hands. This eschatological perspective restores blurred vision in order that the perceiver can become conscious of the distinct presence of the King, through the work of the Holy Spirit, calling his people to a blessed presence in this world and empowering them with his promise of restoration of abundant life for all.

God's eschatological speaking in the last days, as demonstrated here with regard to the Hebrews sermon, underlines the importance of active listening that should culminate in responding to it. The importance of responsible choices based on that responsiveness, is underlined. It is important to realise that the sermon does not offer a one-size-fits-all answer to challenging circumstances. It is clear that the eschatological dimension of preaching should be acknowledged as essential. The eschatological dimension of God's voice in the last days is after all part and parcel of all sermons. Preaching of the eschatological dimension of the last days gives a unique character to sermons, mainly by emphasising the urgency of the act of listening. After all, the centre of focus is God's speaking in Christ who has come but simultaneously is yet to come. The eschatological dimension of preaching places all listeners at the crossing or borders of time. Therefore, functioning between remembrance and

---

92 Tisdale, *Prophetic Preaching*, 10.
93 Long, *Preaching*, 125.

expectation or longing emerges. The eschatological dimension of preaching always reminds listeners of God's deeds in the past and their relevance today. This remembrance inevitably leads to a vivid expectation of the final fulfilment of God's promises. The Hebrews sermon makes it clear that the eschatological dimension is not aimed at creating fear, but rather to put things into perspective, namely that listening to the Gospel should bring responsibility. Eschatology gives meaning to life on earth and provides preachers with the opportunity to guide listeners to deeply reflect on the meaning of life. Consequently, we cannot separate eschatology from the salvation without distorting the meaning of both.

People indeed go to worship services in the hope of hearing something that could help them regain hope. Vos[94] describes this attempt as people looking to a lily in muddy water. This is exactly the uniqueness of hope, namely that it could grow in muddy circumstances, the latter perhaps also a reminder of people's frailty. The Hebrews sermon enables us to realise that preaching is indeed a vessel of hope as soon as God has a face in the sermon. Preaching as the reminding of people of God's eschatological voice in Christ simultaneously takes them to God's future for his children. After all, preaching the hope that emanates from what God has already done in Christ which also embraces that God's future has indeed started today, provides meaningfulness. The element of God's promises, of his grace and also his warnings, is pivotal towards helping listeners experience renewed hope in arduous times, even if it is similar to looking at a lily in muddy water. We agree with Hermelink[95] that, because listeners struggle with challenges in their faith-lives, preaching should be regarded as important communication in which God's promises is communicated. The Hebrews sermon makes it clear, as shown here, that profound hope has to do with God's audible voice in Christ. Therefore, one can say it has to do with God's traces of engagement or concern for today. This sermon further emphasises that preaching God's promises should lead to empowerment that provides listeners with a lifeline of hope[96].

---

94 C.J.A. Vos, "Seeing Visions and Dreaming Dreams: The Imaginative Power of Preaching Hope," in *Preaching as a Language of Hope*, Studia Homiletica 6, eds. C. Vos, L.L. Hogan, and J.H. Cilliers (Zoetermeer: Boekencentrum, 2007), 11.

95 J. Hermelink, "The Theological Understand of Preaching Hope," in *Preaching as a Language of Hope*, Studia Homiletica 6, eds. C. Vos, L.L. Hogan, and J.H. Cilliers (Zoetermeer: Boekencentrum, 2007), 31.

96 Hermelink, "Preaching Hope," 42.

10.3 Conclusion

The present chapter has highlighted that the Hebrews sermon is determined by the all-important fact of God's speaking in and through Christ, which has been realised in the last days. This could well be referred to as an eschatological voice that supposes urgency in the lives of listeners. The sermon relates God's speaking closely with the message of salvation. The Hebrews preacher emphasises this very idea: that the revelation of God's grace in Christ has far-reaching implications for all listeners to sermons. Despite challenging circumstances in arduous times, the act of listening should be meaningful for hearing of the Gospel to be properly mixed into faith-appropriation. The now or today of God's assurance of salvation is simultaneously relevant to listeners' lives. The certainty about God's promises and of the Sabbath-rest awaiting faithful listeners are not issues to be related to the idea of 'maybe, maybe not'. God is speaking in Christ for us to take heed of what he is saying. The most important day according to Hebrews sermon is therefore today. For listeners, every day is in fact today.

REFERENCES

Barton, B.B., D. Veerman, and L.K. Taylor. *Hebrews*. Life Application Bible Commentary. Wheaton: Tyndale House, 1997.

Boyd, R. *The Role of Hebrews 1:1-4 in the Book of Hebrews*. Cambridge: Asberry Technological College, 2017.

Bruce, F.F. *The Epistle to the Hebrews*. The New International Commentary of the New Testament. Grand Rapids: Eerdmans, 1990.

Brueggemann, W. *The Prophetic Imagination*. Philadelphia: Fortress, 1978.

Cilliers, Johan H. *The Living Voice of the Gospel: Revisiting the Basic Principles of Preaching*. Stellenbosch: Sun Press, 2004.

De Leede, Bert and Ciska Stark. *Ontvouwen: Protestantse prediking in de praktijk*. Zoetermeer: Boekencentrum, 2016.

Du Toit, Anrie. *Hebreërs vir vandag [Hebrews for today]*. Vereeniging: CUM boeke, 2004.

Flanigan, J.M. *Hebrews: What the Bible Teaches*. Ritchie New Testament Commentaries. Kilmarnock: John Ritchie, 1997.

Guthrie, Donald. *Hebrews Use of Old Testament*. Washington: Union University, 2003.

Hermelink, J. "The Theological Understand of Preaching Hope." In *Preaching as a Language of Hope*. Studia Homiletica 6, edited by C. Vos, L.L. Hogan, and J.H. Cilliers. Zoetermeer: Boekencentrum, 2007.

Janse van Rensburg, F. "Die eskatologie van 1 Petrus: hoop en vindikasie vir tydelike en permanente uitlanders." *In die Skriflig* 44, no. 1 (2010).

Käsemann, E. *Das wandernde Gottesvolk*. Gottingen: Vandenhoeck & Ruprecht, 1984.

Kater, M.J. "Mark 6:45-52 as a Fear-Increasing and Fear-Decreasing Passage: A Homiletical Analysis from a Biblical-Theological Perspective." *International Journal of Homiletics* 4 (2019).

Kistemaker, Simon J. *Hebrews*. New Testament Commentary. Grand Rapids: Baker Book House, 1994.

Kruger, Ferdi P. "Prediking en gesindheidsverandering: 'n Prakties-teologiese studie in die lig van Hebreërs." ThD thesis. Potchefstroom: North-West University, Dept. Practical Theology, 2002.

Long, Thomas G. *Preaching from Memory to Hope*. Louisville: John Knox Press, 2009.

Lord, C.G. *Social Psychology*. Orlando: Harcourt Brace, 1997.

McMickle, M.A. *Where Have All the Prophets Gone? Reclaiming Prophetic Preaching in America*. Cleveland: Pilgrim, 2006.

Müller, B.A. "Eskatologiese prediking."
In *Riglyne vir eskatologiese prediking*, edited by C.W. Burger, D.J. Smit, and B.J. Müller. Pretoria: N.G. Kerk-Uitgewers, 1995.

Orepeza, B.J. *The Warning Passages in Hebrews*. Tübingen: Mohr Siebeck, 2011.

Oyetade, M.O. "Eschatological Salvation in Hebrews 1:5-2:5." *Ilorin Journal for Religious Studies* 3, no. 1 (2013).

Pieterse, Hennie J.C. *Preaching in the Context of Poverty*. Pretoria: UNISA Press, 2001.

Rabali, T.C. *The Motif of Hastening the Lord's Coming: II Peter 3:11-13 and Its Alleged Parallels and Background*. Pretoria: Unisa, 1992.

Ridderbos, H. *Paul: An Outline of His Theology*. Grand Rapids: Eerdmans, 1985.

Robinson, H.W. *Expository Preaching: Principles and Practice*. Grand Rapids: Baker, 2001.

Russell, B.A. "Fixing Your Eyes on Jesus." *South African Baptist Journal of Theology* 5, no. 1 (1996).

Thomas, G.J. "A Holy God among a Holy People in a Holy Place: The Enduring Eschatological Hope."
In *Eschatology in Bible and Theology: Evangelical Essays at the Dawn of a New Millennium*, edited by K.E. Brower and M.W. Elliot. Downers Grove: InterVarsity, 1997.

Toussaint, S.D. *The Eschatology of the Warning Passages in the Book of Hebrews*. New York: Grace Theological Seminary, 2011.

Tubbs Tisdale, Leonora. *Prophetic Preaching: A Pastoral Approach*. Westminster, Louisville: John Knox, 2010.

Van Wyk, J.H. "Die nuwe hemel en die nuwe aarde: dogmatiese en etiese oorwegings oor 'n aspek van die eskatologie." *In die Skriflig* 32, no. 3 (1998).

Vines, J. *The Believers Guide to Hebrews*. New Jersey: Loizeaux, 1993.

Vos, C.J.A. "Seeing Visions and Dreaming Dreams: The Imaginative Power of Preaching Hope."

In *Preaching as a Language of Hope*. Studia Homiletica 6, edited by C. Vos, L.L. Hogan, and J.H. Cilliers. Zoetermeer: Boekencentrum, 2007.

CHAPTER 11

HOMILETICAL HEADLINES FROM HEBREWS

Maarten Kater and Ferdi Kruger

Now that we have had the sermon to the Hebrews seen from different angles, it is time to offer an overview of a homiletical theory in which we can see at a single glance what contribution this 'canonical sermon' makes to homiletical reflections in the 21st century.

The most obvious classification seems to be the one in which the '*homiletic triangle*' is the starting point. Homiletics constantly reflects on this triangle between speaking through God (text), the conversation with the heard from God by the listeners and speaking for God and the listeners by preacher. Nevertheless, because of their interconnectedness (triangulation) each item could be seen from all three points of view. The most important one is given and aspects which not receive attention explicitly: their silence will be a stimulant for further reflections. The greatest danger for the field of homiletics (and other theological fields) is the idea we have it all and we know it all as if we are able to make a list which contains each and every thing.

11.1 Directions for a homiletical theory to consider and to process are:

- "Jesus Christ is the same yesterday and today and forever." (Hebr. 13:8):
- The three dimensions of time:
  o Contribute to connect in preaching the present with the past and the future:
  o The focus on the present as a "word of exhortation" - the indicative based on the past - motivation from the future.
  o The German homilitician Bohren in his homiletical handbook Predigtlehre for example mentioned these three dimensions as a classification principle: preaching as remembrance (past), promise (future), and a multi-sided "today" (present). Hebrews, however, connects 'remembrance' with "today" and that actually

is what the Hebrew verb *zkr* means and what the Greek word *anamnesis* is about. Remembrance of Christ and past memories is functional in providing hope for the future amid present experiences.
  - Constitute the mode in which the voice of God sounds as pronounced right at the beginning of this sermon (Hebr. 1:1):
  - In these "last days" God speaks "in the Son" *today* (Hebr. 10:25) even by means of words from "long ago" by means of the prophets.
  - Psalms for example actually voices the voice of God today: the *catena* in Hebrews 1: seven Psalms proclaim the superiority of the Son, Ps. 95 sounds "today, when you hear his voice".
- The *exempla* are contemporaries of the people today, addressed in both warning and promise.
- In the "present" the congregation can be addressed by (means of) the example of the desert generation of Israel. In this way the Christian congregation is also taken to or even "in" - which is preferable - the "cloud of witnesses" as given in chapter 11. The use of imitation of *exempla* does not so much direct our gaze backwards to the past, but is particularly intended to attract our view to the future. Moreover, those examples are connected with the Predecessor Jesus. Christ is shown as *exemplum* and *sacramentum*, as his active and passive obedience belong together.
- God speaks to us "today" in our four-dimensional **space-time** by mediate and embodied speech:
- The Scripture text itself has a width and depth and thus forms a space. Certainly, it is a space with walls - we stay within the "fence" of the letter line. In this sense one could also speak of a "space for grace" because of the graciousness of words and texts.
- Each and every text forms a space to which we are invited in when we hear the word of God from within this space in time when we become aware there is much more in it than we see at that very moment.
- There is not a single necessity to set in contrast **Christ-centred** preaching and **listener-orientated** communication. Meaningfulness is integrated within a Person, Jesus Christ. The Christ-centred manner of speaking excludes a so-called Christomonism, because of the analogy which precedes the meaning of each "how much more" (*kreiton*).
- Much of the rhetorical instruments used contribute to glorify Christ and at the same time are of great help to understand and to remember what is said.

- Preaching according to *Hebrews* is to **open eyes by means of listening**: listening accompanied by faith is seeing. The sermon functions as a window on the real world and enables to stand in our world today in the light of the future. Preaching is life support, even in times of great trauma and pandemics. Preaching provides and opens new perspectives and pictures new horizons, a "counter-imagination". The homiletical praxis has to enable listeners in their adaptive capacity to either adjust to possible harm or to embrace dynamic opportunities or to respond to consequences people are currently facing.
- **Persuasive preaching** is not to confuse with a manipulative approach at all. Without pathos there will be no preaching as witness. A sermon needs evocative language. Besides this, the person of the preacher in his vulnerability and his attitudes are at issue (ethos). Of course, persuasive preaching which respect the audience gives logical argumentation as well. It's not as 'Belief, or I shoot'. Moreover, preaching takes place in the last days and as such is a climactic event which causes a strong persuasive urgency.
- **Pastoral preaching is priestly preaching** (Hebrews 5) and deals with real life issues. Being tired of serving the world, tired even of worship, wired of being whispered about in society, tired of spiritual struggle and tired of keeping their prayer life going.
- Preaching is about and on behalf of a **living Person** as *Hebrews* shows us as a common thread during the whole sermon. The firm conviction about what Christ has done, is a prominent milestone in this sermon and offers a solid foundations to stand on amidst of so much tribulations.
- Preaching as **exhortation** (*paraklèsis*) is grounded on the **exhibition** of God's salvation by means of his words and deeds. The bifurcation of explanation and application is not the same as the intertwining of exhibition and exhortation or indicative and imperative.
- To listen has to do with much more than hearing of mere sounds, because it is an **integral activity** of hearing, understanding, remembering, evaluating, and responding to the message.
- The **intrinsic voices** of the hearers are to be exposed by means of an exposure of the threads and dangers the listeners are in. Remembrance is a propellant for the act of seeing in persuasive preaching that evokes a change in attitudes.
- E.g. the distinctive attitude dimensions as illustrated from *Hebrews* and the inner connection of attitudes with ethics.

11.2 Reflections in broader perspective

Besides those overall directions which stem from this 'three-dimensional sermon' there are the following points to process within the homiletical reflection.

- The **value of religious spaces**: in *Hebrews* the Old Testament sanctuary is the abiding background in which the hearers are invited to see the heavenly realities, especially the High Priest Jesus Christ as living and active "today, when we hear his voice".
- Moreover, going to a church building and being in a worship service is not something like being just between four walls and beneath a roof, but is approaching "Zion", is being amongst the heavenly gathering, and still a worship service is connected with the burning bush, even the presence of God. Sermons which downplay these aspects are in the great danger of domesticating God.
- Within the homiletical field an ongoing reflection on **theology of language** will be fruitful. E.g. considerations on 'Voice of God' and the many voices in preaching, the phenomenology of speech and listening, and what communication is about. There will be no real communication without communion. Preaching is about relation.
- There's still a world to be won when it comes to the **use of imagination** in preaching as is clear from the imaginative preaching in *Hebrews*.
- The best preparation of a sermon is the preparation of the **heart of the preacher**. The preacher should be believe in what is communicated from the text(s).
- The awareness of what happens during a sermon in the formation and developing of **attitudes in the various spheres** as cognitive, affective, behavioural, interpersonal, social/political, and spiritual.
- The Latin maxim **lex orandi, lex credenda** could prevent the bifurcation between theology and liturgy and should be enlarged by the *lex orandi* and the *lex vivendi*.
- There is much to consider when thinking about the constituent elements of ecclesiastical experience: hierarchy, immersion, and freedom.

All in all, these headlines are given for reading through *Hebrews* - better to say *listening* to the *Hebrew* sermon - as an ongoing activity, an abiding (re)source for different practical theological issues, serving academy and church.

11.3 Relevance of the Hebrews sermon for the discipline of homiletics

We want to indicate that the Hebrews sermon offers piercing perspectives for the discipline of homiletics. It is clear that it provides a powerful sermon structure within a particular context. The notion of Eswine[1] that preachers should also function like rangers in their preaching in providing assistance to listeners to navigate the terrain of reality, is intriguingly related to this idea. Florence[2] concomitantly refers to Paul Ricoeur and underlines that Christianity itself consists of communication that can be described as a hermeneutics of testimony. One has to suppose that listeners have the responsibility to react to what they have heard. Each sermon then further propels God's people forward, sending them forth to convey this message[3]. So, there consequently has to be some kind of response at the end of the sermon. More concretely formulated, appropriation of the living Word is generally the result of incremental preaching, hence many sermons rather than of a few often is a successful strategy that results listeners making the message their own. In accomplishing preaching that should pinpoint the response to the passage within daily life, it has to be taken into account that preaching is part of a comprehensive process of shaping, also called a nurturing process or a formation process[4].

On the deep level of these matters, one finds that the sermon may reach a formal end, while God's plan of grace in Christ goes further still[5]. Calvin conceives of the preaching of the Gospel as a means of grace because it is the path along which God is pleased to operate to save people[6]. Calvin further boldly states: *'Take away the preaching of the Gospel, and no faith will remain'* (emphasis ours). This means that faith is born of hearing, because the outward preaching is the instrument by which God draws listeners to faith. Faith is after all intimately linked with the act of preaching. In fact, Calvin conceives of the relation between preaching and faith as similar to that between a mother and birth, for the preaching is the mother who conceives and brings forth, and faith is the daughter who ought to be mindful of her origins. Such is the connection between the people's faith and the minister's preaching[7].

---

1 Z. Eswine, *Preaching to a Post-Everything World: Crafting Sermons That Connect with Our Culture* (Grand Rapids: Baker House, 2008), 26.
2 A.C. Florence, *Preaching as Testimony* (London: John Knox Press, 2007), 69.
3 M.W. Goheen, *As the Father Has Sent Me, I Am Sending You: J.E. Leslie Newbigin's Missionary Ecclesiology* (Zoetermeer: Boekencentrum, 2001), 178.
4 S.M. Gibson, *Preaching with a Plan* (Grand Rapids: Baker House, 2012), 18.
5 Gibson, *Preaching*, 95.
6 J.M. Beach, "The Real Presence of Christ Preaching of the Gospel: Luther and Calvin on the Nature of Preaching," *Mid-America Journal of Theology* 10, no. 1 (1999): 110.
7 Beach, "Real Presence," 111.

The relevance of the Hebrews sermon has to do with the fact that it provides homiletics with a perspective that God's voice itself is audible while listening to sermons. The listeners' concrete circumstances often challenges listeners, and the Hebrews sermon helps us understand that preachers have to construct sermons in order for listeners to realise something poignant, namely an exchange of ownership of the sermon. Gaarden[8] refers to meaning that should still be established and be given to the sermon by listeners in the listening process, something that we will term the emerging sermon. Consider in this respect that people's attitudes cannot be separated from the active listening process. This means that preaching the Gospel is aimed at being persuasive. Within a context where scholarly reflection on preaching to a postmodern world is audible, taking note of this research could offer invasive perspectives on the deeper essence of preaching. In this book we will address various aspects related to the Hebrews sermon and our vantage point is to perform this from a homiletical, that is, practical theological viewpoint.

Scholars and preachers who are interested in the relation between preaching and the development and strengthening of a local congregation will find valuable perspectives in this interpretation of this sermon. The sermon makes clear that God's speaking through his Son cannot be separated from a concrete situation and the reality of listeners' lives. This sermon also provides insight around the idea that communication of the Gospel should be delivered in a planned manner and has to be directed in a purposeful manner.

REFERENCES

Beach, J.M. "The Real Presence of Christ Preaching of the Gospel: Luther and Calvin on the Nature of Preaching." *Mid-America Journal of Theology* 10, no. 1 (1999).

Eswine, Z. *Preaching to a Post-Everything World: Crafting Sermons That Connect with Our Culture*. Grand Rapids: Baker House, 2008.

Florence, A.C. *Preaching as Testimony*. London: John Knox Press, 2007.

Gaarden, M.L. *Listeners as Authors in Preaching*. Copenhagen: Aarhus University Press, 2014.

Goheen, M.W. *As the Father Has Sent Me, I Am Sending You: J.E. Leslie Newbigin's Missionary Ecclesiology*. Zoetermeer: Boekencentrum, 2001.

Gibson, S.M. *Preaching with a Plan*. Grand Rapids: Baker House, 2012.

---

8 M.L. Gaarden, *Listeners as Authors in Preaching* (Copenhagen: Aarhus University Press, 2014), 3.

INDEX

Acoustic symbiosis,	36
Active listening,	4, 14, 45, 46, 54, 55, 60, 99, 105, 130, 142, 147, 174, 231, 242
Agogie,	128
Anamnesis,	169, 172, 175, 177, 182, 186, 238
Anaphora,	136, 155
Application,	8, 9, 33, 44, 61, 86, 88, 121, 128, 132, 143, 145, 160, 173, 174, 181, 183, 215, 239
Arduous circumstances,	1, 190
Arduous times,	1
Attitude,	8, 10, 17, 46, 54, 55, 56, 58, 59, 83, 84, 85, 86, 87, 89, 90, 91, 92, 93, 94, 95, 96, 97, 98, 99, 100, 101, 102, 103, 104, 105, 128, 129, 130, 131, 132, 133, 134, 135, 136, 138, 141, 142, 143, 144, 145, 146, 147, 148, 149, 170, 177, 184, 188, 226, 239
Augustine,	50, 67, 68, 69, 70, 80, 118, 178, 183, 184, 185, 186, 193
Better sacrifices,	162
Boldness,	83, 86, 87, 88, 89, 90, 104, 143, 144, 177, 225
Change,	3, 10, 11, 14, 56, 84, 89, 90, 101, 102, 103, 104, 106, 112, 128, 129, 130, 131, 132, 133, 135, 136, 142, 144, 145, 146, 147, 148, 149, 170, 190, 210, 230, 239
Christology,	31, 35, 41, 225
Church,	16, 17, 18, 19, 20, 22, 35, 39, 44, 53, 62, 96, 101, 102, 103, 112, 113, 114, 116, 117, 119, 120, 122, 123, 124, 159, 163, 195, 196, 197, 198, 199, 200, 201, 202, 203, 204, 205, 207, 208, 209, 210, 211, 213, 215, 216, 218, 222, 225, 240
Cognitive,	70, 77, 102, 103, 105, 113, 129, 131, 188, 240
Communicative acts,	2, 12
Community of faith,	17, 18, 45, 46, 142, 144, 173
Corporality,	199

Courage to,	87, 231
Covenant,	10, 56, 131, 153, 160, 162, 163, 174, 176, 177, 178, 179, 180, 181, 203, 208, 209, 220
Covid-19,	2, 16, 20, 22, 92, 115, 149, 190, 195
Daily life,	7, 8, 11, 15, 19, 51, 54, 55, 86, 88, 90, 92, 95, 99, 105, 128, 132, 133, 143, 144, 145, 146, 148, 149, 168, 188, 189, 226, 241
Deliberateness,	132
Dialogue,	14, 30, 31, 50, 123, 141, 142, 167, 170, 181, 188, 196
Diligence,	10, 55, 83, 88, 89, 91, 92, 97, 112
Earnestness,	48, 56, 60, 88, 91, 174, 182
Embodied speech,	37, 41, 238
Encouragement,	6, 7, 8, 10, 48, 60, 61, 85, 87, 92, 104, 123, 127, 128, 130, 134, 137, 172, 173, 226
Eschatological,	10, 63, 95, 96, 97, 141, 160, 215, 216, 217, 218, 219, 220, 221, 222, 223, 224, 227, 229, 231, 232, 233
Ethos,	69, 70, 78, 138, 239
Exempla,	9, 70, 74, 135, 153, 154, 159, 160, 161, 164, 238
Exhortation,	6, 8, 9, 35, 47, 48, 61, 71, 72, 77, 83, 85, 87, 88, 92, 93, 94, 97, 113, 119, 123, 133, 134, 137, 144, 146, 156, 161, 172, 175, 177, 202, 215, 220, 237, 239
Explication,	8, 9, 61, 86, 128, 132, 137, 157, 215
Faithfulness,	104, 141, 142, 152
Forget,	5, 39, 98, 172, 173, 216
God has spoken,	5, 10, 25, 33, 34, 43, 44, 51, 73, 121, 122, 129, 141, 142, 156, 167, 219, 226
God's speech,	31, 35, 50, 155, 158
Habitus,	1
Hearing,	4, 32, 33, 52, 53, 54, 55, 59, 63, 111, 114, 122, 199, 202, 208, 211, 223, 228, 232, 233, 239, 241
Hebrews sermon,	1, 3, 4, 5, 6, 7, 8, 9, 10, 11, 12, 13, 14, 15, 17, 18, 20, 44, 45, 46, 47, 48, 49, 50, 51, 52, 54, 56, 57, 58, 59, 60, 61, 62, 63, 67, 83, 85, 88, 91, 92, 93, 94, 96, 98, 102, 104, 106, 111, 128, 129, 130, 131, 132, 133, 134, 135, 136, 137, 138, 139, 140, 141, 142, 144, 145, 146, 148, 149, 153, 168, 169, 170, 171, 172, 173,

	174, 176, 177, 178, 179, 187, 190, 191, 215, 216, 217, 218, 220, 226, 228, 231, 232, 233, 241, 242
Hold fast,	92, 104, 122, 141, 143
Homiletics,	1, 2, 22, 73, 89, 113, 207, 211, 212, 218, 234, 237
Hortatory,	11, 132, 136, 137, 217
Imagination,	49, 67, 70, 74, 75, 124, 131, 147, 172, 231, 239
Imperative,	8, 28, 44, 47, 48, 57, 88, 89, 102, 133, 239
In memoriam,	57, 169, 170, 180
Indicative,	8, 28, 48, 89, 133, 143, 239
Invisible,	93, 96, 198
Kairos,	224
Kingdom,	48, 74, 231
Language,	25, 26, 27, 28, 29, 31, 33, 37, 39, 44, 67, 70, 72, 73, 75, 78, 79, 84, 91, 104, 120, 130, 131, 132, 137, 146, 147, 148, 185, 186, 187, 205, 208, 209, 210, 211, 222, 239, 240
Last days,	5, 20, 31, 34, 49, 51, 61, 63, 64, 71, 86, 106, 121, 129, 134, 141, 142, 149, 167, 169, 170, 174, 175, 178, 179, 216, 218, 219, 220, 222, 223, 224, 225, 226, 227, 229, 231, 233, 238, 239
Laziness to listen,	94
Legalistic,	6
Lex credendi,	112, 115, 117, 119, 120, 121, 122, 123, 124, 125, 126
Lex orandi,	111, 112, 115, 116, 117, 119, 120, 122, 123, 124, 125, 240
Listening,	2, 3, 4, 11, 14, 25, 33, 38, 39, 43, 44, 46, 48, 51, 52, 53, 54, 55, 56, 57, 59, 60, 61, 63, 68, 83, 93, 94, 95, 99, 111, 112, 113, 122, 123, 124, 125, 128, 132, 142, 145, 148, 156, 165, 170, 173, 179, 186, 187, 188, 189, 190, 195, 201, 203, 204, 211, 215, 219, 220, 221, 222, 223, 226, 231, 232, 233, 239, 240, 242
Liturgy,	16, 18, 19, 44, 54, 79, 84, 93, 102, 103, 115, 116, 117, 118, 119, 120, 124, 125, 130, 131, 132, 142, 144, 145, 146, 147, 148, 169, 173, 176, 178, 182, 189, 195, 196, 205, 206, 207, 208, 209, 240

Index – 247

Liveable life,	2, 128
Living voice,	43, 46, 47, 52, 57, 62, 63, 92, 143, 148, 149, 179, 220, 225, 226, 227
Logos,	57, 69, 70, 78, 124, 138
Longing for,	17, 95, 170, 202, 209
Looking, 52,	114, 154, 157, 197, 207, 232
Meaningfulness,	1, 2, 3, 5, 14, 15, 18, 45, 47, 49, 84, 86, 127, 134, 146, 169, 172, 175, 191, 217, 218, 232
Mediated speech,	34
Memories,	3, 4, 5, 52, 54, 72, 134, 167, 168, 169, 170, 171, 172, 173, 174, 175, 176, 177, 178, 182, 184, 185, 186, 187, 188, 190, 191, 218, 222, 224, 238
Morality,	105, 157, 201, 210
Naming,	29, 101, 156, 159, 165
Old Testament,	9, 14, 31, 32, 34, 35, 42, 50, 52, 53, 75, 77, 80, 87, 134, 138, 140, 153, 154, 160, 163, 164, 165, 168, 173, 174, 176, 179, 180, 181, 187, 192, 203, 204, 205, 206, 207, 209, 212, 213, 220, 222, 230, 233, 240
Pathos,	69, 70, 77, 78, 79, 138, 239
Perseverance,	10, 48, 66, 95, 135, 152
Persuading,	45, 86, 130, 134, 174, 190
Persuasion,	5, 60, 70, 77, 85, 86, 100, 129, 132, 134, 135, 139, 140, 146, 147, 148, 149, 173, 186
Polyphony,	46, 56, 60, 63, 64, 67, 93, 141
Practical reasoning,	1
Practical Theology,	1, 12, 13, 21, 22, 30, 41, 65, 89, 102, 107, 108, 111, 116, 125, 126, 136, 143, 151, 152, 170, 192, 207, 208, 211, 212, 213, 215, 234
Praxis,	1, 3, 4, 6, 8, 11, 12, 13, 15, 16, 17, 59, 91, 98, 106, 111, 171, 172, 174, 239
Preacher,	4, 6, 8, 9, 10, 11, 14, 17, 25, 29, 30, 37, 40, 43, 44, 45, 46, 47, 50, 51, 52, 55, 56, 58, 59, 60, 61, 63, 69, 71, 77, 78, 79, 83, 84, 85, 86, 87, 88, 89, 91, 93, 94, 95, 97, 98, 99, 100, 101, 103, 105, 107, 109, 122, 127, 128, 129, 130, 131, 132, 133, 134, 135, 136, 137, 138, 139, 140, 141, 142, 144, 145, 146, 147, 149, 153, 155, 158, 167, 168, 170, 172, 173, 174, 175, 176, 177, 181, 182, 183, 185, 186, 187, 188, 189, 198, 200, 201, 207, 209, 210, 215,

Preaching,	216, 217, 220, 221, 222, 223, 224, 225, 226, 227, 228, 229, 230, 233, 237, 239, 240 1, 2, 3, 4, 5, 6, 7, 8, 9, 10, 12, 13, 14, 15, 16, 18, 20, 21, 22, 25, 26, 28, 30, 32, 34, 36, 38, 40, 41, 42, 43, 44, 46, 48, 49, 50, 51, 52, 54, 55, 56, 58, 60, 61, 62, 63, 64, 65, 66, 67, 68, 70, 72, 74, 75, 76, 77, 78, 80, 81, 83, 84, 85, 86, 88, 89, 90, 92, 93, 94, 96, 98, 99, 100, 101, 102, 104, 105, 106, 107, 108, 109, 112, 114, 116, 118, 120, 122, 124, 126, 127, 128, 130, 131, 132, 133, 134, 136, 137, 138, 139, 140, 141, 142, 144, 146, 148, 149, 150, 151, 152, 154, 155, 156, 157, 158, 159, 160, 161, 162, 163, 164, 165, 166, 168, 170, 172, 173, 174, 176, 178, 179, 180, 182, 183, 184, 185, 186, 187, 188, 189, 190, 191, 192, 193, 194, 195, 196, 198, 200, 202, 204, 206, 208, 210, 211, 212, 213, 216, 217, 218, 220, 221, 222, 223, 224, 226, 228, 229, 230, 231, 232, 233, 234, 235, 238, 239, 240, 241, 242
Predecessor,	155, 157, 159, 161, 163, 164, 165
Presence of God,	55, 124, 181, 204, 205, 207, 210, 211, 240
Present,	7, 8, 13, 15, 17, 18, 25, 26, 32, 33, 34, 35, 38, 39, 41, 43, 44, 46, 47, 52, 55, 56, 57, 63, 75, 92, 94, 95, 96, 106, 115, 118, 121, 130, 132, 134, 138, 142, 148, 153, 156, 159, 160, 161, 163, 165, 169, 170, 172, 174, 179, 182, 183, 184, 185, 186, 187, 190, 195, 196, 198, 200, 204, 205, 210, 215, 216, 217, 218, 219, 221, 223, 224, 225, 226, 228, 230, 233, 237, 238
Promises,	11, 52, 61, 64, 77, 91, 95, 96, 97, 132, 138, 140, 142, 159, 167, 169, 170, 176, 177, 182, 187, 216, 217, 221, 224, 225, 226, 227, 228, 229, 231, 232, 233
Purposeful structuring,	4
Refusing,	228, 229
Religious spaces,	18, 240
Remembrance,	52, 55, 165, 167, 168, 169, 170, 172, 173, 174, 175, 176, 177, 179, 180, 182, 183, 185, 186, 187, 188, 189, 190, 191, 231, 232, 237
Rhetorical,	35, 60, 67, 69, 70, 71, 72, 73, 78, 79, 94, 135, 136, 138, 159, 183, 238

Saving acts of God,	168, 182, 187
Seeing,	11, 14, 36, 49, 56, 75, 77, 86, 93, 96, 159, 182, 228, 239
Sermon,	3, 4, 5, 6, 7, 8, 9, 11, 13, 14, 15, 17, 18, 20, 25, 31, 33, 34, 35, 37, 39, 40, 44, 45, 46, 47, 48, 49, 50, 51, 54, 55, 56, 60, 61, 62, 63, 67, 71, 72, 73, 74, 75, 77, 79, 83, 85, 86, 87, 89, 92, 94, 95, 97, 98, 99, 100, 101, 105, 113, 114, 116, 119, 121, 122, 127, 128, 129, 130, 131, 132, 133, 134, 135, 136, 137, 138, 139, 140, 141, 142, 145, 146, 148, 149, 154, 155, 157, 158, 160, 161, 162, 164, 167, 168, 169, 170, 171, 172, 173, 174, 175, 179, 180, 181, 182, 183, 185, 187, 188, 189, 190, 195, 198, 200, 201, 206, 207, 210, 211, 215, 216, 217, 219, 221, 222, 223, 224, 225, 227, 229, 231, 232, 233, 237, 238, 239, 240, 241, 242
Stir up,	124, 127
Superior,	49, 71, 72, 121, 162, 163, 165, 173, 180, 181, 220
Tabernacle,	39, 74, 75, 160, 176, 203, 205, 206, 210, 218
Time,	2, 3, 4, 16, 17, 19, 26, 28, 31, 32, 38, 39, 40, 41, 44, 47, 52, 58, 60, 61, 69, 72, 83, 86, 92, 95, 105, 108, 113, 115, 120, 122, 127, 129, 134, 138, 142, 148, 149, 153, 159, 160, 162, 168, 169, 176, 185, 197, 198, 199, 200, 201, 202, 203, 207, 216, 218, 219, 222, 224, 227, 231, 237, 238
Understanding,	1, 4, 5, 6, 12, 15, 27, 45, 46, 50, 53, 54, 63, 64, 68, 69, 76, 84, 87, 90, 91, 94, 97, 98, 128, 131, 132, 144, 146, 156, 167, 170, 171, 172, 173, 179, 181, 183, 188, 189, 201, 211, 222, 224, 239
Visible,	3, 4, 17, 18, 19, 45, 62, 96, 174
Voice,	4, 11, 20, 25, 26, 27, 31, 32, 33, 34, 36, 37, 38, 40, 41, 43, 44, 45, 46, 52, 53, 54, 55, 56, 57, 60, 63, 67, 68, 75, 79, 96, 100, 103, 113, 139, 142, 149, 161, 163, 165, 197, 200, 201, 204, 209, 215, 216, 219, 221, 222, 226, 228, 229, 231, 232, 233, 238, 240, 242
Witnessing,	55, 56, 61

Worship,	2, 3, 4, 10, 16, 19, 38, 54, 84, 99, 100, 112, 113, 115, 116, 117, 118, 120, 121, 122, 124, 128, 140, 141, 144, 147, 148, 154, 155, 182, 187, 189, 195, 196, 199, 200, 201, 202, 203, 204, 206, 207, 208, 209, 210, 211, 232, 239, 240
Zeitgeist,	2, 62